ALSO BY ELIZA GRISWOLD

Wideawake Field
The Tenth Parallel
I Am the Beggar of the World (translator)
Amity and Prosperity
If Men, Then

CIRCLE OF HOPE

CIRCLE OF HOPE

A RECKONING *with*
LOVE, POWER,
and JUSTICE *in an*
AMERICAN CHURCH

ELIZA GRISWOLD

FARRAR, STRAUS AND GIROUX
NEW YORK

Farrar, Straus and Giroux
120 Broadway, New York 10271

Library of Congress Control Number: 2024008257
ISBN: 978-0-374-60168-3

Designed by Gretchen Achilles

Our books may be purchased in bulk for promotional,
educational, or business use. Please contact your local bookseller
or the Macmillan Corporate and Premium Sales Department at 1-800-221-7945,
extension 5442, or by email at MacmillanSpecialMarkets@macmillan.com.

www.fsgbooks.com
Follow us on social media at @fsgbooks

1 3 5 7 9 10 8 6 4 2

FOR FRANK GRISWOLD
1937–2023

The hint half guessed,
the gift half understood, is Incarnation.

—T. S. ELIOT, "The Dry Salvages"

CONTENTS

CONTENTS

CIRCLE OF HOPE

A NOTE

Immersion journalism is unruly. It's like going up to a stranger's car, knocking on the window, and asking to climb into the back seat and ride along for a while. The plan might be to arrive in Vermont in a week's time only to end up in Vegas four years later, with three flat tires. There's no controlling the process, and yet to call this reporting "fly-on-the-wall" isn't intellectually honest. People, like particles, behave differently under observation. Even when they forget someone is in the back seat—still!—the observer remains an irreducible factor of the environment.

As a pastor's kid, a reporter for *The New Yorker*, and a poet, I've spent much of my life at the edge of belief, observing how people organize their lives around what they hold sacred. I was raised to analyze human concepts of the divine—not in order to question their veracity or validity, but to understand their universal principles. Amid moments of transcendence, almost every religious community has to contend with a leaky roof. Inevitably, the outside world bears down.

Churches are harbingers of moral and cultural shifts. From 1998 to 2006, my father, Frank Griswold, served as the presiding bishop of the Episcopal Church, a Protestant denomination of 1.5 million people. When he consecrated the first openly gay bishop in 2003, I watched a modern schism in real time. This wasn't an arcane theological disagreement: it was a profound rift, and it divided the church for good. Some evenings after dinner around our kitchen table, I watched my usually reserved dad put his head in his hands and cry over his failure to hold the church together.

Later that year, as a reporter, I traveled to Sudan with Franklin Graham, son of Billy Graham, the evangelical leader who preached in football stadiums to hundreds of thousands of rapt listeners during the 1950s and '60s. Franklin Graham was different from his father. Billy Graham preached broadly about God; Franklin Graham spoke exclusively of Jesus, exemplifying the rightward political and cultural swing among most evangelicals in the late twentieth century. Like the majority of American evangelicals, who comprise one quarter of the U.S. population, Franklin Graham opposed gay marriage. Many evangelicals viewed the decision by the Episcopal Church and other Protestant denominations to openly accept gay members as a surrender to secular culture and a sign of their demise. Yet it was not hard to see that the same cultural forces buffeting other Protestants would soon confront American evangelicals.

About sixty million Americans consider themselves "evangelical," a term that has always encompassed a range of backgrounds, ideologies, and identities. Evangelicals can belong to any Protestant denomination, or none at all. In general, they hold to several core certainties: they believe that by offering their lives to Jesus, who suffered on the cross and redeemed the world, they are saved; they believe in public witness; and they believe in the centrality of the Bible. They are committed to applying these tenets to all aspects of their lives.

More influential than any other religious tradition in the United States, evangelicals also reflect a larger crisis facing American Christians. Over the past twenty-five years, some forty million Americans have stopped attending church. Scandals over power, money, sex, and abuse have called into question the basic goodness of church leaders and institutions. This exodus from the church is often misunderstood as data-supported evidence of the rise of secularization. However, when people leave their churches they don't always leave their faith.

Evangelicals who align with political conservatives have captured the most national attention. They also represent the majority of the voting block. Yet alongside this more vocal and visible group, a vibrant and visionary cohort has grown in reaction against the religious right. Rejecting their parents' Republican politics, these evangelicals seek to follow Jesus's radically socialist teachings in literal ways. In their willingness to sacrifice comfort and self-seeking in favor of living according to Scripture, they are reclaiming moral authority from the Christian right. Over the past fifty years, this movement has gone by various names. Some adherents and observers have used terms like "progressive evangelicals" and "the evangelical left." Yet most who belong to this movement are trying to move beyond such labels. They are attempting to return to the roots of their faith and the practices of Jesus's first followers. Perhaps a better term to describe them comes from this desire to live from the root (in Latin, *radix*): "radical evangelicals," as some have called themselves for decades.

Their movement began during the 1967 Summer of Love in San Francisco's Haight-Ashbury. Within the secular countercultural revolution, some seekers were drawn to long-haired street preachers who spoke of a deeper purpose and of certain salvation. Surrendering their lives to Jesus, a growing number of hippies became "born again" and in turn birthed a social phenomenon: the Jesus movement. By the early seventies, young people in love beads and bare feet were becoming evangelical Christians in droves, many moving to Christ-centered communes and influencing American popular culture. The Jesus movement captured the public imagination, inspiring, in 1971, the musicals *Godspell* and *Jesus Christ Superstar*. Jesus was so influential that he graced the cover of *Time* that year.

By the nineties, the power of the religious right and the social crises plaguing the United States had revealed essential differences between conservative evangelicals, who viewed belief as individual and the Kingdom of Heaven as eternal life after death, and the radical evangelicals, who believed that Jesus was calling them to transform society in this lifetime, not simply pray for the next. Over the past three decades, these divisions have sharpened, pitting evangelicals against one another, and casting competing visions of the moral call to be a Christian.

No less "Bible-believing" than their parents, today's radical evangelicals aspire to live out Jesus's teachings on love and liberation, building the Kingdom of Heaven on Earth by rejecting capitalism, redistributing resources, and addressing social ills. Turning away from the hypocrisy and hierarchy of the church as an institution, they rely on Jesus's principal moral teaching, the Sermon on the Mount, as a blueprint for their lives. They have established intentional communities in the poorest and most violence-ridden neighborhoods, renounced possessions, set up food pantries, and repurposed school buses to run on vegetable oil. To live out the biblical injunction to forge swords into plowshares, they've melted guns into garden tools.

In 2019, on a street corner in Kensington, the Philadelphia neighborhood hardest hit by opioids, I was standing by one such blacksmith's mobile forge, watching the muzzle of an AK-47 start to glow, when I spotted half a dozen white men and women huddled together on the curb in thrift-store chic. The men wore well-pressed button-down shirts, and the women favored long dirndl skirts and T-shirts with sayings like *There are no good billionaires*. They were punk-rock, but their fresh faces and starry eyes spoke of devotion to something greater: a church, I suspected.

This was Circle of Hope, a vibrant collective of some seven hundred people founded in 1996 by Rod and Gwen White. Hippie church planters from Southern California, the Whites felt called to come east and bring young people to Jesus. So many were abandoning church. Rod and Gwen saw another way: tossing out hypocrisy, GOP politics, rote Bible learning, and hierarchies, the Whites grew Circle of Hope for the next generation of Jesus freaks, building, Rod wrote, "an outpost of his counter rebellion against all the coercion going on in the name of Jesus." Circle, as members called it, attracted all sorts of people—Quakers, Jews, atheists, the occasional Satan worshipper—but mostly it grew into an off-ramp for evangelical Christians fleeing their childhood churches.

Although Rod and Gwen disliked all labels, including the word "church," Circle had, by the time I encountered it, grown into four thriving congregations: three in Philadelphia and one in New Jersey. Rod White had ostensibly stepped away from running the day-to-day. He hated the word "retired," however, so instead he called himself the "development pastor," an informal advisor to the four pastors who had inherited leadership. Ben White, thirty-six when I met him in 2019 and the youngest, by minutes, of Rod and Gwen's four sons, shepherded the smallest and poorest congregation, which met in a former firehouse in Camden County, New Jersey. Julie Hoke, forty-one, and raised in rural Lancaster, Pennsylvania, in a missionary family, pastored a group of young professionals in the historic northwestern Philadelphia neighborhood of Germantown, where Protestants have been dunking new believers in the Wissahickon Creek since Christmas 1723. Rachel Sensenig, forty-two and the first woman to pastor one of Circle's four congregations, had inherited Rod's original crew in South Philly and continued to grow it into something of her own. Jonny Rashid, a thirty-three-year-old Egyptian American, and the only pastor of color, led the congregation in Fishtown, a North Philadelphia enclave of rapidly gentrifying hip.

At one of their Monday-morning pastors' meetings in 2019, I asked Jonny, Julie, Rachel, and Ben if I could immerse myself in their lives as a reporter to follow a group of people attempting to live with Christ at the center of all things. With varying degrees of enthusiasm, they said yes, in the hope that sharing their story might inspire others. Ben, Julie, Rachel, and Jonny also believed in being led by the Holy Spirit. Perhaps my arrival, they reasoned, would mark a new, more expansive direction for the church and allow their message to reach the world. For me, this bright and funny band of Jesus followers served as a microcosm of the radical evangelical movement, which, in its real-life application, promised not only to reclaim the moral heart of evangelicalism but also to serve as Christianity's last, best shot at remaining relevant.

However, as a result of the dislocation caused by the coronavirus pandemic and the crisis of police brutality, a struggle began over privilege and power. Instead of focusing outward on healing the world, as

Jesus called his followers to do, the pastors, and the church, turned in on themselves. Over the next four years, I witnessed the pastors shepherd their beloved community through the most controversial issues of our times. Circle of Hope, once formed of egalitarian ideals and a utopian vision, started to come apart. Amid f-bombs and exegetical arguments, the pastors sparred over the values they'd once shared: who belonged, what beliefs and behaviors could be tolerated, and what Jesus really meant when he called his disciples to love.

PROLOGUE

Ben White was a committed pacifist, but on this July morning in 2021 in South Philadelphia, he thrummed with rage. His beloved and visionary parents were about to be cast out of the community they'd spent their lives building. And he didn't understand why.

"So you're saying it's either you or them," Ben said, glowering at his fellow pastors, who until recently he'd considered to be among his closest friends.

Rachel Sensenig, the eldest and a kind of big sister, leaned forward to listen. Before her, on an open laptop, Julie Hoke was joining the emergency Zoom meeting from her parents' cabin in the Pennsylvania woods. Julie's round face, unadorned, kept glitching, as if her terrible rural internet service mirrored a spiritual disconnect among the four. The final pastor, Jonny Rashid, glanced up from his phone as Ben demanded to know what his parents, Rod and Gwen White, had done wrong.

There was no hint of scandal, no rumor of sexual or financial abuse. (The Whites cared little about money and were independently well-off.) Yet Circle of Hope seemed to be turning against them—"acting as if my parents are a problem to be solved," Ben muttered.

"Every single ethical norm and practice in Christianity says that what Rod did was wrong," Jonny argued. "It's sowing seeds of discord," he explained, a sin according to the Bible's book of Proverbs.

"That's just sanctimonious bullshit, man!" Ben replied.

Rachel slumped at the table's far side. She was tired of their arguing. "This feels like a real masculine power struggle," she offered, a bid for "top dog power." "I really do think you guys need to go have a couple beers."

Ben and Jonny didn't seem to hear her.

Hanging above them, unanswered, was the question of whether the church could survive.

"We need to have a reckoning, to find out who's in the church and who's not," Ben told the other pastors. "I won't kill this church, because it's my whole life, but I could. All I have to do is quit."

Now when Jesus saw the crowds, he went up on a mountainside and sat down. His disciples came to him, and he began to speak and he began to teach them. He said:

PART I

I

BEN

"Blessed are the peacemakers."
—MATTHEW 5:9

Ben White surveyed the darkened strip malls of southern New Jersey through the windshield of his ten-year-old red Prius. Up and down Route 130, scant light shone from the chain stores managing to stay afloat, mostly chicken joints and Family Dollar stores. Many of these strip malls were teetering toward bankruptcy. The post-industrial wasteland of 2020 depressed Ben, who'd been leading Circle of Hope's New Jersey outpost since 2015. Devoting themselves to following Jesus and stripping away the evils of American capitalism, church members called South Jersey "the ruins of empire." Ben hadn't been thrilled to pastor here. He'd wanted to travel afar for the Lord, as an explorer of both interior and exterior landscapes. The belly of his right calf bore a blue tattoo of Reepicheep, a mouse in C. S. Lewis's series The Chronicles of Narnia, with a line of lullaby that Reepicheep's mother sings to him: *There is the utter east*—a call Ben heard to "the undiscovered places of the soul."

Still, Ben had thrown himself into bringing young people into the New Jersey Circle. Cultivating a skater-pastor vibe, the six-foot-four pastor adopted Vans, a hoodie, and a flat-brimmed baseball cap, and struck up a partnership with Kids Alley, a local children's ministry evangelizing out of a van. On Friday nights, he took a small group of teenagers out for pizza. He talked to them about Jesus and personal debt. Inspired by a local evangelist, he trawled a local community college campus, holding up a sign that read, TELL ME YOUR STORY. He was kicked off that campus for proselytizing, so Ben enrolled as a student and redoubled his efforts, inviting people to his church, which occupied a repurposed firehouse along Marlton Pike, a major South Jersey throughway.

The squat yellow building, with four garage doors for long-gone fire engines, came strapped with a $1,200-a-month mortgage, a significant sum for its congregation of one hundred working people. Marlton Pike was the most politically mixed of Circle of Hope's four congregations. Unlike Fishtown, where Jonny Rashid's intellectual band met in a former dentist's office, or Germantown, where Julie Hoke's progressive professionals rented space on Sundays in a Presbyterian church, South Jersey, politically, was bright purple with pockets of red. A handful of people in Ben's congregation loaded pallets in Amazon warehouses and listened to Jordan Peterson, the Canadian psychologist and critic of political correctness. Some had voted for Trump, whom Ben loathed.

But Ben viewed his family's church as beyond politics. In their effort to build the Kingdom of Heaven on Earth, worldly identities, such as conservative and liberal, didn't apply. Circle's radical vision transcended all such markers. In an increasingly fractured world, this aspiration toward unity was a thrilling ideal, and for Ben, it was possible only through Jesus.

Calling himself "evangelical with a lowercase *e*," Ben believed there was one path to salvation. "If it ain't Jesus, it won't save you," as he put it. To him, Circle's mission was clear: "Bringing people to Jesus is our primary goal." Ben also believed in a total commitment to peace. He was an Anabaptist, a member of a five-hundred-year-old Protestant sect to which some two million Christians worldwide belong, including those at Circle of Hope. Anabaptism had, from the start, called for reform. It was born out of the Radical Reformation, a reaction against the corruption of the Catholic Church. Anabaptists insisted only adults could be baptized: those who could make a conscious decision to follow the Lord and demonstrate their commitment to "non-conformity with the world." For this, thousands were persecuted and put to death during the sixteenth and seventeenth centuries. Anabaptists called execution by drowning "the Third Baptism."

For Ben, as for his parents, there was a clear distinction between the radical social reordering Jesus commanded and secular politics. Political protests, including those for the progressive causes Ben agreed with, could get in the way of following Jesus. "'Social justice church' is a brand I've always had misgivings about," Ben said one afternoon in early 2020. He was taking a break from weed-whacking around the firehouse church. Over two dozen years, he'd watched so many fellow Jesus followers drift away from Circle of Hope when their commitment to a cause competed with their commitment to Jesus.

"There's a Venn diagram of the life of faith and the faith of social justice," Ben added. "They're the same until they're different." Herein lay the conundrum. At Circle of Hope, building the Kingdom of Heaven on Earth *required* addressing the world's woes. Being in the world but not of it, as the Bible commanded, meant striking a difficult balance between separateness and engagement. Anabaptists didn't retreat from the world, Ben argued—they showed up at their warehouse jobs at Amazon, Foot Locker, and Nabisco, and served as living examples of Jesus's love. "We're invasive separatists," Ben said. "We're different, in-your-face." Referring to Paul's letter to the Philippians, he said that Anabaptists were called to "shine like lights in a crooked and corrupt generation."

. . .

Ben had always wanted to be a pastor. His mom, Gwen, liked to tell the story of her four-year-old son climbing onto a stool to preach his first babbling sermon at the music stand his father used as a lectern. Unlike the vast number of pastor's kids who resented the strictures of childhood church, Ben relished the shirtless freedom of growing up among Jesus freaks, who established some six hundred peace communes across the United States in the 1970s and '80s as part of the larger Jesus movement. "The counterculture got saved, and they brought their weirdness to Christianity," Ben said. "It was an awakening, a real revival, even if it was a revival for white hippies."

Both Rod and Gwen grew up in 1950s Southern California families who weren't particularly visionary or spiritual. Rod's parents didn't go to church but dropped him off with his sister at a local Baptist congregation for Sunday school, where Rod recalled first feeling the overwhelming presence of Jesus when he was five. Committed to church from then on, he began to catch rides with a kindly elderly lady in her Cadillac. Gwen was sixteen when she first attended Young Life, an evangelical organization that ran youth clubs, sing-alongs, and cookouts around the United States to encourage teens like Gwen to find and follow Jesus. Young Life had its own peer strategy.

"Go find the quarterback, the popular kid," as Gwen put it. "Try to convert that kid. They'll bring a ton of kids along." One afternoon, she joined such a throng outside an overflowing municipal building in Riverside. Standing on tiptoe, she peeked into a window. "On that lawn, I heard that Jesus loved me, and I had never heard that anyone loved me," she said.

Young Life was part of "the new evangelical movement," an ambitious twentieth-century push to reach America with the gospel. Billy Graham, known as "the Protestant pope," feared that Christianity was losing its influence in the United States. He and other evangelical pastors called for a new era of engagement: a revival. Graham's crusades—evangelistic campaigns that were held at stadiums and other large venues and featured both preaching and music—called people forward to give their lives to Christ; attendees included the likes of Johnny Cash, Bob Dylan, and the budding theologian Elaine Pagels. The reach of Graham and other "new evangelicals" would alter American culture and politics. (Graham advised every U.S. president from Truman to Obama.) The new evangelicals created powerful organizations and media outlets, including the National Association of Evangelicals and *Christianity Today*, along with Fuller Theological Seminary in Pasadena, California, which

Rod attended, and Young Life, the youth organization where Gwen found Jesus.

Gwen's conversion experience on the municipal lawn in Riverside, California, transformed every aspect of a childhood marked by loneliness and disappointment. "Coming to Christ blew the doors off my life," Gwen said. A powerful swimmer, she'd missed the 1968 Olympic trials by one one-hundredth of a second. The urgency of sharing her absolute faith in Jesus transformed Gwen's despair into love. She marched against Vietnam and volunteered at a health clinic with Spanish-speaking patients. From a distance, with her cutoff dungarees and sun-bleached hair, she might've appeared as any hippie activist, but Gwen's purpose was spiritual, not political, which she felt was very different. By the early 1970s, college campuses were awash with Jesus freaks, many of whom, including Rod and Gwen, looked like free-love radicals but were in fact enacting what they believed to be an ancient form of rebellion. "We rarely got sucked into the social left," Gwen said. "Because we always wanted to be about Jesus."

When Rod and Gwen met at a Jesus event in 1974 as undergraduates at the University of California, Riverside, Rod invited Gwen to a Bible study in his apartment. Within fifteen minutes, Gwen grew enamored by the ethereal young man with flowing hair and an oversized wooden cross slung around his delicate neck. The next week, she brought homemade cookies. Listening to Rod spin his "grandiose plans to change the fabric of the church," Gwen fell hard. Rod saw evangelization as "just like a sport." He believed the world was due for a new revival, which he would help lead. To prepare, he studied the First Great Awakening, the eighteenth-century evangelical movement that swept the American colonies. He wrote his thesis on one of its leaders, George Whitefield, a fiery Anglican orator. Meanwhile, Rod's Bible study grew so popular that he and his roommates rented a neighboring apartment to accommodate a startling crowd of one hundred students, with Gwen at its center as an eloquent and eager participant.

Falling in love with each other and with Jesus, the two drove around

Riverside. When they spotted Christian fish stickers on other beat-up cars, Rod and Gwen held up their right index fingers, the Jesus freak code that Christ was the "one way" to peace. This was the message of exclusive salvation—that only through Jesus could anyone reach heaven—which Billy Graham and the new evangelicals championed. Graham embraced the Jesus freaks, and they loved Graham. When Graham served as grand marshal of the Rose Parade, beaming Jesus freaks raised their index fingers as his float glided past.

. . .

The 1980s marked a sea change in the image of American evangelicals. With the election of Ronald Reagan, an outspoken Republican, the roomier, soft-spoken evangelicalism of Jimmy Carter faded from view. Over the next forty years, as the term "evangelical" grew more aligned with the Republican Party, the values the Whites lived by came to represent a powerful fracture within the larger faith. Rod called Reagan "the devil," and he believed that Reagan could be the Antichrist, come to signal the Apocalypse. "This could literally be the end-times," Rod said. It wasn't Reagan's conservatism they reacted against; it was his embrace of capitalism in the name of Christianity. "It's the worst capitalist takeover of the system, and he's preaching it like it's gospel," Rod said. To Rod, this was idolatry: "Nancy was doing his horoscope, while he's trying to be a Christian."

For Rod and Gwen, battling the forces of evil didn't mean simply backing progressive political causes. Jesus was calling for a far more radical transformation of society. "Jesus didn't come to earth to dismantle the Roman Empire," Gwen liked to say. "He came to build the Kingdom of Heaven on Earth."

This desire to transcend worldly politics was inspiring but complicated. Although Jesus freaks reflected hippie counterculture, they were also the spiritual children of the new evangelicals, which was, at its core, a fundamentalist movement upholding traditional social values and gender roles. Gwen was as gifted a preacher as Rod. However, as a woman, she was discouraged from preaching and teaching theology at Young Life. Instead, when Gwen married Rod, she taught public school to pay Rod's way through Fuller Theological Seminary in Pasadena. After he graduated, he became a youth pastor at a Baptist church in Riverside, a city of 170,000 about fifty miles east of Los Angeles. Gwen helped him grow the youth group from a handful of kids to over one hundred. Despite Gwen's prodigious gifts with pastoring teens, the head pastor ignored her. He preached from the pulpit about a woman's submission.

"This isn't Jesus," Gwen raged to herself and to Rod. Jesus was love, liberation, and freedom—not female servitude. So they started their own Christ-centered commune. In 1979, Rod and Gwen purchased the Flintstone House, their name for the gloppy brown ranch they bought, with a loan from Gwen's dad, for less than $100,000. (Although Gwen didn't know it until her dad died, she was a soda-bottle heiress; her family had made a small fortune selling their glass bottle company to a large corporation.) On their commune, Rod, then twenty-five, became the visionary leader. Gwen, a year older, organized volleyball matches and swam in their black-bottomed pool, where, over the next several years, Rod also baptized the two dozen members of the radical community they named the Sierra Street Household.

Living according to the Bible's book of Acts and its account of Jesus's early followers, who renounced their worldly possessions to rid themselves of ties to the Roman Empire, Rod dispensed the salary he received as a youth pastor into a common purse, and Gwen cooked communal dinners called Love Feasts, which the Bible refers to (in Jude 1:12) as meals that Jesus's disciples shared with one another. Each year on April 1, they reviewed the principles that bound them to one another and to God and posted them on the fridge.

Many other Jesus communes had no affiliation with a church, but Rod was attracted to the idea of radical reform and wanted to be part of a larger collective, so he ordered a directory of Anabaptist churches and organizations in Southern California and wrote to several. A bishop with the Brethren in Christ (BIC), a denomination of some twenty thousand people that was founded in Pennsylvania in the 1700s and is one of the oldest in the United States, wrote back.

"Before too long, we had the bishop in our living room," Rod said. Observing their statement of formation, their Love Feasts, and their common purse firsthand, the bishop noted to Rod that the Sierra Street Household reminded him of the book of Acts. Rod and Gwen were tickled. The Baptist church where Rod had been serving as youth pastor had told them these same practices were communism. So the Sierra Street Household joined the BIC.

Some of their efforts to follow Scripture were wonderfully zany. To wrest the death and resurrection of Jesus away from both pagan fertility rituals and Hallmark, they outlawed Easter egg hunts. Gwen, who'd given birth to four rambunctious boys in four years, gathered three-year-old Ben and his fraternal twin, Joel; sensitive Luke, five; and Jacob, who at six was already their sharp-eyed leader. She smashed chocolate Easter bunnies with a meat tenderizer and ripped the heads off marshmallow Peeps, while the boys gleefully gobbled the ruined remnants of consumer culture. She also revived a medieval Christian tradition of baking hot cross buns for Easter sunrise, which they tore to represent the breaking of the cross and Jesus's victory over death.

Life on the commune, however, wasn't all swimming and smashing hollow chocolate bunnies. For Gwen, some aspects of building a Jesus-centered utopia proved harder. By the late 1980s, Gwen, who did most of the cooking and caring for people as a spiritual mother, was desperate for a change. Rod asked the Sierra Street Household members for permission to draw on the common purse to take Gwen to Palm Springs, where the Whites set a different course for their marriage and mission. God was calling them on a new adventure. Ben was eight years old when the Whites announced they were quitting communal life in California. Their departure signaled the end of blissful formative years spent tooling around the neighborhood on bikes with his three tow-headed brothers. For Ben, leaving the freedoms of Southern California would always mark an exit from paradise.

In 1991, the Whites headed east to Waynesboro, a former factory town in Central Pennsylvania two miles north of the Mason-Dixon Line, where the Brethren in Christ needed a pastor for a 175-year-old church. For the next four years, the Whites were content, although sometimes, given their SoCal Jesus-freak ways, Rod and Gwen chafed against the culture. America was ascendant. *Wall Street* and Gordon Gekko were hot; *Hair* and hippies were not. Jesus freaks had vanished from the public eye. Locals noted when Rod made the mistake of unwittingly mowing his lawn on a Sunday, the day of rest, wearing only shorts. They were also slightly scandalized when Gwen drove alone to Washington, D.C.

The Whites' eldest, Jacob, turning thirteen, refused to join the Boys' Brigade, the Christian version of the Boy Scouts; during church, he parsed Rod's sermons, scribbling close readings and and handing them down the pew to a highly intelligent girl his age named Aubrey, whom he would eventually marry. Ben didn't like Waynesboro much; he, too, bumped up against its senseless regulations, including enforcements against jaywalking even when no cars were around.

Within several years, Rod and Gwen were ready to move on from Central Pennsylvania. The American church was in the throes of a crisis—"a mass exodus of eighteen-to-thirty-five-year-olds," as Gwen put it. Anabaptists, like most Protestants, were scrambling to fill their pews, which had been emptying since the 1950s. At the dawn of the twenty-first century, the BIC began to abandon its foundational ideal of rejecting the world. To survive, they needed more people, and they were in cities. Ever since Anabaptism had arrived in North America during the 1600s with European settlers, it had remained largely rural, with the exception of service workers, who, fulfilling Jesus's call in the Sermon on the Mount, traveled to cities to work among the poor. Yet, by the nineties, urban decay had exposed the underbelly of American capitalism. God's people were suffering from the disease of poverty.

This call to save the cities coincided with a new call to save the church. Rod and Gwen were determined to do both. They would "build the church for the next generation."

At a 1994 BIC conference, the Whites leapt at the chance to plant a church in a city outside of the United States. They explored options in Kingston, Jamaica; Lagos, Nigeria; and Durban, South Africa. But Jacob, sixteen, the outspoken critic, refused to leave the country, so the Whites explored options closer to home in the Bronx and Philadelphia. Once Gwen determined that public schools were abysmal in the Bronx, the Whites drove three hours from Waynesboro to check out Philadelphia, one of the most racially divided and poorest cities in America.

Heading east along the Pennsylvania Turnpike, Rod and Gwen traded names for their new church. They avoided "church" so as not to scare away the very young people they wanted to attract. Gwen landed first on the word "hope." If other churches were offering "shame," then they'd do the opposite. "Hope was the missing ingredient," Gwen said. Then "circle" arrived on her tongue. "It's a Circle of Hope. That's what we want to offer. That's what we think God wants to offer the world."

. . .

The Whites chose Philadelphia, and, in 1995, as they settled in, Rod set about wandering the aisles of Tower Records, striking up conversations. By a rack of local publications, he spotted a zine about Christian music, tracked down its creators at nearby Drexel University, and invited them to check out his and Gwen's very different vision of church. For too long, American churches had been hotbeds of hypocrisy and abuse, Rod wrote in a self-published volume, *A Circle of Hope: Jesus at Work Among the Next Generation of the Church*. "People," he continued, "have been dominated, abused, bamboozled, threatened and diminished in church for ages." Winning them back was a competitive business: "We are determined to give them a chance to meet Jesus before some other 'missionary' wins them to the other 'gospels' hunting them down."

The Whites' effort benefited from a spirit already afoot in Philadelphia, where the nascent movement born of the Jesus freaks and galvanized in reaction against the religious right thrived. Philadelphia's self-described radical evangelicals, who'd started a magazine called *The Other Side*, were holding conferences and organizing rallies and concerts reminiscent of the Jesus freaks. The Jesus movement had once numbered in the millions, but many had fallen away and no one knew how many like-minded believers were affiliated with this band of boomers, Gen Xers, and, soon, disaffected millennials confronting the world's inequities in the streets of their cities and on their computer screens.

The same year the Whites began to plant Circle of Hope, Philadelphia's radical evangelical leaders helped launch the Call to Renewal, a nationwide revival targeting American cities. Tony Campolo, a pastor and sociologist at Eastern University, and Ronald Sider, who taught at Messiah University's Philadelphia campus and authored *Rich Christians in an Age of Hunger*, which sold 400,000 copies and was published in nine languages, joined Jim Wallis, the founder of *Sojourners* magazine, in rallying young Christians to engage in social justice.

The Call to Renewal, however, wasn't about planting churches. It marked a deliberate effort to contest the growing influence of the religious right among young people by bringing students to postindustrial cities like Philadelphia and Pittsburgh to live and work communally on economic, racial, and environmental injustice. Mission Year, which began in 1999 as part of this reawakening, funneled more than 1,200 young evangelicals from around America to underserved neighborhoods in cities, exposing them to the realities of poverty and solidarity as part of fulfilling Jesus's commandments "Love the Lord your God with all your heart" and "Love your neighbor as yourself." Mission Year was a lived experiment, a *Real World* for young Christians, that led many to shed their parents' politics and commit their lives to justice. Many took up urban farming. By the early 2000s, more than one thousand vacant lots in Philadelphia were transformed into vegetable and flower gardens.

. . .

In the Philadelphia neighborhood known as Center City, Rod rented a raw space at Tenth and Locust. Outside, a large green sign read UNITED FOOD MARKET. Inside, on the second floor, Rod established Circle of Hope's first "rebel outpost," as he called it; the cavernous space was almost deliberately ugly, its plainness a poke in the eye to the pomp of megachurches, and a reminder that a church was about not a building, but people. One of Circle's core teachings held, "The church is not a 'thing' that does things; it is not a building. We are the church and we support one another as Jesus expresses himself through us."

In 1996, on Palm Sunday, Rod led Circle's first official worship meeting with some fifty young people, Gwen, and their four boys. Instead of high-production-value lighting and flat-screen TVs, the meeting consisted simply of Rod, in jeans, speaking at the music stand he'd adopted as his lectern. He didn't use the word "sermon," which implied a formality and preachiness he avoided. Instead, he invited questions and comments, which he called talkback. He welcomed disruption, provocative thinking, and participation. This informal call-and-response was designed to break down hierarchy. Worship wasn't a presentation; it was an experience. For the Whites, the purpose of church was to build a beloved community of those who might disagree about all kinds of particularities but who shared a desire to worship the Lord together and to live according to the tenets of Scripture. Within nine months, they'd grown to a group of one hundred souls climbing the wooden stairs to worship on Sundays.

This flourishing was no accident. It was part of a deliberate strategy developed by the church growth movement, whose tactics Rod had studied at Fuller. Blending corporate marketing with evangelizing, the church growth movement taught young pastors and missionaries how to plant churches as if they were businesses. This spurred a lucrative network of conferences and books, and led to the founding of megachurches and the rise of celebrity pastors, including Rick Warren, founder of the Saddleback Church; John Wimber, a founding leader of the Vineyard Movement; and Bill Hybels, founder of Willow Creek Community Church. Pastors became entrepreneurs, implementing church growth movement strategies to grow churches so large and all-encompassing that they fea-tured travel agencies, dating services, and coffee bars.

One of the most important strategies involved reaching young peo-ple through music, as the Jesus freaks had done so successfully. As part of its spiritual marketing, Circle became home to an alternative music scene, and sometimes the rock show threatened to overpower preach-ing of the Word, which irritated Gwen as a typical display of maleness. During worship, Ben relished being in the midst of it all, sitting on the floor of the raw space, changing transparencies for an overhead projector so that newcomers could read the lyrics and sing along with the songs that Circle's talented musicians and artists wrote themselves, refashioning the poems of Wendell Berry, Mary Oliver, bell hooks, and Rumi (to the Whites' consternation, since Rumi was a Muslim, not a Christian).

Pooh-poohing the idea of liturgy, which Rod and Gwen believed could too easily become rote and stale, they threw out the standard series of scriptural readings of the liturgical calendar. Circle did follow the Christian seasons, including Advent, Lent, and Pentecost, to remind themselves they were part of an ancient tradition.

Yet Circle was undeniably modern. Rod dubbed this the *Friends* model of church planting: share your life in Jesus with a group of strang-ers, and they become your family. At Circle, young people knit their lives together—supporting one another's businesses, forming loose col-lectives to babysit one another's kids, moving into shared houses—all out of a common commitment to love Jesus in every aspect of their lives. Many held jobs as social workers, public school teachers, and health-care professionals, eventually working on the front lines of the HIV and opioid epidemics. All of these seemingly secular helping pro-fessions were, above all, ways to build the Kingdom of Heaven on Earth.

. . .

Among the Victorian homes of West Philadelphia's Spruce Hill neigh-borhood, the Whites purchased a rambling twin with eight bedrooms, original crown molding, and wainscoting. In the backyard, they installed a hot tub that doubled as a vessel for backyard baptisms. In 1995, Gwen went back to school to become a therapist, enrolling in a master's program at Eastern University in psychology and spirituality. On the fridge, she and Rod posted a saying: "The church is the family business." This reflected a teaching at Circle: "Any believer who is not doing their part in the 'family business' of redeeming the world is missing the point of their ongoing existence." Living in community and sharing resources of time, money, labor, and shelter required total commitment from not only Rod and Gwen but also all four of their sons. The Whites invited another Anabaptist family to live with them. They also invited drug users to move in, as long as they didn't shoot up in the house, and they allowed unhoused people to collect mail at their address. It wasn't a sense of service or Christian duty that motivated the Whites. "We were just loving them," Ben said. Although some of Gwen's jewelry went missing, the boys took their housemates in stride. "No one was ever high in the house," Ben said later, "and there weren't any needles."

For Ben, life as a white twelve-year-old pacifist in predominantly Black West Philly proved difficult. Ben and Joel were bullied on their walks to school, with Joel having an egg cracked over his head and Ben running as fast as he could to protect his cardboard model of mitochondria for a science project. The boys sought the protection of their mother, who came onto the porch and invited their tormentors inside. Ben felt put on a path "to be a nerd for the rest of his life."

Joel, the reserved twin, was traumatized. "We were made fun of and randomly punched in the face because we were white," he said. "I became afraid of young Black men, and found people in general dangerous."

Jacob and Luke, who were large and broad, tried to protect Ben and Joel. "I didn't want them to be the punks," Jacob said.

Ben turned the other cheek. "What we should've done is kicked the crap out of those guys," he later said. Instead, teenage Ben sought solace

and belonging among the skaters and punk rockers who were coming
to Circle on Sunday nights to jam.

. . .

The basic building block of Circle of Hope was a "cell," a small group
of up to ten people. Rod adopted the cell model from a church growth
strategy already popular in South Korea. Yoido Full Gospel Church, in
the South Korean capital, Seoul, was a cell-based megachurch hosting roughly 200,000 people every Sunday. With 800,000 worshippers,
Yoido was also the largest congregation in the world. Rod saw each cell
as a microchurch, and by the early 2000s, Circle's dozens of cells were
meeting all over the region in someone's home or dorm room, or at a
dive bar or a skate park. You didn't have to belong to Circle of Hope
to join, so cells attracted a wide range of the spiritually curious. Most
members, however, reflected the church's core demographic: Gen Xers
and millennials who'd been hurt by organized religion or who rejected
right-wing politics, and were seeking more authentic ways to follow
Jesus.

Cells were designed to cross boundaries of neighborhood, age, social class, and race. Rod wanted people to pay no attention to identity
markers that seemed to separate them, in favor of transcending their
narrow confines. "Identity is my bugbear," Rod said. (To define how
Christians were both global and local, Rod also used the portmanteau
word "glocal.") Cell meetings revolved around a question posed by John
Wesley, the eighteenth-century evangelist whose work led to today's
United Methodist Church: How is it with your soul? The responses
broke people open. In one week, in a single cell, a former member of
a Christian cult in South Korea shared the tale of her escape, a young
man raised in a Hindu household recounted seeing Jesus on a hillside in
India, a social worker shared about burnout, and a college student spun
through her fears about failing her upcoming finals.

Cells sparked friendships and conversations among people who wouldn't ordinarily mix. They read the Bible together and bonded around money, work, relationships, or parenting, all through the lens of how Jesus was appearing, or not appearing, in their lives. "It's like being in therapy with Jesus," a member of Circle's South Philly congregation said. As a general practice, every cell left an empty chair, to symbolize a space left open for the next person. The chair was a physical manifestation of Circle's principle that "the church exists for those yet to join."

Once a cell expanded beyond ten, it divided so that the membership could multiply, growing the church and spreading the love of Jesus. Rod intended for congregations to do the same, swarming like bees until they grew to two hundred people. Then forty would "hive off" around a new pastor, selected from among the members to plant a new Circle colony in another ailing neighborhood.

Circle of Hope was flourishing in other ways that served Philadelphia, New Jersey, and Jesus. From the beginning, Rod and Gwen maintained that being part of the church went far beyond worship on Sundays. "You can't have a new church in Philadelphia unless you demonstrate the gospel," Rod said. If you were just naming the world's problems while doing nothing about them, he explained, no one would believe you had anything to offer. To actually change the fabric of the city, and address racial inequity, the Whites started Circle Venture, a nonprofit arm of the church that helped fund worthy start-ups: good businesses that created jobs and contributed to the neighborhood.

The most successful was Circle Thrift, a secondhand store that bought and sold almost everything, including gold, and employed people coming out of prison. Circle Thrift offered necessary items like pots and pans for low prices, or sometimes for free. To redistribute wealth and goods, it hosted a baby and kids' goods exchange, where parents could pick up breast pumps, glass bottles, organic swaddles, and feminist board books, as well as clothes and cribs. Though repeatedly held up at gunpoint, Circle Thrift eventually became so profitable that it funded about 20 percent of the church's budget. However, it sent most of its earnings to the Mennonite Central Committee, a prominent aid and relief organization within the Anabaptist community.

Despite his engagement in social justice, Rod remained vigilant about the spread of political activism at Circle, which he likened to an "infection." He considered himself an activist, but he also taught the risks of not keeping Jesus at the center of one's life. To balance activism and devotion, Rod and Gwen created "compassion teams," which members led out of their own energies and interests. By 2015, these teams included Circle Mobilizing Because Black Lives Matter, which hosted book groups and teach-ins and supported a local participatory defense hub, preparing defendants for court. Circle Mobilizing Because Black Lives Matter redistributed money to Black members of their congregations as a form of reparations, raised tens of thousands of dollars for the Philadelphia Community Bail Fund, and helped Black students start savings accounts. Sustainability and climate experts formed the Watershed Discipleship Team, which hosted workshops with names like "Jesus and Carbon." Others collected food, helped run Mutual Aid in South Jersey, and lobbied the city council to allocate $20 million to affordable housing. One group, calling themselves "financial astronauts," created a "debt annihilation team." Beginning with $10,000 from Circle of Hope, the team members paid down one another's debt collectively. "The currency wasn't money," Ben said. "It was love."

. . .

Circle of Hope also encouraged abstinence, and Ben vowed to remain a virgin until marriage. He didn't lecture his fellow teens at school on the subject, however. He stuck to the dangers of materialism. "I wasn't telling my friends not to have sex," Ben said. "I was telling them not to buy Nikes." Ben met his first girlfriend, Gwyneth, in tenth-grade math class and was totally smitten. By the time they'd finished high school, Ben and Gwyneth had been dating for five years. Deeply in love, Ben knew that he wanted to spend his life with her. But Gwyneth was Jewish, and Ben believed in the biblical injunction to marry a Christian, to be "equally yoked" to the Lord.

During the summer of 2001, following his high school graduation,

Ben was baptized. He waded into the Atlantic Ocean, and Rod dunked him under the waves three times, for the Father, the Son, and the Holy Spirit. Ben emerged salty, sopping, and "ready to do this Jesus thing for real," he said. Soon after, he tried to break up with Gwyneth, but Ben couldn't stand their being apart. A few months later they got back together. Their future remained uncertain. Ben enrolled in Eastern University, a thriving locus of next-generation Jesus followers. Eastern also offered Ben and Joel free tuition, since their mother, who'd graduated from the university's counseling and spirituality program, was teaching psychology there. Ben didn't really need the money; he and his brothers each had about $80,000 in a college fund, from Gwen's family. (Gwen eventually inherited half of a $3 million trust, along with $450,000 in cash.)

Yet Ben, like his parents, lived frugally as part of a commitment to Christ. His role model was one recent graduate, Shane Claiborne, a soft-spoken and bespectacled boy from East Tennessee and a member of Circle of Hope. Claiborne, who'd grown up in a world of right-wing evangelicalism, had renounced his childhood culture and beliefs to follow Jesus, becoming a rising superstar among radical evangelicals. In 1995, Claiborne had occupied St. Ed's—an abandoned Catholic church in Philadelphia—in solidarity with homeless mothers squatting there. Claiborne started the Youth Against Complacency and Homelessness Today (YACHT) club, along with dozens of Eastern students, which Ben joined as soon as he arrived.

During Ben's first week at Eastern, the attacks of September 11, 2001, brought the divisions among evangelicals into sharp relief. Ben listened in horror as his fellow students and Christians called for the head of Osama bin Laden, reprisals against the Taliban members who were harboring him, and against Muslims in general. "Jesus said love your enemies," Ben noted. "No one is even considering this." Since the 1960s and '70s, Anabaptists had traveled as peace workers to war zones in Colombia, Sri Lanka, Guatemala, Bosnia, Chechnya, Chiapas, the Great Lakes region of Africa, and Palestine, where they joined Christian

Peacemaker teams sponsored by the Brethren in Christ, among other denominations. This work also marked a shift in Anabaptist peace theology away from the tradition of separatism. During the 1990–91 Gulf War, Gwen had traveled to Baghdad, Iraq, to join Christian Peacemakers for Thanksgiving. Following 9/11, Shane Claiborne was heading to Afghanistan and later to Iraq to serve as a human shield and to march for peace alongside Afghans.

Protesting alongside other Jesus followers in Philadelphia, Ben slept on the sidewalk in solidarity with Afghan victims of U.S. airstrikes. At Eastern, he also began his prayer life in earnest, waking early and heading to the pond to befriend hostile geese—their hissing a stand-in for the hard-line students who supported America's wars. In early 2003, in the lead-up to the U.S. invasion of Iraq, Ben joined other peace protesters to surround a federal building in Philadelphia, chanting "No business as usual!" As Ben was being arrested, he saw his mom looking on proudly. With George W. Bush almost certain to be reelected, Ben was disgusted with American Christians. He decided to drop out of college and leave the United States. True transformation lay beyond the reach of electoral politics.

"We could change the laws, but we actually needed people to be transformed," he said. "The revolution I wanted to be part of was in the church." Ben found a missionary gig in the hills of Mexico City at a church started by American Mennonites, a branch of Anabaptists. His Spanish was iffy, and he lived with the pastor's impoverished family, sleeping on the floor and, to spare the family added expense, trying not to eat more than his hosts did. He'd envisioned a year in the streets among the poor, but he found himself with little to do. The other young American missionary he knew in Mexico City found a boyfriend and started going to parties, which Ben disdained; they weren't in Mexico to have fun. Mostly, he swept the driveway and memorized the practical precepts of the Sermon on the Mount, which began with the beatitudes—"Blessed are the poor in spirit, for theirs is the Kingdom of Heaven." These provide a how-to guide for Christians, but in particular

Anabaptists, who attempt to follow Jesus's teachings about peace and forgiveness in practical ways.

Ben had been following the Sermon on the Mount all his life. The teachings formed the foundation of Rod and Gwen's commune, as well as Circle of Hope. Ben's parents flew down to Mexico to visit him in the winter of 2003. Back home in Philadelphia, their young church was less than a decade old and already thriving, which was unusual since church plants so often fail. Circle of Hope had reached a church growth goal of three hundred members that year. It was time to expand. They were ready to raise up from among their like-minded community a new pastor who could take along forty members and hive off to create a new Circle colony. One evening, Ben took Rod up to the church roof to show him the view of the neighborhood of Villa de Cortés. Sitting in plastic chairs surrounded by a canopy of palm trees, Rod asked Ben to come home once he had finished his mission year and help him anchor the Center City congregation. Eventually, Ben would become a pastor at Circle of Hope, which Rod hoped to grow into a network of congregations.

Ben received this request not so much as an invitation from his dad, but as a commission from God: to complete his term in Mexico, return to Philadelphia to finish college, attend seminary, and join Circle of Hope as a pastor. Yet there remained the question of Gwyneth. Although she was attending a cell, Gwyneth was still Jewish. Ben longed for her to become a Christian, but he also worried that, through his love, he was pressuring her to convert. This was complicated, since Ben believed wholeheartedly he was called to help people give their lives to Jesus. At the same time, he knew that coercion was awful, wrong, and false. Finally, Gwyneth called Ben in Mexico to tell him that she'd become a Christian. "She is a follower of the Way!!!" he wrote in his journal. Months later, he finished his mission year and returned to Philadelphia, where he joined an intentional community of Eastern students near his parents' twin in West Philadelphia. He finished up college coursework and married Gwyneth in 2005.

Ben used part of his $80,000 trust fund to pay for their honeymoon and to purchase a fixer-upper in West Philly, where he and a friend ap-

plied for community grants to found a collective tool shed—the West
Philly Tool Library—buying a strap wrench and a basin wrench for
communal use in the neighborhood. Ben earned a full scholarship to
attend Princeton Theological Seminary, where several Circle of Hopers had also pursued their master of divinity degrees as precursors to
becoming pastors or teaching theology. Rod prized intelligence and
valued education as a tool of evangelization. "Leaders are readers," he
often said. Ben remained ambivalent. With its billion-dollar endow-
ment, the school reeked of American wealth and empire. He saw little
value in a Princeton diploma. "Fuck this, I don't need your piece of
paper," he said, flipping the bird at Princeton in his mind, refusing to
become "a widget in a church machine."

To graduate, however, Ben had to find an internship outside his
church, so he chose a hospice chaplaincy at Philadelphia's Thomas Jefferson University Hospital, a sprawling concrete complex in Center
City around the corner from Circle of Hope. On his first overnight solo
shift in December 2009, he woke to his pager summoning him to the
neonatal intensive care unit. The medical team was preparing to take a
baby off the ventilator. The child had been declared brain-dead three
weeks earlier. The mother was absent: she couldn't watch her baby be
detached from the machines that made his chest rise and fall, pumping
his heart and filling his lungs. So Ben and the medical professionals
bore witness as a nurse lifted the baby into her own arms. A resident
administered morphine and shut off the last of the life-support machines. Ben asked if he could offer a prayer. The resident nodded.

"You know suffering," he prayed to Jesus, recording his words later
in his journal. "You know death. We know you know this baby, and we
know that you are with him. Be with us now. Amen." When the baby's
heart stopped, two nurses filled a memory box with newborn hats,
swaddling blankets, and a stuffed Elmo.

One spoke about watching a baby die the week before. "I'm not
sure how much of this I can take," she said.

"This isn't exactly what you signed up for, huh?" Ben asked.

"No, it is," she said.

"Well, for what it's worth, what you are doing is really something beautiful and so ancient, you know?" he said.

She thanked him; he realized he was there, as a chaplain, to offer pastoral care not only to the dying, but also to health workers in need of support.

As the nurses swaddled the body, fading from pink to gray, Ben thought of the women who wrapped Jesus's shroud, preparing him for the tomb. "Can I touch him?" Ben asked. The nurses said yes, and he brushed the baby's lukewarm cheek with two fingers, whispering his name. Unsure of how the nurses would feel about the religious gesture, he attempted, in secret, to make the sign of the cross over his body. The nurses zipped the baby into a bag and started down to the basement morgue.

When Ben graduated from Princeton the following year, in 2010, he was eager to fulfill the invitation his dad had offered seven years earlier in Mexico: to pastor at Circle. But there was no full-time role available, so he took a paying job as a hospital chaplain at Jefferson. The night-to-night grew more familiar but not easier. Ben became more accustomed to children rushed in with bullets in their skulls, but he felt no less clumsy and raw. "I was mortified by some of what I said and did," he said. "Literally deathified."

Being a chaplain was mostly about approaching people during the hardest moments of their lives and asking, "Hey, would you like to talk to a stranger?" Often he was met with anger by those furious at God or who didn't believe and found his approach invasive. These unpredictable moments of humiliation sent Ben to the hospital chapel to pray and helped him find a well of inner resilience, which he viewed as a gift from God.

While Ben was working as a chaplain, Rod continued to grow the church. Circle had exploded from 100 members within its first year to 676 by the beginning of 2015. The network was expanding. Circle held worship in four, sometimes five, locations, and each week its some sixty cells met across more and more neighborhoods. But these business-minded notions of growth, which positioned pastors as salespeople attracting new converts, were sometimes at odds with Circle's anti-capitalist, anti-empire vision. Although Rod had little trouble leading amid tension and contradiction, he could be difficult to work for. As Circle grew and attempted different kinds of partnerships and models, more than twenty-three employees quit or were fired. Rod took this in stride, seeing it as the nature of Circle, a church built to welcome misfits and mess, as Jesus had. "Following the Spirit is risky business," one church teaching held.

Circle of Hope stood poised to break the "700 barrier," a church growth measure that Rod embraced for developing a medium-sized church into a large one. When church growth really kicked off, people began to define churches by their sizes to provide pastors with different strategies for each phase. Breaking the 700 barrier required shifting the structure of leadership. "We don't have time to sit in board meetings and argue about who is in charge," wrote Michael Fletcher, the creator of the 700 barrier concept, in his 2003 book, *Overcoming Barriers to Church Growth*. "We have a world to change!"

Rod was also ready to step away from leadership in 2015, planning to "titrate" himself out over the next five years. He called this new phase the Second Act. "Circle of Hope isn't going to be an empire," he said. "It's designed to be given away." After nineteen years at its center, Rod also wanted to end a pastor-led system so that power would be shared more widely among the volunteer teams. This was an admirable ideal that proved challenging to implement. From its inception, to highlight how Circle of Hope was exceptional—different—Rod had rejected the structures and organizational language typical of churches, in favor of developing his own vision.

Rod's vision took shape in a diagram of church polity that he called the Amoeba of Christ. (He rejected the term "organization chart" as too bureaucratic and fixed.) The Amoeba, which was a drawing of five concentric circles, was unfixed by design. Along the inner rings, Rod created six "core" teams to lead the church. "Capacity" team focused on church finances, the "compassion" team focused on activism, the "church-planting" team laid out a vision for growing the church, and "cell coordinators" were one or two people chosen by pastors in each congregation to be the pastor's right hand and to help train leaders of individual cells. At the center of the Amoeba, Rod created a team to advise the pastors; he called it the "leadership team core," and it was made up of one member from all the other teams. The final team consisted of the pastors themselves. In general, when the pastors talked about the "leadership team," they included all of the above, a rough two dozen people who functioned like very young elders.

The Amoeba was intended to be amorphous. It reflected Circle's countercultural principle: "We are living as a created organism, not creating a religious organization." If some aspect proved irrelevant, like a cause the compassion teams took on as activists, for instance, it had "the right to die," Rod wrote.

. . .

Pastors weren't intended to last forever, either. Circle had seen five pastors come and go by 2015. Soon, Ben, Julie, Rachel, and Jonny were meant to take over from Rod as he stepped into the role of development pastor, strategizing growth and advising the pastors. In theory, Rod's loose vision of teams moving together symbiotically was intended to be mutable and collective. In practice, the Amoeba of Christ obscured the reality that, despite his protests and stated desires, Circle still adhered to Rod's vision. This attempt to create a community without hierarchy could obscure how power really worked at Circle of Hope. It could be called a tyranny of structurelessness.

Ben was hoping to plant a fifth Circle of Hope in West Philadelphia, cell by cell. "The plan was that I build a kingdom of my own," he said. "That's the grandiosity of it: if you multiply cells, you make disciples." But drawing new followers was harder than it looked. "I suck at multiplying," he said. Maybe he was better at bringing Jesus to the dying than to the living. Finally, in 2015, the opportunity arose to pastor full-time at Circle of Hope in New Jersey. To listen to God and to pray for guidance, Ben went on a hiking retreat in the wilds of a state park along the Jersey Shore. Dropping his map and losing his way in the salt marshes, he saw that God was asking him to surrender his grand plans for elsewhere and to follow the path his father had already blazed—to become, in essence, "a bitch and heir to my dad's church."

2

JULIE

"Blessed are those who hunger and thirst for righteousness,
for they will be filled."
—MATTHEW 5:6

A plague of bedbugs made sheltering in their row home nearly unbearable for Julie Hoke, her husband Steve, and their two kids, Isaiah and Alliyah, eight and eleven. Feeling the bugs crawl on her skin was keeping Julie awake at night. She itched and tried not to scratch on camera when she joined Rachel, Jonny, and Ben for their first awkward attempt at virtual church on March 15, 2020. Until the coronavirus pandemic drove them online, forcing them to act as one congregation, each was accustomed to leading worship alone.

In a blaze of high energy, Jonny—bald, baby-faced, and clad in a tan twill suit—set the tone. "Tonight is a special evening! It's an exciting opportunity for us to continue to *be* the church!" he exclaimed.

"We've never been a church where you show up to a building in order to participate. We're a body, right?" he asked, echoing the teaching that their church was made of people, not wood and brick.

Facing the viewers square on, Ben scrolled through his phone, reading the names of those joining online. "This moment is kind of tragic and poetic and kind of beautiful," he offered. "I'm looking at all of you here together in the chat. I'm sending as many heart emojis as I can!" At first, Ben had opposed virtual church. As Anabaptists, they were called to follow Jesus, not the mandates issued by the governors of New Jersey and Pennsylvania. (To draw a sharp line between their faith and their country, many Anabaptists don't celebrate the Fourth of July.) Ben had argued with Jonny, "If you can go to Home Depot, you should be able to go to church." But Jonny used Scripture to convince Ben that this was the best way to follow Jesus's call to love your neighbor. To care for one another, they had to stay apart.

Rachel stepped into the frame from behind the camera. She took a seat next to Julie, who, for the time being, remained quiet. This marked the third Sunday of Lent, the forty-day season of reflection and repentance in preparation for Jesus's death and resurrection at Easter. A decade earlier, on Good Friday, led by Shane Claiborne and others, Circle of Hope members marched behind an eight-foot wooden cross to Colosimo's Gun Center, a Philadelphia gun shop that sold illegal weapons. Their protests succeeded in shutting the shop down for good. On other Good Fridays, Circle of Hope had gathered outside the U.S. military base in Horsham, Pennsylvania, calling for an end to lethal drone strikes. Ben still kept a cardboard sign in his basement that read, in red letters, DRONE ASSASSINATION IS IMMORAL.

Circle of Hope was exceptionally good at this Lenten work of calling out the world's ills, or, as Ben put it to viewers during that first virtual meeting, "seeing things for what they are, and saying something about it."

But Julie turned toward Ben to correct him. Lent wasn't only about addressing wrongs in the external world. It required turning inward, naming your sins, and repenting. Here were the stirrings of what would soon openly divide them: this question of what following Jesus required, focusing outward on healing the world or addressing first the sins within yourself.

For a long time, well-meaning white people at Circle had engaged in social justice without stopping to acknowledge their own privileges. Self-examination was well overdue.

"We have to make room to analyze resentment," Julie told Ben.

"Speak up!" Jonny prompted Julie, in a brotherly chide. "They can't hear you as well as Ben and I!"

Julie was an introvert. Until three and a half years earlier, she'd been a social worker. Leading online worship seemed to require centering herself and creating some zippy, peppy persona that was false and made her self-conscious. "I feel so out of my element," she said later.

Over the coming months, some women worshippers began to complain about what they were seeing on-screen. Jonny and Ben co-opted the informal liturgy, bouncing off each other, with the women silent. The four pastors responded by planning out their repartee beat by beat so that Julie and Rachel, who spoke more deliberately, were able to get a word in. Each week remained a trudge.

"It feels like a discipline of love to keep showing up," Julie said. She pastored Circle of Hope in Germantown, a historic neighborhood founded on land granted to the Quaker colonist William Penn in 1681. It had once served as Penn's "peaceable kingdom," a model for religious freedom. In 1688, it became the birthplace of America's anti-slavery movement. Anabaptism thrived. (The Brethren in Christ held their first Love Feast there on Christmas Day in 1723.) In 2020, its cobbled streets were lined with landmark Black-owned businesses like Uncle Bobbie's, a coffee shop and bookstore, and FarmerJawn Greenery, an agricultural greenhouse. Germantown remained a rare hub of Black-led development and of organizing. Germantown's population was 80 percent Black. Julie's congregation of 135 people was mostly white.

. . .

As lockdown deepened from weeks to months, Julie was spending her days leading the church from a desk in her unfinished basement. On the wall, a map of India hung next to a shelf of musical instruments, including a wooden xylophone, hand drums, and a bansuri, an Indian flute. (Her husband, Steve, had studied ethnomusicology at Messiah, and his family had a long history of missionary work in India.) Steve was also doing his job under duress. He worked for the city of Philadelphia processing applications for public assistance. Suddenly, from a desk he'd set up in their dining room, he was fielding a crush of applications from people in immediate need. Alliyah and Isaiah had little to do: Philadelphia's public schools, already facing a budget crisis, were struggling to start classes online. Every day during his lunch break, Steve took the kids on a walk across the street in Fernhill Park, a large green space where Alliyah collected pine cones for nature crafts and Isaiah played basketball until the city, citing public health concerns, took the nets away.

. . .

The demands of being a pastor sometimes collided with being a mother. Throw global chaos into the mix, along with mass deaths, the politics polarizing families, including hers, and the anxiety of making high stakes collective decisions alone and in a vacuum. Then add a reporter who arrived at the worst possible time asking for more of Julie's overscheduled hours, probing the church's dynamics, and poking around in the most difficult stories of her childhood, with the intent of sharing them with the world. Who wouldn't want to hide?

When she could find a rare moment alone, she worked in her garden, a tangle that covered every inch of their front yard: hosta, sweet potato vine, Russian sage, zinnias, black-eyed Susans, and ferns. She created Google photo albums to track their growth. "Or death!" she quipped. Most of the plants came from swaps and cuttings, and some in her care were at least eighteen years old; she'd planted one as a teenager while at Lancaster Christian School.

Julie had grown up only seventy-five miles from Philadelphia but in a different world. She was born a Bitterman, a family of conservative evangelical missionaries well-known in Lancaster County. Lancaster was home to a large number of the nearly half a million Anabaptists in the United States, including the Amish, who still clattered past her family's house in their horses and buggies. But, like millions of other evangelicals in America, the Bittermans didn't belong to any sect or denomination. They belonged to a church, Calvary Independent, which had been sending out missionaries since the 1800s. Around the altar, a map of the globe was lit with tiny electric lights in every country where the church supported missionaries. Their principal aim was to fulfill Jesus's command known as the Great Commission (Matthew 28:19–20): "Therefore go and make disciples of all nations, baptizing them in the name of the Father and of the Son and of the Holy Spirit, and teaching them to obey everything I have commanded you."

Julie's grandfather Chester Allen Bitterman Jr., a strict authoritarian and father of eight, sent his five sons into the mission field, which could be dangerous work. Beginning with Dwight D. Eisenhower, successive American presidents rallied evangelical Christians to oppose the Soviet empire, framing the Cold War as an existential battle against atheism. In 1975, Gerald Ford made an offhand comment at a press conference, dropping the fact that the CIA sometimes used missionaries in the field. The remark had unfortunate reverberations: it linked U.S. intelligence operations to missionaries, which placed the latter in further peril.

Since the 1970s, her father, Curt, had volunteered every summer at a missionary boot camp in Florida, teaching teens how to lay bricks to build churches and hospitals, and taking them on short-term mission trips to remote places all over the world. Curt's brother, Julie's uncle Chester Allen "Chet" Bitterman III, had joined Wycliffe Bible Translators, an organization founded in 1942 as part of the new evangelical movement, which was committed to translating the New Testament into every language on earth.

In 1981, while working as a radio operator in the Colombian jungle, Chet was kidnapped by leftist guerrillas who demanded that Wycliffe Bible Translators leave the country immediately to respect indigenous people and the sovereignty of Colombia. When Wycliffe's leaders refused, the guerrillas shot and killed Chet. His murder became international news and galvanized a young generation of Cold War missionaries. After Chet's murder, Wycliffe Bible Translators received an unprecedented number of applications. The family ordeal became a popular Christian book, *Called to Die*, as well as a play, *Martyred: The Chet Bitterman Story*. The Bittermans, who'd prayed fervently for Chet's release, spoke little of their loss. But silence didn't diminish its power.

"Chet's death became an undercurrent of our entire childhood," Julie said.

At home in Lancaster, Julie's grandfather put his four surviving boys to work at his industrial weight and measurement company, Bitterman Scales. On the flank of every truck, he painted the Bible verse Proverbs 11:1: "A false balance is abomination to the Lord." He distrusted most secular institutions, including the federal government and the medical establishment. Instead, he relied on a Christian chiropractor, who prescribed unconventional treatments, including taking dozens of vitamins a day and drinking from thick plastic cups that he claimed would ionize water.

At Sunday school, Julie was taught how to evangelize among other children, stringing bracelets of colored beads—"black for sin, white for a heart washed like snow, red for the blood of Christ, green for new life, gold for the streets in heaven"—as a gift and a conversational gambit to introduce Jesus. She didn't remember how old she was, three, maybe, when she'd first recited "the sinner's prayer": "Dear Lord Jesus, I know that I am a sinner, and I ask for Your forgiveness. I believe You died for my sins and rose from the dead. I turn from my sins and invite You to come into my heart and life. I want to trust and follow You as my Lord and Savior." The prayer was intended to guarantee eternal life, but Julie was always plagued by the fear she'd done it wrong.

To reassure herself, she recorded each time she'd prayed the sinner's prayer on a scrap of paper, tucking the scraps into a red tin with teddy bears on its lid as talismans: "Kneeling at my bed (at night). I exsepped Jesus. I think I was 3 yrs old. And now I Love Him. <3."

At twelve, Julie made her first trip with her parents, sister, and brothers to the Lord's Boot Camp, set in a 250-acre swamp on Merritt Island, an hour east of Orlando, Florida. The missionary training camp was founded in the seventies by Teen Missions International, which would grow into a $3.7 million outfit. The Lord's Boot Camp would train as many as forty-two thousand children from ages four or five to eighteen, sending them to at least nineteen countries. That summer of 1991, Julie and her family were preparing thirty-four teenagers for a trip to Papua New Guinea.

The Bittermans' day began at 5:30 a.m. with physical fitness and Bible memorization. Julie raced along with the teens, stacking sixty-six wooden crates painted with Genesis, Exodus, Leviticus, Numbers, Deuteronomy, Joshua, Judges, Ruth, and so on—the names of the books in the Bible, in canonical order. Sometimes they did it backward, boosting themselves over a wooden wall painted with the words "Doubt," "Confusion," and "Anxiety," and rope-swinging over a stone-lined pit filled with swamp water, the "Slough of Despond." The pit was named for the greatest ordeal endured by the hero of the seventeenth-century Christian allegory *The Pilgrim's Progress*, which Julie's dad, Curt, read to his kids before bed. Sometimes Julie fell in.

Along with ditch digging and cement pouring, classes offered basics in disaster relief, since mission trips included caring for refugee kids and children who'd lost their parents to HIV/AIDS. Although they were devoted to fulfilling the Great Commission, Curt and other leaders understood that the hearts they were most likely to change were those of their campers. Curt hoped that, for their campers, coming face-to-face with hunger and loss would alter their consciousness. "You can't eat in front of a starving person and be the same ever again," Curt explained.

Sweating in her kid-sized steel-toe work boots and bathing in the alligator-infested swamp, Julie made it through training. On their last night in Florida, the lights in the big top went off, and the teens, each holding an unlit candle, were invited to make a decision: Did they want to become a light in the dark world?

Lighting her candle alongside everyone else, Julie said yes, but she doubted herself. At night, in the mosquito-ridden tent, she was haunted by questions: "If Jesus gave his life for me, I have to be willing to do whatever whenever for him. Am I actually doing that?" she asked in her journal. What if Jesus called her to go to a dangerous country? What if Jesus called her to die, as he had her uncle Chet?

. . .

These fears proved hard to shake, and since the Bittermans' conception of faith didn't allow for doubt, Julie felt like something must be wrong with her. The trip that summer to Papua New Guinea was also harrowing and strange. To save money on flights, Curt drove his family, along with thirty-four uncomfortable teens, clad in their bush gear, from Florida to Los Angeles in a clunker of a school bus with TEEN MISSIONS on the side.

Every time the bus broke down, he led the teens in prayer, and every time they fixed the bus became a miracle. Once, a woman spotted the broken-down bus by the side of the road, and knowing Teen Missions, she took all the kids home to her trailer for sodas. That was a miracle, too.

When they finally reached Port Moresby, the capital of Papua New Guinea, the team traveled upriver by raft to arrive at a hard-to-reach mission station. For the next six weeks, Julie climbed a nearby mountain every day with the teens to hack an airstrip out of the jungle using machetes so that missionary planes could deliver supplies. At the end of the trip, Julie contracted a mysterious rash so severe that she had to deplane on the way home to be hospitalized in Australia. The experience left Julie uncertain about her path.

As a teenager, Julie was supposed to evangelize among non-Christian friends. "The problem was, I didn't know anyone who wasn't Christian," she said. Every year, Calvary Independent Church hosted a conference for some two hundred missionaries who showed indigenous handiwork and shared foreign customs. Her mom gathered hundreds of china plates so that the missionaries, on furlough, didn't have to eat their enormous homestyle meals on paper plates. Designed to inspire young people like Julie, the conference hosted celebrities from the multimillion-dollar world of contemporary Christian music, which emerged out of the folksy twang of the Jesus freaks.

However, instead of calling for an end to injustice and promoting peace, this new strain of contemporary Christian music promoted the ideal that America was God's chosen nation. The greatest star of the conference was Scott Wesley Brown, who sang ballads about how a believer's duty was to brave the benighted places of the world. Julie particularly loved his hit song "Please Don't Send Me to Africa." Listening among the teens, she felt proud of its message, and her family's willingness to sacrifice:

I'll serve you here in suburbia
In my comfortable middle class life
But please don't send me out into the bush
Where the natives are restless at night

. . .

Heartbreak and betrayal first led Julie to question her upbringing. At eighteen, she was cutting out pictures of wedding dresses from magazines and tucking them into a journal given to her by her first love, Beau. She had grown up at her Lancaster church alongside him and had imagined her future serving with him as a missionary. A year into their relationship, however, Beau dumped her, then briefly dated her sister. How was he allowed to act that way? Looking for someone to help hold Beau accountable, Julie approached one of the pastors at her family's church, all of them men who upheld fidelity as an integral aspect of following Jesus. It wasn't okay for Beau to throw her over, she asked, and then take up with her sister, was it? But the pastor said nothing to Beau. Julie felt twice betrayed; the church's teachings didn't seem to apply to boys. Later, Beau became the lead pastor at their church.

At Eastern University, Julie confronted more of her own questions. She'd never considered the role that the Bittermans, or any missionaries, played in geopolitics. She was learning that for centuries, missionaries had furthered the ambitions of nations and empires. Emphasizing hygiene, education, and enterprise, missionaries worked alongside colonists to instill Western values.

"There's a lot more to consider than giving people God's Word, and helping them make a decision to follow Jesus," she wrote in her college journal. As a teenager, she'd gone on short-term trips to the Dominican Republic, Mexico, and Kenya. Still, she wasn't ready to leave all she knew behind, and in early 2001 she signed up to lead a Teen Missions trip to Ethiopia with both of her parents as chaperones. "Father, use me this summer to help prepare and raise up laborers for the harvest," Julie prayed.

Before leaving, she attended a conference at Eastern hosted by the Institute for Global Engagement—a center for critical study—where academics and missiologists were studying the role of missionaries. The conference shook her. One speaker described "white saviorism": the idea that international do-gooders, in the name of digging wells or delivering polio vaccines, were spreading the harmful disease of neocolonialism. Saving souls and building churches across the Global South destroyed indigenous cultures and laid the groundwork for rich countries to extract resources. In the audience, Julie felt her stomach give way to the sickening truth. This was the first she heard of the Hippocratic principle "Do no harm" being applied to the world of missionaries. When conference participants broke up into small discussion groups, Julie confessed that she wanted to cancel her upcoming trip to Ethiopia. The others suggested, instead, that she still go even while carrying these tensions within her. "They met me with a lot of grace," she said.

She returned to the Florida boot camp that summer to prepare for Ethiopia with her team. On commissioning night, she stood outside the big-top tent, thinking, "What we are doing with these kids is not okay; none of this is okay."

Despite her mounting unease, she took her team on to Gambela, Ethiopia, off the lower headwaters of the Nile. A few weeks later, they were building a cement-block church to double as a health clinic. On weekends, they traveled to villages to screen *Jesus*, an influential film used to share the gospel since 1979, and to perform evangelical puppet shows. Most of the time, their local contacts did the preaching, and the American teenagers served as the attraction. "We basically drew the crowd," Julie said. The trip was going smoothly until a local pastor gave the team an ox.

Julie already found it uncomfortable to watch hungry teenagers who'd been working all day beneath a punishing sun load their dinner plates with more food than the villagers typically consumed in a day. Meat was so precious that the villagers rarely ate it. She wanted to return the ox, but another American missionary told her they couldn't. It would be unspeakably rude to reject such a generous gift. Outside the newly built church, Julie's team had constructed a concrete-block font, which they called the baptistry. After Curt helped slaughter and butcher the ox, they cooked the meat on a spit in the baptismal font, which the team renamed the "baptisserie." Although the term was supposed to be funny, the spectacle intensified the tensions and questions Julie was already carrying. She wasn't okay with this. The meat tasted sour and chewy, but she choked it down.

. . .

Wrestling with disillusionment, Julie returned from Ethiopia in the fall of 2001, moved to Philadelphia, and became a social worker, paying home visits to teen moms. The moms, who frequently had no fixed addresses and were constantly being kicked out of difficult living situations, could be hard to locate. Julie still believed that Christians were uniquely gifted with grace and generosity. Yet as she plodded along Philadelphia's hot summer sidewalks knocking on doors and searching for her clients, she observed that her coworkers' capacity for endurance and grace exceeded her own. "They're better Christians than I am, and they aren't even Christians," she thought. Yet she still believed faith played a unique role in her work. Soon, she moved on to counseling mothers and children transitioning from shelters into affordable housing. "I wanted these women to have Jesus, not just a healthy community," Julie said. "That was the seed of my calling."

At a Halloween party in 2002, Julie met Steve Hoke, a talented percussionist who came from a long line of missionaries and bishops in the Brethren in Christ. His brother, Bryan Hoke, would soon become bishop of the Atlantic Regional Conference, overseeing churches in Delaware, New Jersey, and Central and Eastern Pennsylvania, including Circle of Hope, where Steve was going to church. Steve was a gentle soul and pretty wonderful, so one Sunday evening in 2002, Julie tagged along with him to Circle. She was appalled. At home in Lancaster, churchgoers carried Bibles under their arms and in purses. No one brought Bibles to Circle of Hope. As Rod argued against the war in Iraq, she wondered if he was preaching the gospel. When one member invited everyone to strip off their shoes and walk around barefoot, Julie thought it was wacko.

No, Julie wasn't sure about Circle of Hope, but she was sure about Steve Hoke, so she decided to check out a cell. Sitting in someone's home with other young professionals—a teacher and a lawyer, not the barefoot punks—Julie heard people talk about the intimate challenges of their lives, as well as the role of doubt in their faith. Her cell read the Bible together, but they also celebrated birthdays and taught one another to make café con leche and a grandmother's soup. Week after week, she felt that Jesus's love proved more expansive and inclusive than her childhood faith allowed. Finally, Julie could ask questions.

. . .

Joining Circle and marrying Steve, Julie did her best to keep up with the demands of weekly cell and worship and becoming a mom to Alliyah. She'd recently returned to work when her dad, Curt, called one night in 2009. A family scandal was on the verge of breaking. Bitterman Scales was about to be indicted for criminal activity and tax fraud. Along with Julie's uncles Craig and Grant, and her grandfather Chester, her dad was facing federal prison. For nine years, the U.S. government charged in its suit, the Bittermans hid their earnings in offshore trusts and bogus liens, which cost the IRS $437,000.

The Bittermans hadn't concocted this complicated scheme on their own. They'd been duped by a snake-oil businessman named John Michael "Red" Crim, who ran Commonwealth Trust, a Texas-based investment firm that turned out to be a tax fraud outfit. Crim had earned the Bittermans' trust by quoting Scripture and claiming to be a former pastor. He was, it turns out, the head of a criminal enterprise that taught people to hide their money in offshore accounts while paying Crim hefty processing fees. Crim was preying on Old Order Mennonites, the Amish, and conservative evangelicals like the Bittermans, whose faith rendered them suspicious of secular institutions and open to conspiracy theories. Commonwealth Trust peddled myths about God versus the federal government, using Scripture to justify its scams. Crim was, in some ways, a proto–Alex Jones, and Commonwealth Trust traded on the kind of fears that came to be part of the QAnon conspiracy theory: that the government was out to get people, and believers were protected by relying on the Bible to break phony government codes.

Julie, who'd never met Crim, had always thought he sounded suspicious. She remembered an instance in the mid-1990s when she was in high school and the Bittermans hosted a family meeting to explain some of their company's tax-evasion schemes. Watching a short sales video that attempted to lay out how it was legal not to pay taxes, Julie felt unsettled. The schemes had struck her as wrong, maybe illegal. Money and Bitterman Scales, however, were in the men's realm, so she'd raised no questions.

When the case went to trial that summer of 2010, Julie drove to the federal courthouse in Allentown. Entering the courtroom, she spied the Great Seal of the United States, emblazoned with an eagle, and was struck by the gravity of what had transpired: her family was in serious trouble. From her uncomfortable place on a wooden bench, Julie listened to detailed accounts of offshore holdings that sounded implausible until the prosecution played secret recordings of family conversations. She couldn't believe that her family had been caught up in a sting operation. It did seem to Julie that the IRS was targeting her family: Why had the government spent a decade investigating a small family business? The trial lasted three weeks. In the end, a jury convicted the four Bittermans of conspiracy to defraud the United States.

But the Bittermans didn't believe they were guilty, because they'd been following God's law, not that of the federal government. For the next five years, they launched appeals while the judge continued to deny their request for a new trial. Finally, on July 22, 2015, Julie found herself back in the same federal courtroom awaiting their sentencing. The Bittermans were ordered to pay $437,000 in restitution, and Julie's dad received twenty-one months in federal prison with a fine of $7,100. As the bailiff read out the verdict, Julie scribbled notes. Curt was a "consistently hard-working and respectable man of society," she wrote. "We are all broken. Lord restore us. Lord listen to your children praying."

Curt, for his part, was baffled by the verdict. How could God have allowed him, his brothers, and his father to be punished for doing His will? He and his brothers worked out a deal to surrender themselves over time, so that at least one of them would be able to keep running what was left of the business. As his court-appointed date approached, Curt prayed for guidance: "Lord, I'm supposed to get in my car and drive myself to prison and get out and walk in. And I still don't have an answer to how this is all gonna work." The answer was simple, God told him: there were plenty of men in prison who desperately needed to be saved.

"I'm not asking you to be Billy Graham. Just be yourself," he heard God say. After lights-out that first night in prison, Curt lay in the bottom bunk in a large open room and prayed aloud, telling the story of Moses and the burning bush. He didn't yet know that he was supposed to be silent. From the darkness, another man replied, "That's not how I remember the story." The man turned out to be Muslim, and although he didn't prove keen on giving his heart to Jesus, Curt loved their conversations.

In prison, Curt led a Bible study and befriended a guard—a fellow believer. He asked for the guard's help enacting a miracle. In the Bible, the army of the faithful brought down the walls of Jericho by marching around the city in circles. Curt read about a prayer practice that promised something similar: a believer could encircle a place three times and vanquish the forces of evil. Curt wanted to try it. He approached the warden to ask if he could be driven around the prison in a paddy wagon to pray. Curt was willing to wear a straight jacket. But the warden said no, so Curt asked the friendly guard to loop around the prison three times, in a vehicle, praying for a revival. When the guard agreed, Curt was delighted, believing with all his heart that God had sent him to prison to evangelize, and that he was doing his best to fulfill the Great Commission.

. . .

The day after Curt was sentenced to federal prison, Julie went on a pilgrimage to the John Heinz National Wildlife Refuge to ask God what he wanted her to do. "You call me out upon the waters," she prayed, quoting a contemporary tune by Hillsong United, a worship band born of the charismatic megachurch Hillsong, based in Australia.

As everything in her family was turning upside down, Julie felt God calling her to become a pastor. In the mission field, she'd watch formidable women direct field hospitals and hack paths into the jungle, but standing in front of a church teaching the Bible was different. Before coming to Circle and being awed by Gwen White's articulate gift, she'd never heard a woman preach. It wasn't just a matter of her childhood theology: Julie wasn't sure she had the expertise or personality for the role. She hated being the focus of attention, and few in the church knew what her family was going through, which made her feel like she didn't fit in.

In the safety of her cell, however, Julie did share her family's ordeal. Over time, she felt her shame lighten into compassion for herself. She also shared the story with Rachel, who was soon to become the first woman at Circle to lead a congregation. Listening to Julie's family secrets and her questions about whether the Holy Spirit was calling her friend to become a pastor also, Rachel encouraged Julie to go forward with the process. She was already leading, standing up in front of everyone and directing cells as a cell coordinator, a position that served as an informal pipeline for potential pastors.

When a congregation grew large enough to multiply, the cell coordinators who'd proven their capacity to lead were usually put forward as the next apprentice pastors. Becoming an apprentice wasn't like filling out a job application, Rachel told Julie. Instead, she'd be joining the group of three or four apprentices who met with Rod once a week, usually at the Broad Street Diner, to talk about Scripture and to inquire about what God was doing in their lives. The selection process was one of collective discernment. According to Rod's vision, pastors were only part of a larger whole. But Julie had seen Rod in action, and these claims about equality didn't ring true. She wasn't sure she could follow in his charismatic, entrepreneurial footsteps, or that she wanted to.

"I don't know how to use PowerPoint," Julie wrote in her journal. But she also loved Circle of Hope, so she kept going forward in the apprentice process. One Sunday after Thanksgiving in 2015, she addressed the whole church and risked sharing the shame of her family scandal, recounting her first visit to her dad in federal prison. The orange jumpsuit had shocked her, she told the congregation, and brought up a stir of emotions: "sorrow and fear and powerlessness, coupled with my anger with the realities of the prison industrial complex." She shared that her dad, however, displayed none of these negative feelings. "In this environment, my dad said he is looking to the Scriptures for answers and finding God there," Julie went on. Citing Old Testament prophets and warriors like Daniel and Gideon, who battled the forces of evil, Curt had been gifted with absolute certainty that he was where God wanted and needed him to be. Julie no longer believed that sin and salvation worked quite so tidily, or in the kind of magical thinking in which prayer instantly fixed broken-down school buses.

In 2016, when Circle's regular attenders (or RAs in church growth–speak) hit a high of 712 people, the community decided to plant a new congregation. By this point, Circle of Hope was flourishing in three locations: Center City, Fishtown, and South Jersey. Circle was ready to multiply a fourth in Germantown. As an apprentice pastor, Julie found it daunting to listen to Rod, Jonny, Ben, and others strategizing about numbers and expansion. (Rachel, with her natural gift for growing cells, said little in such discussions.) Julie had never fully ascribed to the male pastors' preoccupation with breaking the 700 barrier. The idea of being a CEO and selling the church made her feel inadequate. When Julie sensed something wasn't right, she often turned her misgivings on herself.

Initially, Rachel was supposed to hive off to begin the new church in Germantown. But then Rod handed her his congregation, and planting Germantown suddenly fell to Julie and her fellow apprentice pastor, Jerome, one of Circle's few Black male members. At the beginning, when they'd first planted Circle, Rod and Gwen attempted to tackle the issue of race by seeking advice from Spencer Perkins and Chris Rice, two young pastors and peace builders whose book, *More Than Equals*, chronicled their common struggle to dismantle racism. Unless the Whites were willing to make racial reconciliation their church's sole purpose, Perkins and Rice advised, their effort was likely to fail.

Disheartened, the Whites had envisioned Circle of Hope addressing all manner of social ills, not solely racism. So they came up with creative solutions on their own, one of which involved buying a house not far from their own in West Philly, and right next to Malcolm X Memorial Park, to establish Shalom House, a racially diverse intentional community of peace builders. The social experiment lasted for several years but ultimately fell apart. Over twenty years, Circle also hired three Black pastors—Gerry West, Joe Snell, and Bryan Robinson—with the hope that they could help build a more racially diverse church. Each of these partnerships ended for various reasons, which Rod saw as personal and individual, and others would come to see as part of a problematic pattern at Circle.

Julie and Jerome spent several months walking and driving around

Germantown looking for church space to rent or buy. They didn't have an office, so they met in coffee shops. Buying a church, however, was tough in Germantown, where they had to vie with developers already snapping up distressed real estate. Instead, as a temporary solution, they found a building five minutes away, in Northwest Philly, for rent. Rod hoped that, together, Julie and Jerome could help fulfill his dream of building a transracial church. Despite such intentions, growing a church of young, mostly white do-gooders was much easier.

Of the four White sons, Jacob, the eldest, was a curmudgeonly sage who questioned certain aspects of Circle's theology. "My dad started the church to pastor to young professionals," he said. "That's who he was trying to attract." Jacob was allergic to the white saviorism he saw among many of the earnest urban homesteaders at Circle of Hope. Jacob taught middle school math at General George G. Meade School, an underperforming school in Philadelphia (in 2020, zero percent of its eighth graders were reading at grade level), yet he harbored no illusions that he was saving anyone. Jacob saw the gap between his parents' utopian teachings about being transracial and healing neighborhoods, and the reality embedded in the church growth movement, which planted new churches by targeting educated transplants, who were almost entirely white people.

The church growth movement, which had become popular in the 1970s and '80s, evolved from the strategies used by the American missionary Donald McGavran in India during the 1930s to target potential converts according to caste. The movement's concept of "people groups" categorized "the unreached" according to socioeconomic determinants, including race and class. As McGavran wrote, "Peoples become Christian fastest when least change of race or clan is involved." McGavran authored, along with Win C. Arn, a 1973 book titled *How to Grow a Church*. (Billy Graham wrote the foreword to the book.) McGavran's mentee, C. Peter Wagner, a former missionary in Bolivia, taught Rod at Fuller. Wagner's books, including *Your Church Can Grow* and *Our Kind of People*, justified racism under the guise of evangelization. He attempted to cast the segregation of churches as "a dynamic tool for assuring Christian growth." To apt observers, it was clear that these strategies reinforced class and race structures in America. The Black evangelical activist John Perkins wrote in his 1982 book, *With Justice for All*, "How convenient it is that our 'church growth experts' tell us that homogenous churches grow fastest!"

Despite the fact that Philadelphia, home to 1.6 million people, was almost evenly split between white and Black residents, Circle of Hope could only count 15 to 25 percent of its some seven hundred members as people of color. Circle still held that dividing people according to the color of their skin was antithetical to creating the Kingdom of Heaven on Earth, which transcended all earthly identities. "Don't bean-count us" became a Circle principle for a time, a rejoinder against critiques that the church had failed to tackle its overwhelming whiteness.

In Germantown, Julie and Jerome were failing to draw a diverse new crowd to their church plant. Julie recalled sitting next to Jerome on a couch and cringing when she heard Rod ask, "Where are all your Black friends?" Jerome told Julie that he was feeling discouraged. But she refused to entertain his doubts. "I see God working through you," she replied. By the end of 2017, Jerome quit anyway, saying at his exit interview that he "didn't feel listened to by Julie." Julie didn't get it: in all those coffee shops, she felt, she'd listened intently. It wasn't until the crucible of 2020 that Julie understood her role in ignoring the mounting problems Jerome was trying to show her. Although he'd told Julie he wanted to go, she'd pushed him to stay. "My personal encouragement, without bigger systemic change," she reasoned, "made pastoring in Circle of Hope difficult for him and left him feeling unheard."

. . .

Julie had been hardwired in church to believe that every action she took served a greater purpose. When George Floyd was murdered by a police officer on May 25, 2020, in Minneapolis, Minnesota, this purpose became anti-racism. But determining the relationship between anti-racism and following Jesus would threaten to destroy the church. In May 2020 mass protests in Philadelphia and across the country in support of the Black Lives Matter movement heightened the challenges of pastoring for Julie and the others. They were forced to face the gap between their visionary principles and the painful reality that, when it came to race, Circle of Hope was no different from other churches. In 1960, Martin Luther King Jr. had declared that "eleven o'clock on Sunday morning is one of the most segregated hours if not *the most* segregated hour in Christian America." Sixty years later, 80 percent of churchgoing Americans still belonged to racially homogenous congregations. Circle of Hope was among them.

At first, led by Circle Peacemakers, a compassion team that Rod and Gwen had begun years earlier to help draw young people's attention to far-flung injustices, church members turned up to protests, marching behind a long white banner trimmed in black, with CIRCLE OF HOPE in inch-thick black letters. At one protest, Julie ran into Jasmine and Iboro Umana, who were married and had recently moved to Germantown from Chicago, where they attended Willow Creek, a megachurch founded by Bill Hybels. Jasmine and Iboro were both medical doctors. They had discovered Circle of Hope online and come along one Sunday. Since the Germantown flock didn't own a building, they found space in other churches, eventually renting the Longstreth auditorium at the First Presbyterian Church for $400 a week. They met on Sundays at 3:00 p.m. The church building, with its Tiffany stained-glass windows and murals by Violet Oakley, an American artist famous at the turn of the century, spoke to Germantown's earlier era of prosperity, as well as the larger role that church had once played in the lives of Americans.

The Umanas decided to join Circle and began to attend Julie's cell, where, when necessary, people supported one another in spiritual and material ways. (When one single mom and longtime Germantown resident faced eviction, the cell shared enough money to keep her in her apartment.) During lockdowns and citywide curfews, people of color in the cell talked through how to shuttle their kids safely around Philadelphia using white friends as drivers, since their kids were safer with a white driver at the wheel. Jasmine shared how hurtful it was that, during her shift at the hospital, only a few white doctors mentioned the murders of Breonna Taylor and Ahmaud Arbery, which had occurred a few months before that of George Floyd.

To educate his medical colleagues at the hospital, Iboro compiled a history of how racialized trauma affected the health of patients of color. When Julie invited him to present this history to the cell, Iboro quoted Marc Lamont Hill, an abolitionist and an author who taught at Philadelphia's Temple University and cautioned against describing the recent unrest as a "riot"; the organized resistance, he argued, was a "rebellion." Hill's argument was part of a hotly contested theological debate regarding the nature of protest and violence, and another cell member, a white nurse, took issue. Christians couldn't condone violence, the nurse argued, especially not Anabaptists, who were pacifists. In cells, disagreement was welcome. Circle of Hope held that God was present in such dialogue. The disconnection over the George Floyd protests, however, revealed what Julie and some others feared was an irreconcilable theological difference.

When the nurse left the church some months later, Julie saw his unwillingness to remain as a reflection of new fissures: Circle's mostly white Gen Xers, from skaters to social workers, considered engaging in secular political struggle antithetical to their core identity as Anabaptists. As Ben had put it, "Anabaptists would say don't mess with politics. That's the Kingdom of the World." For younger and newer members, including Jasmine and Iboro, following Jesus required political and social action. Within months, it was clear to Julie, the Umanas, and many others, that the church had to do more in response to racial injustice than merely attending protests.

Church wasn't a place of business, or a school or hospital, Jasmine explained. Church was a place people came for the care of their souls. This, after all, was the organizing principle and first question of cells: "How is it with your soul?" How much, Jasmine, Iboro, and others began to wonder, was Circle of Hope willing to change in order to care for their souls?

In their cell, Julie heard people of color asking questions about Circle of Hope that she didn't know how to answer. For instance, the church held to core teachings, called proverbs, which were intended to arise organically from the community. As one proverb read, "We are called out to be a living organism, building community together in love." Circle described the proverbs as the "convictions that drive us." Each year, the pastors added more, until, by 2020, there were 105 proverbs listed on the church website. Some were slogan-y sayings, like "Leadership is a team effort." Others embodied Circle's in-your-face rebel culture, like "Jesus is our agenda." (Some members felt uneasy about these pithy sayings, which occasionally bordered on heresy.) As responses to a shifting outside world, the proverbs weren't intended to last forever. They were meant to live and die.

Yet those that endured were to be taken seriously. One long-standing proverb vowed, "We will do what it takes to be an anti-racist diverse community that represents the new humanity." To Julie and others, however, Circle's commitment to anti-racism seemed pretty thin. In a church that remained so white, she wondered if they were following the proverb and doing "what it takes to be an anti-racist diverse community."

Every year, Circle of Hope underwent a process called mapping. Together as a church, the members discussed the direction in which the Holy Spirit was leading them, and how to get there through a common set of goals for the year, fulfilling the proverb "We are called to move with what the Spirit is doing next." Mapping usually began in the spring with pastors sending open-ended questions to cell leaders to discuss in their weekly groups. Informed by these discussions, the pastors and cell leaders came up with common goals for the year, some of which were specific, like finding jobs for people struggling in the church, and others more ephemeral, such as "Expand our understanding of how we can take care of one another in difficult times."

In 2020, with the country aflame, Julie, Jonny, Rachel, and Ben decided to direct a churchwide conversation toward identifying what needed to change at Circle. This was a shift: Circle members used the map not to criticize themselves, but to broaden God's kingdom. At first, Rod urged the four pastors not to go forward with making the map until members could be together in person. But they dismissed Rod's reservations. "We are in uncharted territory as a world and as a church," as Julie put it. For the first time, the pastors sent out specific, targeted questions about how Circle needed to respond to racism both outside and inside the church. They asked each of their sixty cells to answer the following questions: "We have been stretched in so many ways in a very short period of time. What do we hold on to and what do we change? We are grateful for this new burgeoning world-wide anti-racist movement in response to George Floyd's murder. What are we going to do to keep the anti-racist movement going in deeper and wider ways?"

. . .

The issues arising at Circle of Hope weren't just about race; they swirled around all kinds of marginal identities, including who Jesus meant when he said "the least of these." No matter how much Circle viewed itself as revolutionary, it had fallen behind the culture on same-sex marriage and affirmation: the policy of publicly declaring the acceptance of LGBTQ people in both membership and leadership in the church. For nearly twenty years, Circle had played a theological version of "Don't ask, don't tell," refusing to issue any kind of statement. Meanwhile, LGBTQ affirmation had become one of the most polarizing factors in American Protestantism. Pews became trenches in the culture wars. Beginning in the 1970s, several of the more progressive denominations—including the United Church of Christ, the Episcopal Church, the Evangelical Lutheran Church in America, and the Presbyterian Church USA—had gradually come to celebrate the marriage and ordination of lesbian and gay members. Other mainline denominations, including the American Baptist Churches USA, the United Methodist Church, and the Reformed Church in America faced schisms from conservative factions.

Yet the Brethren in Christ, the denomination to which Circle of Hope belonged, continued to vehemently oppose same-sex marriage. "The practices of premarital sex, extramarital sex, adultery, lesbianism, or homosexuality have no place in the life in Christ," read the 2020 edition of *The Manual of Doctrine and Government,* in which the BIC defined its current practices, values, and organizational structure. To outside ears, this sounded shocking, but the sentiment was in step with most evangelical churches. For the BIC, as for so many, holding the line against homosexuality had become the most important bulwark in defending faith against secular culture.

Circle of Hope, in contrast, attempted to welcome everybody who wanted to follow Jesus, no matter what they believed. "We are called to love people where they are," he argued. Rod, who rejected words like "policy," as having nothing to do with Jesus, refused to play by the world's rules.

Avoiding a stand on affirmation also allowed Circle to remain part of the Brethren in Christ, which cosigned mortgages and deeds. According to its guidelines, the BIC had the right to claim all assets of a church that strayed from its core theology. Circle had a lot to lose: it was surprisingly well-off. The success of its thrift stores and the tithing of some long-standing members, including the White family, added up to accounts with $1,225,496 in cash and another $2.3 million in real estate, which Circle might be forced to forfeit if it violated BIC doctrine. Having a policy to have no policy worked well enough until 2020.

To become a minister in the Brethren in Christ also required a license. Yet no one at Circle of Hope cared about such bureaucratic dealings. The authority to pastor came not from a piece of paper, but from the beloved community, and from God. Nor did Circle follow the tradition of ordination, in which religious authority is conferred on a pastor—that was so much pomp and nonsense—and Jesus said nothing of it in the Bible. Julie said, "We didn't esteem ordination as a necessary right step." However, the BIC did require its pastors to sign a contract saying they upheld its teachings, including those on sexuality.

Julie knew that, in good conscience, she couldn't sign such a form, yet she refused to lie. And despite the fact that each of the pastors supported affirmation to varying degrees, they'd gone ahead and signed their names to this exclusionary document. Julie asked Rachel, Jonny, and Ben how they could put their name to something they didn't believe in. But their answers amounted to "mental gymnastics I knew I couldn't follow," as she put it. She was under additional pressure to sign. Her brother-in-law, Bryan Hoke, was also her bishop. For several years, he'd encouraged her to get licensed. By 2020, he was pressing harder and asking why she was dragging her feet. "You need to get credentialed," he wrote in an email. "Anything holding you back from doing so?" Bishop Hoke had a record of enforcing the Brethren in Christ's policy of casting out those who didn't uphold their teachings. In 2019, he had defrocked the pastor of the Bridge, a church Hoke once led in Hummelstown, Pennsylvania. Although the Bridge's pastor hadn't yet performed a same-sex marriage, he'd said he'd be willing to do so. That declaration was enough for Hoke to shut down the church, close the building, and lock it. Closing the church was painful. Hoke cried as he turned the key in the lock, and for a time he worked with those who remained to reopen the church, but the Bridge stayed closed.

Bryan Hoke was a soft-spoken bishop and a known champion of women in the church. Still, Julie knew if she were to tell him the truth about how she felt, his role might require him not only to dismiss her as pastor but also to shutter Circle of Hope and seize its assets. In fact, Julie had done more than affirm the idea of same-sex marriage. On one drenchingly hot afternoon in August 2020, she had gone to Laurel Hill Cemetery and met two friends who were beloved leaders of her congregation. She walked with them to a shaded slope facing the Schuylkill River, a meditative place near where Julie took her kids to collect weeping willow boughs for wreaths, as her mother had taught her to make. With a longtime friend of the couple acting as witness and videographer, Julie conducted the first queer wedding in Circle's history. "The Spirit of God is at work in the lives of these people," she said. As a result, the couple worried for Julie about what might happen to her for going "completely rogue." Julie, however, didn't view her role in performing the rite of marriage as an individual act. She was following the collective will of her congregation, with the support of her fellow pastors. "I'd do it again," she said.

3

RACHEL

"Blessed are the meek."

—MATTHEW 5:5

Standing by her pink bathtub, Rachel Sensenig prepared to baptize her daughter, Cori, foal-like and wearing a black Virginia Beach T-shirt. "I'm here in South Philly with my daughter, and I just have a few questions to ask her," Rachel said, speaking into the camera of the phone her husband, Jeff, was holding. "Cor, do you know that Jesus has forgiven you of your sins and that He's your Lord?" Rachel asked her daughter.

Cori said yes. Although she was only fourteen, young to be baptized according to Anabaptists, she felt ready. "I used to be a really anxious person," Cori explained. "And now I feel like I have a new understanding of peace, and that's been really amazing. I feel a lot of freedom in that, and I pray a lot more. I'm hungry for the word of God, and I'm excited."

"Shall we baptize her?" Rachel asked the virtual congregation. A chorus of yeses appeared in the chat. "All right, let's do it. So you can tell we're just here at home in the bathtub, but God is with us, and you are, too. So we're gonna go forward three times all the way under."

Cori climbed into the bath and knelt in the water. Rachel bowed her daughter's head gently forward and into the bathwater. Then Cori popped out of the tub and prayed with her parents.

"This is the apex of parenting, Jeff and Rach," Gwen White typed in the chat. "Rejoicing."

Zoom Baptism was Rachel's creative solution during the coronavirus lockdown, when it proved too dangerous to gather together as one body. Rod had urged holding off on baptisms altogether. "I ran the church as anti-virtual," he said. Circle of Hope had a proverb to this effect: "As the world pulls us toward 'virtual' we will keep struggling to live rooted, in real time." Ben had seconded him. Rachel paid little attention to their dissent, reminding them that as Anabaptists, they didn't need pastors to conduct baptism. They belonged to "the priesthood of all believers," a term derived from the early church in the Bible, and a core belief for Anabaptists and many other Protestants. Unlike, say, the Catholic Church, with its hierarchies and robes, this ideal spoke to a form of worship in which everyone shared authority. One believer could dunk another safely at home or in a nearby creek.

"By the banks of the (live) stream we gather," one member typed. The baptism smash cut from Rachel's South Philly bathroom to the bottle-green Wissahickon Creek. The frigid murk swept past the brown-eyed and nervous Danny P., shivering in shorts and white plastic slides. Danny P. was a brand-new thirty-something member of Rachel's congregation, and a heroin addict trying to get clean. He'd found Circle through attending recovery meetings there, and I'd met him several months earlier in cell. Danny P. and I became friends, and he'd invited me to come along in person to his baptism. Danny P. had been battling depression and addiction since high school, and, for him, a lot was riding on this moment's potential for transformation. A powerful chill rose off the freezing creek. It reached the bank where I stood in a puffy coat. I couldn't imagine dipping a toe in that water, let alone immersing myself in it.

"I've never felt so much love in myself, and trust in God," Danny P. said. He sloshed in, bare chested, up to his knees. By being baptized, he was taking the third of Alcoholics Anonymous's Twelve Steps, turning his will and his life over to the care of God as he understood him. The top of his buzz cut disappeared beneath the creek's surface.

. . .

Circle of Hope celebrated baptisms and communion four times a year at their seasonal Love Feasts, funky loaves-and-fishes potlucks reminiscent of the book of Acts. New members joined Circle's covenant and shared their testimony of coming to know Jesus. "Living in covenant, like a family with a common Father, is basic to being a Christian," one proverb held. The covenant wasn't a list of rules to follow or a code of belief—it was "a symbolic summary of the heart of what keeps us together." It required action and participation in becoming "a movement of cells to multiply congregations."

In summer, pastors baptized members in the Wissahickon Creek or the Delaware River, as in a scene out of Garth Davis's 2018 film, *Mary Magdalene*, in which Rooney Mara costarred as the faithful follower alongside Joaquin Phoenix as Jesus. Rachel, with high cheekbones and sun-kissed hair, resembled Mara and identified with this version of Magdalene, who was portrayed not as in the familiar myth of the fallen prostitute tagging along behind Jesus, but as a fisher of women, wading into the sea to baptize her sisters in Christ.

For Circle's winter Love Feasts, Rachel baptized new members in an inflatable birthing tub she'd bought online for $100. She relied on her right-hand guy, Jimmy Weitzel, an affable recovering heroin addict who wore Adidas Sambas and occasionally highlighted his shoulder-length hair, to fill the tub with warm water so that the baptisms were pleasant. For the feast that followed, she roasted pumpkin and cooked pasta e fagioli, Italian comfort food she'd learned to make from her father's family, coal miners who left Italy and arrived in Pennsylvania during the 1900s.

Rachel grew up in the Poconos, on a defunct coal mine at Mauch

Chunk Lake, a three-thousand-acre reserve where her father served as the ranger. A voracious reader, she often climbed a wild pear tree with books she picked up from a borrowing shelf at her church, losing herself in tales of undercover missionaries smuggling Bibles into communist countries. The story of Amy Carmichael, an evangelical missionary in India who rescued and cared for child prostitutes, led Rachel to dream of becoming a missionary doctor. Poring over an illustrated Bible, she reread accounts of Jesus's first followers, men and women risking their lives traveling around the Roman Empire, smuggled in baskets and preaching a message of love. As a child, she grew inspired by this imagined vision of the past.

Rachel's born-again parents, Dennis and Susan DeMara, were former Jesus freaks who, like many members of the movement, tacked hard to the right during the 1980s and '90s, allying themselves with the politics and principles of the emerging Christian right. Living off the land, Dennis and Susan raised their children out of the pages of *Little House on the Prairie*, which Susan read aloud to them. As a park ranger, Dennis, who graduated from Penn State with a degree in landscape architecture and served as a lieutenant colonel in the U.S. Army, earned $6,000 a year. At Christmastime, he worked on a tree farm so they could afford to buy presents. Susan stretched the family's $80 food budget to feed four children, serving watered-down orange juice, and then only on Saturdays. For protein, the DeMaras raised and hunted rabbits.

Around them, the land was changing. As coal mines receded, the earth returned to itself. For the first time in nearly two centuries, borage and mustard plants were sprouting from the scarred mouths of mining tunnels. Surrounded by bright yellow forsythia bushes and the sweetness of lilac, her pockets laden with sour cherries and crab-apples that she baked into pies, Rachel never imagined that her family was poor. Her father taught her to make sumac tea, stalk a deer, catch and cook crayfish, and distinguish edible mushrooms from deadly ones. He also taught her how to balance a checkbook and insisted that she learn to change a car's oil before getting a driver's license. He didn't like feminists, whom he called "feminazis," and he didn't believe that women should be leaders in church. That a woman could be a pastor was beyond imagination. Yet he didn't see the contradiction between his disdain for women and his devotion to his eldest daughter. Half-jokingly, Dennis referred to Rachel as his first son, until it became impossible to ignore that she was a girl.

The most important lesson that Susan offered Rachel and her two younger sisters was that of her past: on her own since the age of fifteen, Susan had become a cute petty thief in white go-go boots with a daisy painted on her cheek. She'd done so many drugs that she didn't know she'd been at Woodstock until she saw a documentary many years later and remembered the rain, tab after tab of acid, another girl slipping in the mud, and wetting her pants. Falling in with the lower rungs of the New Jersey mafia, Susan became a goomah, a girl on the side. Then one evening in 1974, three years before Rachel was born, Susan's mafia boyfriend called to say he was coming over to break her legs. Desperate, she opened a Gideon Bible, dropped to her knees, and flipped through the pages to find John 3:16, the verse she'd caught sight of on a billboard along the Pennsylvania Turnpike: "For God so loved the world, that he gave his only begotten Son, that whosoever believeth in him should not perish, but have everlasting life."

"Jesus, if you're real, please help me," Susan begged. In an instant, she knew she was safe. Soon after, she left the guy for good. Newly sober, she became Carbon County's resident artist, designing a rainbow patch for the park rangers' uniform. Dennis DeMara was cute and soon followed her everywhere, including to her Bible church. Within a year of their first meeting, in 1975, Dennis was saved; soon they were married and raising four children next to a dam in a little yellow cabin.

As a textbook for their Christian life, the DeMaras turned to the lessons of James Dobson, who, in 1977, the year Rachel was born, founded Focus on the Family, a broadcasting empire that reached millions of American families over the radio, as well as in books and magazines. Dobson's teachings, formed in direct reaction against the women's liberation movement, upheld traditional domestic roles for women. Using Scripture to ground his claims, Dobson argued that keeping a woman at home was the foundation of a family's success against the corrosive forces of modernity. Susan adopted these teachings. She worried about the acid she'd dropped, avoided baby formula as expensive and unnatural, and used home remedies, such as placing onions on her children's feet and chests for fevers.

When Susan felt overwhelmed, Rachel stepped in to mother her siblings. From an early age, she was her parents' closest confidante. On the rare afternoons that she wasn't caring for her siblings, she hid in the woods to escape the crush of adult responsibilities, sometimes running into black bears or swimming with water snakes coiling around her. She wasn't afraid.

To her younger siblings, Rachel cast an impossible shadow. In high school, she was both National Honor Society president and a 1991 finalist in the Miss Teen Pennsylvania competition, which was judged "on the basis of poise, personality, and beauty of face and figure." A child evangelist, she even succeeded in bringing her friends to church, and to Jesus. And she followed the Christian ideal of maintaining her virginity until marriage. Purity culture—an abstinence movement for teenagers that arose as the Christian right's solution to rising rates of teen pregnancy, sexually transmitted diseases (STDs), and the AIDS crisis in the early 1990s—was at its zenith.

Her parents were tough on Rachel, expecting her to be both a faultless beauty and a model of self-sufficiency for her two little sisters to follow. Yet Rachel's success was also a challenge for her youngest sister, Rebecca. Three years younger and a rebel from the start, Rebecca was the opposite of everything demure called for by James Dobson.

In a nearby Poconos town, Susan ran Care Net of Carbon County, one of a network of crisis pregnancy centers. Such centers began to spring up in the 1960s mostly in small, poor towns across Canada and the United States as rivals to Planned Parenthood clinics. In lieu of abortion, Care Net and other crisis pregnancy centers offered pregnant women counseling, cribs, parenting classes, sonograms, as well as introductions to adoption services. But not abortion. At night in their cabin, over spaghetti, Susan shared cautionary tales with her daughters about the teenagers who'd wandered into the centers with STDs, unwanted pregnancies, or botched abortions. She sprinkled in questionable assertions about the dangers of having sex before marriage, including the claim that it led to higher rates of suicide. "It isn't the healthiest choice physically or emotionally," she told her daughters.

In 1996, Rachel headed off to Messiah University. The Christian college was only an hour away and offered her a partial scholarship. Since 1968, Messiah, a historically Anabaptist institution founded by the Brethren in Christ church, had also pioneered a program to introduce its wealthy white students to Philadelphia's poverty and racism. Rachel didn't know any Anabaptists—or any pacifists. In her home, her father, who'd commanded a military base in Uzbekistan during the conflict in Afghanistan, staunchly believed in the American military. Rachel quietly disagreed, and in some ways Messiah began to open her eyes to roomier takes on the Bible and faith.

But the community also disappointed her. Even with her partial scholarship, Rachel still had to take out $80,000 in student loans to pay for Messiah. She worked three jobs and watched her fellow students, who seemed stuck-up and spoiled, have plenty of time to study, which Rachel wanted to do. Messiah's motto was "Christ Preeminent"; its nickname was "Cash Preeminent." "Where is their struggle?" Rachel asked herself as she scrounged leftover pizza from her delivery job for dinner and discounted day-old Dunkin' Donuts for breakfast. She was itching to go into the world and "do the work of Jesus," as she put it. She spent the summer of 1997 after freshman year as a counselor at a wilderness camp, mountain biking thirty miles before dawn, then teaching caving and rock climbing without eating more than a few bites all day.

Returning to Messiah in the fall deeply ambivalent, she'd dropped below one hundred pounds. Although she was trying to disappear, her diminishing figure earned admiration in a culture of perfectionism.

In a class on political violence, she spied Jeff Sensenig, a good-looking soccer player. He was dating a blond, blue-eyed American who was also the model for the girl on the Swiss Miss hot chocolate box. From a distance, Rachel wrote them both off as problem-free until she heard Jeff say smart, thoughtful things in class and eventually he asked her out. Rachel went once, but she'd just read the classic text of purity culture, Joshua Harris's *I Kissed Dating Goodbye*. (Harris, whose book sold over one million copies, has since denounced the book, apologized for the pain it caused, and no longer considers himself a Christian.) After reading Harris's book, Rachel had decided that even innocent dinners distracted her from God, and she avoided Jeff—until she ran into him again in the fall of 1997 on Messiah's Philadelphia campus and, soon, they became a couple.

In 1999, Rachel and Jeff got married at Rachel's childhood Evangelical Free Church in the Poconos, and moved to a racially mixed part of South Philly, making friends with the sex workers on their corner and a local dope dealer who came to parties in the tumble-down home with a three-story roof deck they'd purchased from a Christian friend for $60,000. Many of their Messiah friends attended Circle of Hope, but, at first, Rachel and Jeff remained skeptical of what looked to them like a "white, idealistic, extension of college thing: hanging out with one another and not getting involved in Black and brown churches in their neighborhoods." She and Jeff considered this "selling out." From the outside, it smacked of classic white saviorism: Circle members were living the picture of helping others without truly offering themselves in solidarity and equality. The young couple decided they were going to be more authentic, living *among*—not as saviors but as neighbors.

Striving to do things differently, Rachel went back to school to earn her master's in social work, and found her dream job. As a counselor at the Community Living Room, a psychiatric rehabilitation program, she created a model for group therapy that introduced art and spirituality. Her clients, mostly transgender people and queer people of color living with HIV, called her "pastor," a term she'd never really heard applied to a woman. She marched with the AIDS Coalition to Unleash Power (ACT UP), the grassroots advocacy organization founded in 1987 to bring attention to the deadly epidemic. She also helped start a candlelight Narcotics Anonymous meeting at eleven o'clock on Friday nights. That meeting—dubbed the Eleventh Hour—grew to become one of the largest in the city.

At home with Jeff, she'd never experienced such loneliness. She was working full-time while at school to pay back student loans, which her new husband didn't have, thanks to his family. She was also doing all the cooking and cleaning, keeping house as she'd been raised to do. But it was tough at night, after working and studying all day, to fold laundry while Jeff played video games. Marriage, in the world Rachel had inherited, was supposed to answer a woman's every need and desire. Instead, her hungers surprised her.

For help, Rachel turned back to James Dobson and other authors of Christian how-to books. They made her feel worse. She didn't identify with the female role of submission so much as with the male role of the seeker of adventure and desire. Rachel's solution was to make herself smaller. "I just need to disappear," she told herself. Seeking oblivion, she ran for hours, dozens of miles, and drank too much. At times, she found herself tempted to walk into traffic. Admitting that she needed help was excruciating. But one year into the marriage, she turned to a friend, who told Rachel to call Gwen White.

Gwen had graduated from her psychology and spirituality program at Eastern, and become a therapist in 1997. Turning a church closet with a window into her office, she started Circle Counseling. Offering "professional mental health services grounded in faith" she wanted to create a safe place to help clients explore emotional and mental health. Gwen's practice at Circle Counseling became her passion and focus, as the church was Rod's. Both, in complementary ways, were helping mostly evangelical kids shed the harmful culture in which they'd been raised, without abandoning Jesus. Gwen tried to keep a strict policy that she didn't counsel Circle's members, but, to some, the boundaries grew fuzzy between psychotherapy and what might qualify as spiritual direction. There were other blurred boundaries between the family and the church. When Rod and Gwen's second son, Luke, faced marital trouble, he and his wife went to Circle Counseling, where they saw a therapist friend of the Whites. Eventually, Rod and Luke secured degrees in counseling and became therapists at Circle Counseling, where Luke lived above the office.

The church also subsidized counseling for its members, with therapists at Circle Counseling working out individual rates with prospective clients, and the pastors signing off to pay the bills from church funds. Gwen was especially proud of this subsidy program, which made therapy possible for all who wanted it. In theory, members could receive the subsidy for going to any kind of counseling, but most relied on Circle Counseling.

When Rachel arrived in Gwen's cozy nook, Gwen mistook her wide-eyed slightness for meekness. Soon, however, Gwen saw parallels between Rachel's domestic struggles and her own. Before the Whites left California, Gwen had suffered from a deep depression. On their Jesus commune, Gwen felt overlooked by Rod. Devoted to ushering in a new Great Awakening, he could be pretty grandiose and single-minded. People thanked Rod for offering them teachings that really came from Gwen, and the pattern of being cast in his shadow left her feeling erased and wildly lonely.

Seeking connection, Gwen struck up an intimate friendship with a young married woman on the commune. They swam and talked for hours, until Gwen's growing dependence caused the young woman to pull away. Devastated, Gwen turned to Rod, but he proved too busy pastoring others. One day in 1986, feeling overworked and overlooked, Gwen told Rod she wanted a divorce. "Call a lawyer!" she shouted, tossing a rotary phone at him. When Rod stood up, unexpectedly, the phone clocked him in the head, and Gwen rushed him to the hospital for a stitch.

Gwen knew she had to keep pursuing her independent spiritual growth and therapy. During one session, she noticed a book on her therapist's shelf that she'd been searching for: *The Other Side of Silence*, in which Morton Kelsey, an Episcopal priest and Jungian analyst, explored contemplation, an ancient form of meditation. "Some people call it a waking dream," she explained. "Basically my spirit and the Spirit of God were interacting together." Mornings before the boys woke, Gwen sat in the quiet of an unfinished outbuilding where the commune was constructing a church, and repeated the "Jesus prayer," a form of supplication dating back to the fourth century: "Lord Jesus Christ, Son of God, have mercy on me, a sinner." One image kept resurfacing: she was swimming with Jesus, and for a long desperate second, she realized she was starting to drown. Jesus stood by and let her go under. As the 1990s began, Gwen was drowning under the demands of caring for her own four kids and two dozen more needy members of the Sierra Street Household while Rod was often nowhere to be found. When Rod attempted to read a letter of apology to Gwen, she dumped a bowl of Grape-Nuts in his lap.

Nearly a decade later, in her closet office, Gwen helped Rachel find a pathway out from the Christian patriarchy that both women had internalized. She introduced Rachel to the Catholic theologian Henri Nouwen, whose book *Life of the Beloved* focuses on "Belovedness," the idea that God's unconditional love stands at the core of our being no matter what. As Rachel cast off the damaging teachings that led women to hate and hurt themselves, Belovedness became her lodestar.

After a year in therapy, as her work with Gwen was winding down, Rachel began to visit Circle for worship on Sundays at 5:00 p.m., climbing the stairs above the supermarket and finding a place in the back. Gwen served as Circle's "teaching pastor," a title that challenged the shibboleth that women weren't allowed to teach in church. An inspiring speaker, Gwen guided Rachel and many women to reconsider other received "Christian" ideas. "So much of the Christian witness in our time has drifted to proclamations of success and excellence," she preached. "The God of the strong. The God of the American dream where we choose rightly and fight justly."

Standing before the ragtag Sunday evening crew, Gwen exemplified to Rachel, as to others, that women could be gifted preachers, which Rachel had been raised to think impossible. Then there were Circle's radical readings of Scripture that transformed Rachel's understanding of the role women played in the Bible. In Matthew 15:21–28, when a gentile woman implores Jesus to heal her daughter, he dismisses her, comparing her to a dog. But she pushes back, arguing that even dogs are allowed crumbs from their master's table. Jesus capitulates, praising her faith and healing her daughter. A woman changes Jesus's mind. Intrigued by this teaching and others, Rachel kept coming back. On another Sunday evening, a woman shared her struggles with fertility, quoting Isaiah 54, which begins: "Sing, barren woman, you who never bore a child; burst into song, shout for joy, you who were never in labor." Then, in front of everyone, the woman sobbed. Rachel couldn't imagine sharing such raw emotion in church, or anywhere. Yet in this dingy space, tears weren't simply tolerated; they were holy.

Rachel was still encountering new ideas about women and Scripture when her youngest sister, Rebecca, the blue-eyed troublemaker, arrived in Philadelphia. Rebecca had followed Rachel to Messiah, where, a few months into her first semester, she found out she was pregnant. The stigma of walking around a Christian campus while her belly emerged proved unendurable, so Rebecca transferred to Temple University and moved in with Rachel and Jeff. Her options were to marry the boyfriend she didn't love or put the baby up for adoption. Their mother, Susan, introduced Rebecca to an adoption counselor, and the sisters spent hours sitting together on her bed, poring over prospective adoptive parents. Rebecca chose an open process so that the baby would know who she was. Filling a memory box with family photos, she slipped a message inside that read, "I love you fully!" Late on New Year's Eve 2000, Rebecca woke Rachel. She was in labor. The two headed to the hospital, where Rachel watched awestruck as her little sister, who in her mind was still a child, gave birth to a son. Leaving him in the hospital two days later proved more soul crushing than either could have imagined.

"We'd been fed this heroism in giving up your baby," Rachel said. "But this was too much to give away." The crisis pregnancy center taught the solution of adoption without considering the psychological ramifications. When they returned home, Rachel's mother-in-law bound Rebecca's breasts with frozen cabbage leaves to discourage the flow of her milk. For a few years, Rebecca stayed in touch with the adoptive family, but eventually she received a letter from the father saying that God, and his wife, had directed him to end communication. Although Rebecca eventually married and had other children, she never fully recovered from giving her son up for adoption.

. . .

Witnessing Rebecca give birth opened something in Rachel. She became an informal doula to women at Circle, spending all night on house calls with young and scared expectant moms. She saw Jesus as a mother. "In a sense, we are birthed out of his impermanent death," Rachel wrote. She read *Revelations of Divine Love*, in which the fourteenth-century mystic Julian of Norwich described Jesus giving birth to humankind from the cross. *Revelations of Divine Love* is also the earliest surviving English work by a woman. There were ancient historical examples of this image of being born again, through Jesus, including a sixth-century vulva-shaped baptismal font that archaeologists found in Tunisia.

Yet for Rachel, the sense of Jesus as mother was not ancient or medieval. In 2003, Rachel gave birth to her son, Zach, and then, in 2005, to her daughter, Cori. She took her kids everywhere. On Sunday evenings when Rachel played violin at church, she stashed baby Cori in her instrument's open case. She brought both children to Circle's Mother Blessings, ceremonies in which women came together to support the sacred work of motherhood. Mother Blessings were the antithesis of typical baby showers. Instead of bringing electric warmers for baby wipes, or other trendy must-haves, they offered one another real-life stories of what lay ahead. "The message wasn't 'This is your destiny,'" Rachel said. "It was more 'This shit is difficult and you're going to have really hard moments.'"

Although Jeff remained critical and at the edge, Rachel was drawing deeper inside the community. In 2005, Rod invited her to lead a cell. With her warmth and charm, Rachel was naturally adept at inviting others into the intimate groups of ten. Beginning with strangers she met at the playground, cells multiplied effortlessly under her care. Rachel reached out to neighborhood outcasts, including drug dealers and sex workers, to welcome those Jesus called "the least of these," in Matthew 25:40. A year later, Rod asked her to give her first talk during worship. In the shower as she got ready, Rachel realized that she, a woman, was going to be preaching. She sunk to the bathroom floor. "God doesn't want me to make myself small at all," she realized. "God wants to overflow out of me." That evening she offered a parallel between the temple described in the Old Testament and a woman's body. Both were made to house others, and sacred. "It's about the temple being us," she said.

Beneath these expansive ideals, however, there were subtle but restrictive realities at Circle. Women might lead services or cells, but most were married and many were raising children in playgrounds strewn with needles, or in unfinished houses with lead paint in the windowsills. Renovating on the cheap could kick lead dust into the air. For Rachel, who found God in nature, raising kids in the city involved a sacrifice, and one night in 2009, when Jeff was away on retreat, a housing inspector came by to evaluate their refinancing application. He discovered a carbon monoxide leak in the basement.

"I don't know how you guys are still alive," he told Rachel. She panicked: the leak could already have caused irreparable brain damage to Zach and Cori. What the heck have I done to my kids by raising them here? she asked herself. She took the kids to another Circle home. Lying awake praying while her kids were sleeping next to her, she saw a figure kneeling in the corner. She thought at first that the figure must be an angel, but then she understood it to be Jesus. She was floored. "I knew we were going to be okay," she added, "that the Bible was actually true and that Jesus was advocating for us before the Father night and day."

In 2007, while working her shift at Circle Thrift, Rachel met a high-strung and hilarious hipster, Jonny Rashid. Eight years younger than Rachel, and with bushy black hair, Jonny was audacious by nature. His arrival marked the third generation of Jesus followers: millennials. He'd grown up in the Lebanon Area Evangelical Free Church, a congregation much like her own in a county much like her own, too. Yet his manner was different. Jonny loved pushing boundaries and nattering about politics as they poked around aisles that smelled of sawdust and ironed sweat. As a counselor leading LGBTQ groups at the time, Rachel wondered about Jonny's sexuality. He slipped on outfits playfully, like identities. Once at Circle Thrift when he tried on a pair of women's skinny jeans, she let a weighty moment hang between them, not wanting to venture further into a tender realm with complicated repercussions.

Several years later, when Jonny got married to a woman he met at Circle, Rachel looked on with concern as she watched him weep through the wedding. For Rachel, God revealed herself through these relationships. Before she, Jonny, Julie, and Ben became pastors, they were friends who relied on one another. When Rachel and her kids got lice, for instance, Julie came over to comb the nits out of their hair.

Although she didn't use the term, Rachel was already serving as a pastor at Circle. She was attending births, leading cells, and teaching, and yet she still wasn't sure a woman should lead a congregation. Eventually, in 2011, Rod asked Rachel to become the church's administrative pastor, a job held almost exclusively by women—in other words, his secretary.

"It was a revolving door and it paid crap," Rachel said later. She knew that taking the job meant being mentored by Rod, and was a likely step in becoming a pastor. But she still loved her job as a counselor at the Living Room, where she earned a good salary, and traveled around the country speaking at conferences. Turning over the decision to become an administrative pastor, she spent a night awake and in prayer. "I was embarking on this journey of dying to myself," she said years later. "I know that sounds really martyrish."

Upon taking the job, she found that being Rod's secretary was as awful as she'd feared. Berated for her lack of clerical skills, she cried every day for three years. Rachel had gone from presenting at conferences to getting snapped at for making spreadsheets that Rod didn't like. "I went from feeling pretty accomplished to just feeling like a ding-dong," as she put it. And if God wanted her to start new churches—church-planting was still a male role, including at Circle—she needed a clearer sign.

To wrestle this out with God, she signed up for a women's conference in Colorado's Rocky Mountain National Park. Deciding to go required a new kind of commitment. "To find childcare, book the flight, and say to Jeff, 'We're paying for this, since I need to figure this out,' was huge," she said. At the conference, she waited for a sign. Finally, Jesus came to her in a vision, his arms open wide, asking, "Are you so enslaved to the culture that you can't find this new way that I am bringing?"

She returned to Philadelphia and the next time Rod excluded her from a pastors' meeting, asking her to go get some donuts, Rachel told Rod she wasn't that person anymore. Women at Circle were already calling Rachel a pastor, and she was ready to step forward and fill the role. "I was a serious player," she said. "I was a disciple."

. . .

Rachel, like Julie, never attended seminary. Rod claimed not to value academic degrees, but he could be mercurial. Sometimes the women felt he used their lack of formal theological training against them. Once, Rod snarkily called into question whether Rachel thought she was "qualified" to be pastor. No, she said. This was never about being *qualified*—this was about being *called*. The authority was from God, not from any school or certification.

"If you read the book of Acts, the first church planters were idiots. Luke even records that these guys were so uneducated that people knew that they had been with Jesus," Rachel said. Their qualification was love.

Such freighted moments inscribed themselves on Rachel, but not on Rod, who could miss the effect of his comments on others. Above all, he admired the pastor Rachel was becoming. When he stepped back in 2015, he decided to bestow leadership of his 250-person congregation in Center City, the original Circle of Hope, on Rachel. At the same large meeting in which Rod formally set forth the community's decision to send Ben to South Jersey, he announced that Rachel would become the new pastor of his congregation, which was the largest in the church.

Rachel's husband, Jeff, remained silent. He was not pleased. He resented Circle's claim on his wife, the overcommitment that "doing life" together required.

Rachel couldn't ignore what she felt the Spirit asking her to do. "That call from God kind of stole my heart," she said. Enduring the church for her sake, Jeff attended regularly to support Rachel and to listen to her preach. Yet he remained suspicious of Circle's whiteness and its lore. And having a wife as a pastor came with more personal costs. By default, Jeff would become the primary caretaker of their two kids. After lengthy discussions, Jeff agreed to support her decision, and to lead cells and men's retreats, which he and Rachel called, jokingly, his "manistry."

With Rachel as their pastor, Rod and Gwen intended to remain members and keep participating in the beloved community they'd created. Although in many churches, ethical professional guidelines required departing pastors to take at least a year away from their former congregation, Rod believed such legalistic strictures were unnecessary. Did building the Kingdom of Heaven on Earth require a manual of bureaucratic rules?

Still, Rachel observed, ceding leadership to her could be challenging for Rod. For the next several years, although he'd ostensibly stepped out of day-to-day managing in favor of casting a longer vision as "development pastor," he was still prone to micromanaging her, along with Julie, Jonny, and Ben. Visiting congregations, he offered real-time notes on Google Chat during worship about how to preach. When he didn't like what Rachel was doing, he made his displeasure known. "He'd be there on Sunday evening chatting people up, and send an email the next day on tips and what he thought could be improved," Rachel said. Rachel didn't battle Rod; she didn't feel the need to. She skimmed his tips. "I would take them or leave them," she said.

· · ·

In Center City, gentrification had caused the rent to triple at their loft space, and in 2017 the community dispatched Rachel to find a new building to buy. Just over a mile away, at 2212 South Broad Street in the neighborhood of South Philly, she found out that Carto, an Italian American funeral home, was going on the market. One day in April, with Rod's encouragement, Rachel rang the doorbell, and the owner's daughter, Natalie Guercio, came to the door wearing a bustier and stilettos. She was a local celebrity for her role on the TV series *Mob Wives*. Her bodyguard, in a suit, stood behind her.

"I know this is up for sale," Rachel began, and although Natalie eyed her through heavy synthetic lashes, she allowed Rachel inside and walked her around. In the basement, where Rachel wanted to open a preschool, banks of cameras blinked. Although Natalie was reluctant to let go of the place, the two women became friends over time, and Rachel became a kind of pastor to Natalie. When the deal finally closed, Rachel arrived with a handful of enthusiastic young members to clean up. There was dog poo everywhere, and vats of formaldehyde and containers labeled MEDICAL WASTE in one of the back rooms. In the former viewing room, behind a heavy curtain, the cleanup crew discovered a horse mask, a gun, and a pentagram painted on the wall. Rachel wondered if someone had intended to scare them or if the previous occupants had truly tried to summon evil. The team set about scrubbing the heavy brown carpet, and painting the walls and dentil molding a fresh new coat of white. To be certain they'd vanquished any possible spirits, Jeff spent the night and prayed with other men. Later they learned that Natalie had hosted a purgatory-themed Halloween party there. On *Mob Wives*, she swans around on the same ugly carpet, and Rachel wasn't sure whether the Satan theme was real, or made for reality TV.

. . .

It was exciting for Circle of Hope to have a new pastor who happened to be a gorgeous forty-year old woman from Pennsylvania. One member of Rachel's flock, Bethany Stewart, a chic legal aide who was twenty-six and a budding Black Lives Matter activist, migrated from Center City to South Broad because she wanted to be pastored by a woman.

Not everyone landed at Circle from rural, white evangelical backgrounds. A handful, like Bethany, hailed from Spirit-filled Black evangelical churches. She was raised as the child of a strict fundamentalist pastor, her mother, who'd homeschooled Bethany, teaching her to read at the kitchen table out of the King James Version of the Bible. She'd been taught its diction as well as to accept its verses as literal truth, like a history book. Beginning in Genesis, Bethany had memorized verses about how God created the earth in six days and Eve emerged from Adam's rib, which confused her. "The idea of a woman coming from a man, when women bring life, always felt kind of wack to me," she said. But she had been taught that the Bible was infallible and that there was no questioning its logic.

Homeschool was lonely; outside of tennis camp and dance class, church was Bethany's only real chance to see people. She loved the spectacle of people filled with the Holy Spirit. Women in fine hats babbled in tongues and swooned. "If no one saw you fall out, you might fall out again," she said. Once, a traveling healer laid hands on a woman with a broken leg, telling her she could walk. Bethany watched the woman hobble into a wincing run across the sanctuary. "Her leg was still fucking broken," Bethany said. "That's what I enjoyed seeing at church. Bullshit like that."

By her twenties, Bethany had fallen away from church, until, in 2014, her cousin Jerome introduced her to Circle. (Jerome, who was leading a cell alongside Ben at the time, later became an apprentice pastor alongside Julie.) When Bethany had first attended Ben and Jerome's cell, she'd anticipated a traditional Bible study. But cell was nothing like that. Instead, it was more like therapy, with people sharing their most intimate struggles, and how they related to Jesus. Bethany had struggles of her own. Since childhood, Bethany had been starving herself as an extreme form of fasting to mortify the flesh. Capable of going days without eating, she'd developed severe body dysmorphia. Sharing her story with Rachel had helped Bethany let go of the painful belief that faith required rigid discipline. The idea that God could be kind, and feel alongside her, be *for* her, was freeing and new.

"Maybe God doesn't have to be so hard," as Bethany put it. She also thought it was cool that Circle held worship services at five o'clock on Sunday evenings. "It was almost like they wanted you to go out and party the night before," she said. Although Circle of Hope was nearly entirely white, and worship could be weird, it was very welcoming. "They were the kindest people I've ever met," Bethany said. Rod, however, had a tendency to speak bluntly, which Bethany respected. She'd never seen a pastor wear blue jeans while railing against Disney and the American dream. "Rod is a wild motherfucker," she said.

In 2016, Bethany became the head of Circle Mobilizing Because Black Lives Matter, the compassion team that connected the church to the BLM movement. Although Bethany led Circle's anti-racism efforts, as well as a cell, she wasn't sure about joining the church and becoming a covenant member. Rachel encouraged her. Being a leader, Rachel explained, wasn't just about cells; it included showing up on Sundays and joining the covenant.

So, for Circle's 2018 spring Love Feast, Bethany waded hip-high with Rachel into the Delaware River below the Tacony-Palmyra Bridge. Wearing a pair of black leggings and a T-shirt with stylish rips, she allowed Rachel to dunk her three times under the filthy water. Afterward, she was so grossed out and embarrassed by her clingy wet tee that while everyone else joined the potluck feast, Bethany headed home to shower.

As a new covenant member, Bethany found photographs of herself on Circle's website and social media, which bothered her for a couple of reasons. First, photographs could trigger Bethany's body dysmorphia. Second, the repeated use of her image smacked of tokenism. "I feel like we're taking my picture to make the church look more diverse than it is," she told fellow Circle members. "It's not about seeing Black people as individuals but using them to recruit other Black folks." Bethany assumed that, given how vocal she was, everyone knew how she felt. Rachel, her pastor, didn't.

At an axe-throwing party that Rachel organized for Jimmy Weitzel's thirtieth birthday, someone made a joke that Bethany should pretend that the target was Rachel trying to take her picture. Rachel, who wasn't there, didn't hear the quip. Soon after, Rachel sent Bethany a photograph of herself from another Sunday meeting. Bethany texted back, reminding Rachel of her dysmorphia, and that photos she found unflattering could stop her from eating for days.

"Rachel, I feel like I've tried to explain this before and maybe I've never done it well. But pictures can REALLY ruin my day. I was having a really good day and feeling like I kinda come down and this picture has kinda ruined it. I'm sure that's not your intention, but honestly sometimes pictures of me make me cry, and it's so painful for me. If you're gonna take pictures of me, please don't send them to me, or post them."

Soon after, without Rachel's knowledge, a Circle communications team staffer reposted yet another photograph of Bethany, alongside a pastoral message from Rachel. Incandescent with rage, Bethany texted Rachel, "I hope this wasn't you."

Then Bethany fired off a cease-and-desist letter, demanding that Circle never use her image again without written permission. Attempting to reassure Bethany, Rachel replied with Scripture, quoting Matthew 5:14–16: "You are the light of the world. A town built on a hill cannot be hidden. Neither do people light a lamp and put it under a bowl. Instead they put it on its stand, and it gives light to everyone in the house. In the same way, let your light shine before others, that they may see your good deeds and glorify your Father in heaven."

"You're weaponizing the Bible against me," Bethany wrote back.

Their discussion went back and forth. Bethany was so upset she couldn't sleep. Rachel put the matter aside for the morning, later regretting that she hadn't called the staffer right away to take the post down. For Bethany, this exchange marked the end of their friendship. Rachel kept trying to reach out, but Bethany didn't want to engage. Eventually, at Bethany's request, she and Rachel sat down together, with a church member acting as an informal mediator. Despite Rachel's willingness to repent, Bethany didn't feel ready to forgive. Bethany remained at Circle, but she didn't see Rachel as her pastor anymore. Rachel, who loved Bethany, regretted missing the post before it went up and then arguing with Bethany using the Bible.

Rachel agonized over the incident, especially given the other racial tensions emerging at church. She also felt called to pastor to young women, and to help deconstruct the toxic theology that burdened so many. She wanted to help free them of inherited ideas about God and shame, and she was good at it. I'd seen this firsthand in her cell of Temple University students. Many shared an evangelical background similar to Rachel's, including a sense of themselves as second-class Christians because they were women. They'd been raised on complementarianism, a word not all of them knew, although many lived its implications. Complementarians held that, according to Scripture, men and women were divinely ordained to fulfill distinct roles in society and the church. Women were instructed to submit to their husbands, and not to lead in church.

Without spending a lot of time defining or debating academic terms, she read the Bible alongside her cell, reconsidering powerful Old Testament heroines and seeing new kinds of leadership in their stories. When anyone balked at different interpretations, Rachel didn't push. Ideological debate wasn't her thing. She thought preachiness and finger-wagging would only drive away these young women, and she was right. Along with Rachel, I'd met their parents. They trusted Rachel and were drawn in by her warmth and presence, as well as her fluency in their church-y language. Bare of trendy progressive trappings, she could travel between worlds with ease and authenticity. She could listen gracefully to a cell member's mom argue against abortion without having to assert that she was pro-choice. She could sunbathe with Temple students on a New Jersey beach, wearing a floppy hat and cat-eye sunglasses, trading Rooney Mara's Magdalene for Audrey Hepburn out of *Roman Holiday*.

Chatting about their classes, she dropped nods to Scripture about love and self-forgiveness.

For her Temple cell, their weekly Zoom meetings during the coronavirus pandemic became a lifeline. Many, who'd just escaped from the strictures of their conservative families when they enrolled in Temple, were thrown backward into their childhood homes, whispering from their girlish bedrooms about how hard it was to be trapped in lives they'd already left behind. They made care packages for one another and drove around dropping them off. For Rachel, the care packages and giggling deliveries were a playful and positive form of beloved community. This was following Jesus. However, when she shared a video of one delivery during YouTube church, Ben and Jonny, among others, began to comment with dismay that the girls weren't properly masked and were not staying six feet apart. They were hugging!

This bothered Rachel in the extreme: here were young women unlearning an evangelical culture of shame, only to be scolded by men. She was delighted when a woman who'd been at Circle of Hope for decades quoted Scripture in their defense, typing into the chat a paraphrase of what Jesus said to his disciples who scolded a woman for anointing him with expensive perfume (Mark 14:6): "Leave them alone, they've done a beautiful thing."

4

JONNY

"Blessed are those who are persecuted because of righteousness."
—MATTHEW 5:10

On Sundays in Fishtown, Jonny Rashid preached the news. "I like holding the Bible in one hand and the newspaper in the other," Jonny said, echoing the twentieth-century Swiss theologian Karl Barth, who opposed the Nazis. Leading his congregation of theology students and activists from his music-stand lectern, a style inherited from Rod, he shifted his weight from leg to leg, casting himself as a modern-day prophet. Being a prophet wasn't about ladling soup; it was taking on, and taking down, the powerful and popular voices of conservative pundits and theologians. He sought the gospel everywhere and rarely went more than a few moments without checking email or Twitter or Reddit or Facebook or Trello or Slack. Jonny compared himself to the apostle Paul, who sought to become "all things to all people" for the sake of sharing the gospel. "To those on Instagram, I got on Instagram to win them," he said.

. . .

Jonny had grown up steeped in this language of winning souls, and battling the forces of evil through spiritual warfare. His Egyptian parents were evangelical Christians who had fled religious persecution in Cairo, arriving in the United States in 1982, three years before Jonny was born. The Rashids moved first to Allentown, Pennsylvania, where they joined Jonny's uncle, who, along with his grandfather, had established the Christian Evangelical Arabic Church, an independent church that held services in Arabic and welcomed primarily Syrian and Egyptian Christian immigrants. Many were fleeing the Middle East in search of religious freedom and economic opportunity increasingly denied them in their traditional homelands. Jonny's father, Samuel Rashid, a medical doctor in Egypt, got a job at a McDonald's while he searched for a residency. Eventually, he found one, and when Jonny was four, the Rashids moved to Lebanon County; while his father worked on his medical career, his mother, Rebecca, started Sphinx Cuisine, a catering business.

Few in Lebanon County knew the long history of Christianity in North Africa and the Middle East, the birthplace of the faith. Most of their neighbors assumed, given their skin color, that the Rashids were Muslims. Jonny was one of the few brown kids in a county where nine out of ten of the 150,000 residents were white. Until the 1990s, the Ku Klux Klan held sway in neighboring Dauphin County; in 1999, when Jonny was thirteen, the Klan held a rally in the heart of Lebanon City. Ignoring the racism, the Rashids hewed tightly to right-wing politics, in accordance with their evangelical principles.

Although Christianity existed in Egypt since ancient times, the Rashids traced their evangelical faith to the 1940s, when Jonny's grandfather Fawzy Rashid met American evangelical missionaries and joined them, becoming a pastor. Fawzy managed to build three churches in the predominantly Muslim country. "It was hard to get the government to permit you to even fix a toilet in a church," Jonny's father, Samuel, told me. The family revered Fawzy and believed God had given him special powers against evil. In one story, Fawzy woke one night to find the devil standing next to his bed. "Oh, it's you!" Fawzy said, unperturbed, going back to sleep. Jonny suffered from severe migraines, which he believed were divine punishment for lying, embellishing his academic success to please his parents.

Like so many other kids of his generation, Jonny was terrified of not making the cut when Jesus returned at the rapture, a pseudo-scriptural event that stemmed from the early 1800s and swept through evangelical subculture during the 1970s. The 1973 Christian horror film *A Thief in the Night* featured a popular song used by the Jesus movement, "I Wish We'd All Been Ready." These narratives had profound, if often unseen, impact on American culture. The rapture reemerged in the Christian pop culture of the 1990s thanks to the mega-popular Left Behind book franchise by Tim LaHaye and Jerry B. Jenkins, which sold sixty-five million copies and laid out in graphic detail exactly what would happen to those whom Jesus didn't welcome up to heaven on Judgment Day. The terror of not being a good enough Christian to be raptured gave birth to a new anxiety among young evangelicals. When they were tweens, Jonny's sister, Debra, two years older, checked his bed in the morning to make sure that he hadn't been raptured and she left behind. Jonny's childhood fear that demons "were alive and well" didn't leave him. Although he'd never seen a demon personally, once he became a pastor he counseled others to "look away" and "not engage" such evil if they encountered it. "It could kill you," he said. Into his thirties, whenever he got a creepy vibe about a place, he spoke aloud the name of Jesus.

. . .

As a teenager who didn't fit in Lebanon County, Jonny became a self-described asshole. Wearing a T-shirt with the slogan GORE IS AN OGRE—a swipe at the presidential candidate Al Gore—he argued with his classmates about what being a Christian entailed. He'd been raised to believe that the Bible was the inerrant and infallible word of God, and he used his encyclopedic knowledge of Scripture to set himself above others, since he so often felt set apart. "I didn't want to convert people," he said later. "I wanted to win."

He was fifteen when his teacher wheeled a rickety TV into the classroom of Cedar Crest High School to watch events unfold on 9/11. That morning, Jonny told a friend, "Muslims did this." As fellow Christians who believed they'd suffered under Muslims, the Rashids assumed the attacks would bond them to their community. Instead, they felt singled out, suspect. Samuel started wearing an American flag pin on his white doctor's coat. Jonny had always been embarrassed by his mother's poor English in public, and the fact that she made their PB&Js on pita, but her failure to assimilate made them stand out, and felt like a threat to their survival.

"We thought if we hated Muslims enough and draped ourselves in enough American flags, we'd be spared," Jonny said. "That just wasn't the case." At school, bullying became explicit and racialized. "Jonny, you look like Osama bin Laden," one classmate told him. And the list went on: "Jonny, you're a camel fucker." "Jonny, you're a sand n——." "Jonny, does your family live in a pyramid?"

"For my parents, 9/11 felt like what they were escaping came to the U.S. to attack them," Jonny wrote later. "For me, it felt like who I was, and what I looked like, was under attack in the U.S." It didn't matter that Jonny's family had suffered for their faith over centuries, or that he could quote almost any letter that the apostle Paul sent to anyone. Jonny wasn't white enough to be a Christian.

This experience of rejection sparked Jonny's first doubts about his evangelical faith. At his youth group, Jonny and the other teenagers sat in a circle at the back of the church, talking about how God created the earth in six days—a tenet of young-earth creationism—and how not to masturbate. He vehemently supported America's invasion of Afghanistan in October 2001, but over the next few years, his feelings changed. As the Bush administration, in 2002 and 2003, set an open course toward invading Iraq, Jonny startled his youth group by saying, "I really believe Jesus has another way," and raising questions about Christianity and militarism.

In other areas, too, Jonny's hard-line ideas were softening. In 2004, the spring of his senior year, a gay-straight alliance started at Cedar Crest, and members of the fundamentalist Westboro Baptist Church showed up from Kansas to protest with signs that said GOD HATES FAGS. Dimly aware of his own budding and complicated sexuality, Jonny risked speaking out against the protesters. "Hate really doesn't have a place in school or in America, it truly doesn't," he wrote on the personal blog he kept during high school.

At the edges of evangelical subculture, other young Christians were asking about the morality of war and the American empire. Many of these questions were influenced by alternative bands within contemporary Christian music. To parents, these alt Christian bands sounded much the same as popular contemporary Christian music, which was conservative. Instead, the subversive lyrics functioned as code, vanishing before they reached adult ears.

Rocketing around the hills of Lebanon County in his Volkswagen Golf GTI, Jonny became a devotee of these punk Christian practitioners. With his youth group, Jonny rode in a van to Creation, an annual Christian music festival that drew crowds of as many as a hundred thousand people. Creation boasted a petting zoo, fireworks, extreme sports, and baptisms. (One of its founders, the Reverend Dr. Harry Thomas Jr., was convicted in 2018 of sexually assaulting minors and sentenced to eighteen years; he died in prison in 2022.) On the festival's main stage, the celebrities of contemporary Christian music played familiar songs. Yet Jonny was drawn to the smaller stages, where alternative bands sowed seeds of deconstruction. In "Get Your Riot Gear," Five Iron Frenzy, a Christian ska band, called out police brutality. In "The Old West," they took aim at the racism and violence embedded in the historical American doctrine of manifest destiny:

> West or bust, in God we trust, "Let's rape, let's kill, let's steal"
> We can almost justify anything we feel . . .
>
> Said one cowboy to another, "I think it would be nice
> if we could take these injuns and convert them all to Christ"

. . .

In summers during high school, Jonny ran the Coal Cracker water ride at Hersheypark, a chocolate-themed amusement park in Hershey, Pennsylvania, the town founded in 1903 by the Mennonite-born Milton S. Hershey for the workers at his chocolate factory. Even at a crowded amusement park, Jonny, wearing sideburns and short shorts, stood out. Mornings, he and his friends carpooled to work together, often stopping on the way at a Turkey Hill convenience store. One morning in 2004, while Jonny's friends stocked up on chocolate milk and breakfast sandwiches, the middle-aged employee behind the cash register told Jonny that he couldn't come into the store if he wasn't buying anything.

"I don't want to accuse you of stealing," the employee threatened, as Jonny recalled it.

"I don't want to accuse you of discrimination," Jonny shot back.

The mother of one of Jonny's friends was a Turkey Hill executive. After Jonny reported the incident to her, the employee was fired. That fall, from his Temple University dorm room in Philadelphia, Jonny testified in a hearing to determine the employee's eligibility for unemployment benefits. For Jonny, the experience of calling someone to task for discrimination proved formative.

Jonny, who hoped to become a journalist, didn't want to go to a Christian college like Liberty University, where his sister had enrolled. Although his mother feared that it would cost Jonny his faith, he instead chose Temple, a public college with no religious affiliation. Still, he heeded his mother's admonitions and drove three hours round-trip almost every weekend to attend the Lebanon Evangelical Free Church with his parents. He also joined Crosswalk, an on-campus evangelical ministry.

With one foot in progressive activism and another in conservative evangelicalism, Jonny participated in some of Crosswalk's activities but not all. When his fellow Crosswalk Christians carried crosses on their backs to class on Good Friday to remind students that Jesus had died for their sins, Jonny demurred, opting instead to cover the event for a school paper. He still donned a blazer for worship, but he grew his hair big and long, which set him apart from the cleaner-cut Christian crew at Temple, where his classes were rapidly reordering his priorities. He

attended progressive teach-ins called Dissent in America, which decon-
structed George W. Bush's use of the word "crusade" and the growing
wave of American militarism. The teach-in attendees discussed the hypocrisy of Pat Robertson, the Christian right leader, who claimed to be
pro-life yet prayed publicly for the death of a Supreme Court justice.
Christians weren't the problem in America, one aging hippie speaker
told the students. Evangelicals were. Inwardly, Jonny cringed. He de-
voured Angela Davis's 2003 book, *Are Prisons Obsolete?*, and wrote a
sociology paper about how punk music and 9/11 had shifted his politics. Income inequality and the environment were the real Christian issues, he argued; supporting war and opposing abortion were not. Jonny
came to believe that he and his fellow evangelicals were worshipping
different gods. When Crosswalk sang hymns or prayed to "our God,"
Jonny sang "my God" instead.

Jonny was joining an evolving generation of Jesus followers. Calling
themselves by a variety of terms—"exvangelical," "deconstructionist,"
"spiritual but not religious"—some attempted to reclaim Jesus, disentangling the Bible from conservative politics. Others abandoned the Bible altogether. Beginning in the late 1990s, this burgeoning movement
drove a market for popular books and podcasts, as well as celebrity
speakers, eventually including the likes of the author Glennon Doyle
and the podcaster Blake Chastain. In addition, alternative forms of
spirituality were emerging. The massive wellness market began to take
hold; yoga became a billion-dollar industry; and meditation gyms with
expensive memberships, like MNDFL, sprang up around the country.
Millennials who'd been raised in secular homes started reading the book
of Ezra and debating Harry Potter, the sacred text of their childhoods.
Disaffected young Christians were dabbling in new movements, including one called the emergent church.

Concerned with the diminishing number of young believers remaining in the church, the emergent church sought to make worship
more relatable and relevant. Led by figures such as Brian McLaren,
Doug Pagitt, and Rob Bell, the emergent church movement provided an
alternative to right-wing evangelicalism. Moving beyond old-fashioned

worship practices and dogmatics, many flirted with the postmodern idea that there was no such thing as objective truth. Suddenly young people could ask questions previously verboten about whether everything in the Bible had actually happened. Emergent churches tried to woo a young generation of skeptics by having fun. They held pub nights, rented warehouses and movie theaters, placed sofas in their sanctuaries (modeling the grunge look of *MTV Unplugged*), and hosted fringe Christian rock shows that blurred the lines between sacred and secular.

Circle of Hope didn't view itself as part of the emergent church movement. Its members weren't joiners and insisted on doing their own thing. Yet its unchurch-y churches featured couches and Circle hosted fringe Christian rock shows at Fishtown, its coolest location.

Fishtown lay only a few blocks away from the North Philadelphia neighborhood of Kensington, which was a stop on the East Coast's heroin highway, and suffering the ravages of the opioid crisis. Its parks were open-air drug markets frequented not only by sellers and users but also by people trying to help them. Along Kensington Avenue, various faith-based storefronts had sprung up, such as On the Rock Ministries, which advertised boxing and Jesus, and Cast Your Cares Ministries—the latter's sign depicting two steaming mugs of coffee, a Bible, and the inscription "Cast your cares on the LORD and He will sustain you." There was also the long-standing Jesuit presence of St. Francis Inn, serving hot meals and brown-bag lunches, and the House of Grace Catholic Worker health clinic.

Among the arrivals in Kensington, in 1998, the emerging radical evangelical leader Shane Claiborne, along with six other students at Eastern, started an intentional community called the Simple Way. Part of a movement known as "new monasticism," the members of the Simple Way grew their own vegetables, ran a food pantry, and refused to pay taxes and thereby fund military spending. On the Simple Way's door, a prayer was painted over a dripping heart:

HEAL ALL THAT IS BROKEN . . .

IN OUR HEARTS

IN OUR STREETS

IN OUR WORLD

AMEN

During his first year at Temple, in 2005, Jonny heard about Circle when he learned that one of his favorite Christian punk bands was playing at the Fishtown location. Curious about a church that would host his kind of bands, he went to check out worship. He donned a blazer, tucked a Bible under his arm, and took the train to Kensington. Walking the sketchy half mile from the station to Circle's Fishtown location, he entered the former dentist's office and warehouse with smeary plate-glass windows, mismatched wine-colored drapes, and exposed brick walls. The interior was club-like and dim; dust motes floated through what rare sun could reach the room. A praise band was singing, with lyrics projected on the wall so that everyone could sing along. There were the familiar uplifted hands and outstretched arms.

Outfitted with its own recording studio, Circle was home to folk-punk bands like mewithoutYou and the Psalters. Painting their faces like a hippie version of the rock band Kiss, they called for revival. Modeling their new sound on "where Christ is found, and where Christ calls us to be—among the least of these," the Psalters visited refugee camps in Turkey, Israel, and Iraq to share music and instruments with people from different cultures. Music was only part of a larger way of life that revolved around seeking Jesus and justice—members worked in homeless shelters and lived in a bus that ran on vegetable oil.

Some funkier members practiced anarcho-primitivism. Believing that civilization was the primary engine of alienation, they rejected modern hygiene, including showering and changing clothes. On Sunday evenings, visitors could sniff out the church on their way up the stairs to worship. Instead of High Church "smells and bells," such as frankincense smoking from thuribles, the sacred aroma was the human body.

On that first visit to Circle of Hope, Jonny, who didn't know any of the songs, felt out of place until he spied a sticker on an open laptop that read WAR IN IRAQ? NO! It was the first sign he'd ever seen of Christian pacifism. When the music stopped, a raggedy twenty-something guy with a nose ring stood up. Jonny noticed that beneath his denim jacket, he wore a ripped maroon sweatshirt. While wondering what kind of church leader would wear torn clothing to worship, Jonny realized that he was the pastor, Joshua Grace.

Skimming past Scripture, which wasn't really part of his talk, Joshua launched into a poorly constructed ramble. Jonny was dismayed. It didn't follow the sermon model to which Jonny was accustomed: first, the male pastor laid out the Bible in simple, literal terms, then offered direct exposition, often with a practical application for a Christian life. He was a world away from Rick Warren and Tim LaHaye. After the meeting, Jonny recalled approaching Joshua and asking, "Do you believe the Bible is the inerrant word of God?" he asked, testing. If the pastor said no, then he wasn't really a Christian. In response, Joshua posed a question of his own: "Are you asking me if I believe that Jesus miraculously fed five thousand people, or that five thousand people shared what they had?" Jonny was disappointed. To answer a question with a question was an apologetic trick. It was proof enough that Circle of Hope was a scam. Jonny left, telling people that he didn't much like Circle's theology, which didn't adhere strictly enough to the Bible. Later, back at Temple, the Crosswalk pastor warned that "Circle of Hope doesn't preach the word of God."

During his sophomore year at Temple, he visited Circle only sporadically. That changed the following summer after he traveled to Cairo with his parents in 2006. This was his third trip to Egypt: he'd gone as a toddler and in middle school to visit family and to see the sights. This visit was different: Jonny, Debra, and their parents were going on their own mission trip to provide health care and food to poor and persecuted Christians. Most days, the Rashids' minivan climbed the steep hill of a slum near the old city, where the Zabbaleen ("Garbage People" in Egyptian Arabic) lived. In Cairo, as a sign of their low status, Christians collected garbage. They also kept pigs, which, according to Islam, were considered unclean. In Garbage City, pigs clattered through a narrow warren of streets leading up to a massive cave church carved into a cliff. In this community, Jonny witnessed suffering and poverty he hadn't accounted for or anticipated, along with unexpected acts of humility and grace. Watching their driver tenderly bathe an old man, he was overcome.

Recently, Jonny had become a vegan. In Cairo, every afternoon around three, cousins hosted the Rashids for lunch, honoring their American family by placing extravagant meals of suckling pig and stuffed chicken before them. Too young and concerned with displaying his principles to think about the cost of this hospitality, Jonny rejected the meat out of hand, offering lectures about the evils of capitalism and the merits of socialism. His Egyptian family started good-naturedly calling him *shmaal*, "eccentric."

In Egypt, Jonny was reading Shane Claiborne's popular 2006 book, *Irresistible Revolution*. Published only six months earlier, it was becoming a phenomenon, selling 300,000 copies and inspiring disaffected evangelical kids to commit their lives to global service. As Jonny read about Claiborne's experiences with Mother Teresa in India, he saw reflections of the poverty and grace that he was witnessing in Egypt. His parents defined the adversity facing Egyptian Christians in terms of religious persecution by Muslims. But Jonny could see the enemy wasn't Islam; it was economic injustice.

Claiborne also wrote about attending Circle of Hope. So Jonny decided to give the unconventional church a more committed try when he returned to Philadelphia in the fall. On this visit, when Jonny raised his hand to ask a question during worship, which Circle encouraged, Joshua called on him, saying, "Oh, Jonny, I was just praying for you the other day." Jonny was thrilled to be remembered. When he told Joshua afterward that the conservative Crossroads pastor had tried to warn him away from Circle of Hope, Joshua replied, "They probably want to keep you around, because if you were in my church I'd want to keep you around." For Jonny, this was transformative: he wasn't just welcome, but wanted.

From that day on, he was all in. During worship, he looked around the crowd and made lists of people he wanted to befriend, taking them to Atlantis, the dive bar down the street where Circle members hung out and drank PBRs. People at Circle shared cars, and Jonny lent his beloved VW to anyone who needed it. "I wanted to be that person," he said. For his entire life, Jonny had longed to belong—to be part of something righteous. Dumpster diving outside a Dunkin' Donuts with other Circle folks, he fished for a dinner party of bagels and donuts. Hanging out with Circle's anarcho-primitivists, Jonny didn't stop wearing deodorant, but he did take a job at Circle Thrift, where he shared his shift with Rachel, to whom Jonny was drawn as a warm friend and cool older sister. At parties that Rachel and Jeff hosted, Jonny stumbled around the third-story roof-deck with older hipsters who got a kick out of his humor and his nervous charm.

Rachel took Jonny under her wing, making him feel part of Circle, and he adored her, calling her "radical and daring and courageous" in a blog post he wrote years later for the church website titled "What I Love About Circle of Hope: Rachel Sensenig." By then, many blogs, which had in the 1990s so effectively allowed unconventional figures at the edge of evangelicalism to find new influence and platforms, had gone the way of the Blackberry. Still, Rod—intent on reaching others with his message and building influence—continued to blog relentlessly. Circle of Hope had all kinds of blogs, many offering daily prayers and messages from the pastors.

As a strategy of church growth, Circle encouraged cell leaders to keep a "Love List," of people to target for evangelization and prayer. Many approached their gym trainers or baristas. Casting himself as Circle's "company man," Jonny went up to strangers and acquaintances, relentlessly pursuing them with invitations to come to his cell. He'd moved away from a career in journalism; the print market was collapsing, and he wagered that teaching in a public school would prove a more stable profession. After graduating from Temple with a master's in education, he taught high school social studies in Kensington for a couple of years. A career as a public high school teacher, however, didn't hold enough potential for the vision and leadership to which he felt called. Joshua asked Jonny to join the 2008 apprentice pastor program. It was Jonny's dream come true.

Rod, however, harbored reservations about Jonny. He'd seen Jonny from a distance over the past several years, and he wasn't impressed. Rod had watched many kids shed their parents' conservatism and find new freedom in following Jesus. Jonny, though, wasn't like that. For one, he treated Rod with a deference that irritated him. "I don't know what you're doing," Rod recalled telling Jonny, but "we're not doing that here." In addition, Jonny had a fire-and-brimstone tone that wasn't Rod's vibe.

Yet both men were glued to the news and shared similar takes. Along with Ben, they disagreed with David Brooks, the conservative *New York Times* columnist who, they felt, positioned his right-wing arguments in seemingly reasonable language. They also disdained the punishing, albeit popular, theology of neo-Calvinist pastors like Mark Driscoll, the polarizing cofounder of the failed Mars Hill megachurch who preached damnation while clad in a flannel shirt, drawing tens of thousands under his influence. At Circle, Jesus was love, love, love and forgiveness, not excoriation and hellfire.

Still, despite their similarities in taste, Rod thought that Jonny did little more than talk, or Tweet, about injustice, which wasn't the Circle way. "We are united in demonstrating the gospel by acting for justice, not merely talking about it," one proverb held.

And Rod, moreover, didn't trust Jonny's ambition. In group settings, he'd observed Jonny asserting himself in ways that Rod felt reflected Jonny's ego rather than a commitment to Jesus. Rod, who could be brutal in his characterological assessments, told Jonny that he was "a narcissist" and that he was "passive-aggressive." Rod also labeled Jonny with one of his most damning monikers: "You're not really Egyptian," he said. "You're more Central Pennsylvanian." He was referring to the self-righteous mindset that masqueraded as faith, and from which he'd been trying to help young people escape. For Rod, labeling someone "Central Pennsylvanian" was a way to call them small-minded and moralistic—too tied to the rural towns and evangelical churches in which they were raised.

All this led Rod to dismiss Jonny early in the monthslong apprenticeship, calling him too unstable to be a pastor. Jonny, however, didn't give up. The next spring, when Joshua again invited him to become an apprentice, Jonny put himself forward. This time, despite his reservations, Rod, who trusted in the process and the Holy Spirit, kept his objections to himself.

· · ·

By 2010, when Jonny became a pastor, most progressive Christians were openly embracing LGBTQ affirmation, but Circle of Hope was not. Instead, the church was becoming known as the city's "progressive, homophobic church." As a pastor, Jonny was toeing a complicated line: he wanted to welcome everyone to Circle, without understanding how he was setting up queer people for rejection.

That year, Andy Stahler, a social worker in his thirties who worked with the aging, arrived at Fishtown curious about the place. Andy, who'd grown up in an evangelical church in the Philadelphia suburbs, came out when he was a teenager. As a result, he'd suffered religious abuse, and since then, avoided church altogether. But Circle of Hope looked to be different. People were dedicating their lives to the poor and choosing to live in Kensington. "They're doing some pretty hardcore stuff for Philadelphia that I'm not doing," he'd said. If their attitude about serving the poor was radical and different, Andy assumed they must be open around issues of sexuality.

In Fishtown, Jonny took him to the dive Atlantis for PBRs. When the issue of Andy's sexuality arose, Jonny assured him it wouldn't be a problem. Rod and Joshua weren't concerned about Andy's sexuality. There'd been queer members in the past. But they warned Jonny against allowing campaigns around sexual identity. Jonny didn't take this warning seriously.

In July, Andy attended OutFest, an annual LGBTQ block party, where he and a friend handed out flyers they'd made listing churches that welcomed queer people. Wanting to add Circle to this list, he emailed the entire church, asking, "We want to welcome any and all people to our congregation, no?"

Rod issued a swift and direct rebuke. "We do not want to be divided up by gay political activism," he replied. "You are not in covenant with us, certainly not enough to resist promoting a divisive issue we have been successful at avoiding, so far." Rod blocked Andy from the church listserv, then warned Jonny against allowing the church to be used as a political platform for gay rights. This was the kind of activity that Rod sometimes referred to as "infection." "Do not wait," he wrote to Jonny in an email. "Get into it before the infection takes root."

In response, Jonny apologized to Rod for causing some of the "infection" by waiting too long to talk to Andy, which he was going to do that evening. Inviting Andy to his house, Jonny offered him a choice: "Stop talking about homosexuality or leave the church."

"I wasn't willing to do either one," Andy told me years later. "The church is a place for all people, and so is God's love." Instead, he wrote to Rod, bidding to remain part of Circle, "I spent so many lonely years thinking that the very thing I was inside was bad—that in my being, I was an abomination . . . It made me feel like, why do any good at all? I was very lost for a very, very long time. Now, I have joy and purpose and other Christian friends who really love Jesus. I do not condone promiscuity. It's about accepting people's identity."

Rod tempered his tone in reply: "You are on a rare journey, especially among so-called gay people, don't you think? I am so glad God found you and convinced you he loves you as you are. You're right. I was protecting the church, as is my duty. But I was also protecting you from the church, since email dialogue about sensitive subjects, especially sexual, are almost impossible not to misunderstand." He went on: "I knew your intentions were good and I can support your goals in many ways, I think. My interests were order, mutuality, unity, clarity and the big picture of living as the organism we call Circle of Hope."

Andy, however, kept trying to win over Rod so that he would not be ushered out. "Thank you for your kindness," he wrote back. "I never thought of it as you protecting me but that means a lot." He went on: "I just want to reiterate that I am not at Circle to push a gay-affirming position. I have already agreed to back off on that one. I am here because I love Jesus." Andy pleaded with Rod to be allowed to keep attending Jonny's cell so that he didn't "stumble," he wrote, adopting a word he'd heard at Circle.

Jonny received a voicemail informing him that his cell had been "dissolved." It wasn't clear to Jonny whether Rod and Joshua had decided to shut it down to stop Andy from returning. This wasn't the last time that a cell was dissolved for going rogue or harboring dissent. "There was nothing for him to come back to," Jonny said. Andy had no other choice but to leave. Although Jonny had apologized to Rod and carried out his directives, he felt uneasy about what he and the church had done. "I was carrying a lot of water for something I didn't believe," Jonny reflected years later. Andy eventually joined the Green Church, a welcoming congregation that met in a Philadelphia-area arboretum, and where a friend's mom was the pastor. Andy became a deacon.

With Andy gone, the issue of sexuality receded for a time, and Jonny focused on building his career at Circle of Hope. He wanted to get married, a decision he would later see as influenced by the heteronormative pressure on pastors at Circle of Hope. With his allure and determination, Jonny was known as a flirt among the young women in the church, and soon he paired off with a woman who he thought was awesome. By the end of 2010, they were married and hiving off to form a new congregation with fifty young people, including college students, in North Philadelphia near Temple University. The vibrant crew, which met at first in a parking lot, came together to jam and drink beer. For a time, they kept the congregation's sound equipment in a van, since the congregation had no permanent home. Jonny pastored and baked cookies.

For all the countercultural trappings, however, the church remained socially conservative when it came to gender roles and power. And it remained ambivalent about affirmation. In 2012, Jonny was approached by a queer couple to officiate at their wedding; he refused, saying that although he "personally accepted them," Circle of Hope wasn't "there yet." "Better no conversation than a bad conversation," he hedged. "At least that's what I'm saying for now." Privately, he tried to set himself apart from the Whites, venting to friends about Ben's white privilege and singling him out for problems at the church. "*You are an educated, employed, white, tall, man!*" he wrote to one friend, using italics for his imaginary conversation with Ben. "*You almost never have to think of any 'category' and it's easier for you to graduate to the 'New Humanity' because you were the emperor of the old one!*" In a church that spoke derisively of empire, calling the founder's son an emperor was a pointed attack.

Ben, who knew nothing of Jonny's opinion, assumed the two were close friends.

In 2013, as his theology on sexuality evolved, Jonny made an unusual admission on his pastor's blog on the church's website: "Being forced to identify sexually, for example, when no adequate label exists is painful—one might say, I'm not totally gay or totally straight, but I feel like I need to fit somewhere. And I feel that pain personally."

Outside of Circle of Hope, both secular and mainstream Protestant culture around affirmation had shifted. In 2013, the Supreme Court struck down part of the antigay Defense of Marriage Act, declaring the 1996 law signed by Bill Clinton unconstitutional. Among progressives, the new moral call was an increasingly loud drumbeat to pass a federal law to legalize gay marriage. According to Gallup, 50 percent of Americans agreed. For a rebel outpost of Jesus followers claiming to be radical and visionary, Circle had fallen woefully behind and was attracting public censure. A local paper ran an article that year, claiming that the seemingly progressive church was "silencing gay congregants." The reporter, Ryan Briggs, who had been Jonny's debating partner in college, quoted Andy Stahler as saying that Jonny was "doing Rod's dirty work." When cornered for comment four years after the incident, Jonny stonewalled, telling Ryan that he didn't really remember Andy, which was untrue. "Rod told me to deny it, and I did," Jonny said.

Soon after the article was published, Jonny spotted Ryan across the room at a city council meeting on affordable housing, an issue particularly rife in Fishtown, which Circle of Hope had helped inadvertently to gentrify. Jonny, who sat on the steering committee of the Philadelphia Coalition for Affordable Communities, was there to advocate for a land bank. He turned to a fellow activist and pointed out Ryan.

"That dude just wrote an article saying that I hate gay people," he said.

"Do you hate gay people?" the activist asked.

Jonny replied with a vehement no.

When Ryan Briggs approached Rod White about Andy's complaint, Rod invoked Matthew 18:15–17, which many evangelical churches use as a model for discipline: "If your brother or sister sins [against you], go and point out their fault, just between the two of you. If they listen to you, you have won them over. But if they will not listen, take one or two others along, so that 'every matter may be established by the testimony of two or three witnesses.' If they still refuse to listen, tell it to the church." Here's how it was supposed to work: if someone in his church had an issue with Rod's behavior, he explained, then, according to these verses from Matthew, that person should come to Rod alone at first and in private. But Andy had broadcast his complaint in the newspapers.

As Jonny explained it in a blog post at the time, the advice in Matthew 18 is like the opposite of what Kelly Clarkson does in her song "Since U Been Gone." He cautioned against the public callout. "Sometimes writing an angry breakup song isn't best," he wrote. The best way to contain conflict was to go to the offender in private, one-on-one. "We need to move on beyond the rage, I think," he continued. "Especially when it comes to relationships within the church." Later, he would come to view this post as one more way in which he was acting as Circle's company man.

In some ways, the direct approach to conflict in Matthew 18:15–17 limited the corrosive power of gossip, since one believer first went to another in person and alone. But a problem around power was built into the teaching: applying Scripture in this way also helped maintain the status quo by silencing dissent. To confront a pastor about his wrong-doing required not only courage, but also positional power.

Several weeks later, a second article appeared in another paper saying that Circle of Hope was phony: "Their target demographic is millennials. Yet today, in 2014, it is demonstrably their position that they will not even talk about the place (if any) of gay people in their church." For all the talk about rejection of worldly culture and of out-siders, Circle of Hope didn't like being called behind the times, es-pecially on issues of justice and including people at the margins, like same-sex couples. Finally, unprompted one day in a meeting, Rod asked Jonny and others, "Why don't we let them get married?"

Several months later, Rod wrote an addendum to the church's teachings that fell under the title "Marriage in the New Creation." It was a first and halting effort to acknowledge queerness. "Sexual arousal is a characteristic of a person, not their identity," he wrote. "How we respond to our arousal and the feelings themselves tend to be fluid and are subject to the same temptations and maturation as are all our ways." In other words, it was natural for someone to be attracted to people of the same gender but choose not to act on it and enter into a heterosex-ual marriage anyway.

This idea resonated with Jonny. He could be attracted to people of both genders and choose to stay in his marriage.

. . .

Jonny was close to Rachel and to Ben, but he didn't know Julie very well for the first several years they pastored together. Their personali-ties couldn't have been more different: where Julie was quiet and seri-ous, Jonny was everything but. Still, they had much in common. Julie's parents lived only a few minutes from Eli's Place, the wood-paneled diner that Jonny's parents opened after his dad lost his medical license. Curiously, the Rashids also endured a local scandal during exactly the same years as the Bittermans did. In 2013 and 2014, Samuel Rashid was indicted on multiple charges of indecent assault of four female patients, including a teenage girl. More than thirty women had come forward, willing to testify. In court, his accusers said that Samuel had conducted unnecessary breast and pelvic exams for unrelated complaints, such as a sore throat.

Samuel Rashid pleaded no contest. He lost his medical license, and received a sentence of six months to two years in Lebanon County Correctional Facility. Still, Jonny's family didn't think he was guilty; they maintained instead that he was following the advice of his attorney. Being a person of color in such a white county, the family held, made it impossible for Samuel to get a fair trial. Racism, Jonny believed, was a main factor. How could it not be in a county where the KKK had been embraced and where schoolkids called him a "sand n——"?

"The only real possibility I held out for my dad's innocence was the racism of Lebanon County," Jonny recalled. "The jury was likely to fry him."

When Samuel was incarcerated, Jonny drove to Lebanon County Correctional Facility once a month to visit. "To see him wearing a jumpsuit was as hard as you'd imagine," he said. But in terms of weighing the veracity of the charges, to Jonny, his dad's case wasn't as clear-cut as innocence or guilt. "My dad thought that he could do what he wanted and was invincible," Jonny said. Harder still was the public dishonor. Although his mother, Rebecca, believed her husband had been falsely accused, Jonny suspected the women were telling the truth. "I didn't think they were fabricating the story," he said.

After serving six months of his sentence, Samuel Rashid was released for good behavior, and once he was out of jail, the Rashids didn't speak about the ordeal. Over the next ten years, however, as the #MeToo movement informed public consciousness, Jonny's perspective shifted. It didn't matter if the women had misunderstood Samuel's actions. "What matters is how many accusers he had. I decided to believe the women's stories," he said.

"Would a white doctor have gotten in less trouble? Maybe. But I still believe that for what he was charged with, the sentence that he ended up serving was fairly minor."

In an effort to compartmentalize, Jonny focused instead on the dismal state of American politics. When Donald Trump was elected president in 2016, with the decisive support of Pennsylvania, including his home county, Jonny was disgusted. When Trump enacted the Muslim ban, barring kids who looked like his own from entering the United States in 2017, and lawyers rushed to the Philadelphia airport to help them, Jonny began to argue partisan politics in the pulpit, issuing a prayer that his mentor Joshua said cut off the heads of all the white people. Although the Whites agreed with most of Jonny's positions, Rod and Ben didn't like his tone, hearing in it the platforming and political side-taking that Circle of Hope strove to avoid.

Later that year, when a white supremacist murdered the counterprotester Heather Heyer during the Unite the Right rally in Charlottesville, Virginia, and Trump declared that there were "very fine people on both sides," Jonny heard echoes of the Anabaptist teaching of a concept called the third way. For centuries, Anabaptists had taught that following Jesus transcended politics and other worldly divisions. If two sides were in conflict, there was always a third way, which Jesus revealed when telling his followers to turn the other cheek or writing in the dirt instead of sentencing an adulterous woman to death. But Jonny was beginning to think that avoiding political conflict in the name of the third way was a means to condone racism. "It was becoming clear how hollow the theology was," he said. Knowing that he would risk Rod's displeasure if he wrote in such starkly partisan terms, Jonny decided to take a stand.

That week, Jonny blogged under the title "How to Make an Anti-Fascist a Follower of Jesus." Online, Jonny was learning to wage theological debates in a new community of Facebook groups that formed out of r/Christianity, a discussion on Reddit. "It felt like youth group," he said. Jonny had met very few of his new friends and enemies in real life, but that didn't matter.

This embrace of the moral merits of social media marked a departure. Four years earlier, in 2013, he'd blogged, "Twitter, Instagram, and other social media not only makes us more self-conscious, it also makes criticism of each other easy." But now these online conversations were his most stimulating, and they were taking place beyond Circle.

In these virtual communities, Jonny created a new role for himself. He policed chat rooms and threads, making sure that amid debate, no one was inflicting racial harm. When someone violated the safety of others, Jonny tried to drive the offender out.

"How long do you need before people of color can feel safe?" he wrote angrily to a white woman administrator of the r/Christianity group's offshoot on Facebook who wouldn't kick a member out of their group.

"Back the fuck off," she told him.

He didn't. The woman called him sexist, but in the end she left the virtual community and Jonny dismissed the incident. "It was white woman's tears," he said.

As Jonny's tone sharpened online, so did his sermons and blog posts. Ben began to call them "too intellectual." As Ben saw it, the Christian circles on Twitter, which Jonny frequented, were less about following Jesus than they were about gaining followers. "The pointy-headed Twitter people don't want to follow Jesus," Ben said. They were, he felt, interested in garnering clicks and likes based on saying the right thing. "And that's how Americans work, but I'm not an American," Ben groused. "I'm a Christian."

In Ben's critiques, Jonny heard echoes of Rod, and feared he was risking his position at Circle. "I might be targeted," he realized.

Jonny's church plant was also foundering. By 2017, it was clear that college kids' lives were too peripatetic to help Jonny establish a new Circle near Temple University. So many of the contradictions Circle had contained for more than a decade were also pulling the church in different directions. In Fishtown, the "good businesses" they'd seeded were thriving. Those businesses included Pizza Brain and Franny Lou's Coffee Shop (named for both the abolitionist and poet Frances Ellen Watkins Harper and the faith-based civil rights activist Fannie Lou Hamer), "the only organic and conflict-free coffee shop in town." Yet their success, which helped transform Fishtown from a ravaged neighborhood to one of the hippest in Philadelphia, ushered in a complex dynamic. By creating jobs and businesses, which made a place more habitable, they had also made it more expensive. Circle's idea of "healing neighborhoods" by "occupying the places of empire" sounded inspirational, but the presence of young white professionals purchasing dilapidated homes and planting vegetables in empty lots that they bought for a song at city auctions had severe consequences, however unintended, for others. They drove up property values and drove out longtime residents.

"We talked about gentrification as if it was someone else, but it was us," said Dawn Smelser, the owner of the local yoga studio MotherHeart and a former Fishtown covenant member. Dawn had arrived at Circle's Fishtown location in 2010, by accident, while attending an African drumming class at the back of the space. Circle was so emergent that Dawn hadn't known it was a church. Inspired by their justice-oriented mission, she'd come to Sunday meetings and, soon after, decided to start her studio nearby, hanging a sign with MOTHERHEART in a Sanskrit-like font above a set of prayer flags, which grew tattered and faded. But leaders opposed her teaching yoga, as it meant promoting Eastern traditions. The pastors asked her to steer Circle members away from Hinduism, toward a "Christ-centered" practice. Circle of Hope was also opposed to all forms of self-help if they weren't focused on Jesus. "We are discipled for mission, not just for personal growth," one proverb instructed.

The Fishtown community began to come apart in 2017, after Dawn's friend Sarah divorced the Whites' second son Luke. After the split, Luke remained at Fishtown, heading the little kids team for those under four. He eventually dropped away, although he still belonged to the covenant. Dawn received a blind carbon copy of an email that leaders sent to Sarah, forbidding Sarah from attending Circle meetings, including the cell she led. Sarah was instructed not to invite friends of more than a decade over to her house for spiritual practices, like morning prayer, or social ones, like brunch.

"She was shunned," Dawn said. "But I didn't understand that until I tried to leave the covenant a few months later and people refused to talk to me on the street. Finally, someone explained that I was being shunned, too." Shunning was an old-fashioned discipline—an Anabaptist tradition since the 1500s, when it was called the ban. Circle didn't officially practice shunning, but in its tight-knit community, it was clear who was in and who was out.

For all the countercultural trappings, members tended to marry one another young, and Circle placed a high value on monogamy and abstinence. The understanding wasn't that sex was sinful. It carried responsibilities. "How we relate sexually is a spiritual, communal matter and can't be reduced purely to a discussion of private expression or individual rights," one proverb read. So, the thinking followed, breaking the bonds of a marriage endangered the community.

When a Circle couple faced a split, it was often the woman who no longer wanted to stay in the marriage. Several of those women felt cast as harlots, treated as if their departures posed a danger to others. Distaste for this undercurrent, disaffection due to divorce, and the absence of affirmation—as well as a swift and mysterious departure by Joshua Grace from Fishtown—left members uneasy. Although Joshua resigned, ostensibly to take a sabbatical, many friends and congregants felt he had been pushed out. (To speed Joshua's exit, Jonny was empowered to hand him a severance check for $25,000.)

When Jonny took over in the fall of 2018, some of the old heads, as longtime members were called, blamed Jonny for displacing their beloved pastor. It was a difficult time for Jonny and the Fishtown congregation, but through humor and goodness, he prevailed. He quietly changed the emergent culture, which had wooed people without making it clear what Circle actually was. On the glass door of their Frankford Avenue building, beneath the sign reading Circle of Hope, Jonny added (WE ARE A CHURCH).

For Andrew Yang, a Taiwanese American musician and attorney who'd already been at the church for a decade, Jonny's grace as a leader intent on bringing people together amid these divisions became the reason to stay. "I admired his compassion and his humility and his ability to accept criticism that he didn't deserve and kind of absorb it," Andrew said. "He worked with the people willing to work with him and was charitable to people that didn't." He then added, "That version of Jonny, I would've followed him anywhere."

. . .

Jonny still got caught sometimes between being a company man and being himself. In 2018, Circle continued to wrestle with some aspects of LGBTQ affirmation, but Jonny was eager to publicly signal that queer people were welcome, so he asked Rod and his fellow pastors if he could post a picture of himself with a rainbow flag on the church's Instagram to signify the church was inclusive. Rod, who disliked the political implications of the rainbow flag, went along begrudgingly. Jonny also contacted Church Clarity, a crowdsourced website that scored churches according to their stance on LGBTQ inclusion, and listed the Fishtown location as affirming.

On issues of race, Jonny also sometimes found himself caught in between. In advance of Black History Month in February 2020, Bethany Stewart asked Rod if she and her fellow activists on the Circle Mobilizing Because Black Lives Matter compassion team could write prayers for the church website. Rod said no. Circle didn't need prayers for Black History Month, he'd told her, since church teachings were already "naturally anti-racist."

But Bethany had grown tired of being told no. She was familiar with Circle's lack of commitment to teaching anti-racism. When she led book groups and teach-ins on behalf of Circle Mobilizing Because Black Lives Matter, all were opt-in. Compassion teams could go out into the world and help change things, but they weren't supposed to turn inward and try to teach or change things at the church. Leading discussions, she found that although members were willing to hold forth on racism elsewhere, they were incapable of owning the problem in their own lives, or in their church. They assumed that by calling themselves anti-racist, they'd already done the necessary work of dismantling racism, which was a cultural construct anyway.

Rod's claim that Circle's teachings were "naturally anti-racist" seemed more of the same. "We're really good at looking at other churches and seeing their racism, but we don't see it in ourselves because we have this attitude that we've arrived," Bethany said.

So she went ahead and posted prayers for Black History Month on the Circle Mobilizing Because Black Lives Matter Facebook page. She wrote about the secret language embedded in the spiritual "Follow the Drinking Gourd," by which slaves mapped their trip north using the Big Dipper to guide them; she wrote about loving Cardi B and how the biblical invocation "Oh! May the God of green hope fill you up with joy!" could apply to being an ally during Black History Month: "Ask yourself how you can support and celebrate revolutionary black joy."

People began to read the prayers and share them in cells, and soon after, Jonny asked her to come to his office in Fishtown for a meeting. Bethany didn't know Jonny well, but she'd noticed that Rod had cc'd him in their discussion about the prayers for Black History Month.

"They called me to the Black principal's office," she said later.

Jonny greeted her warmly, and offered her a La Croix from the mini-fridge he kept stocked for visitors. She remained reserved, and glanced at his office bookcases, which tracked two thousand years of Christian thought and practice: Bible concordances; *Christ & Culture*, by H. Richard Niebuhr; more recent offerings such as *The Naked Anabaptist*, by Stuart Murray; and a leadership book that Rod had instructed the pastors to read, Edwin H. Friedman's *A Failure of Nerve*.

Finally, Jonny worked around to telling Bethany that her daily prayers were proving "divisive." He explained, "I don't want to have to choose between the Black prayer blog and the white prayer blog."

To Bethany, this sounded like convoluted white logic: here was Jonny, a brown man, serving as henchman for the white pastors. Still, they chatted amiably, sharing frustrations about why the church wasn't further along in its anti-racism efforts.

Jonny recalled offering his opinion that Circle should hire an outside diversity, equity, and inclusion consultant. By the end of the meeting, he thought he'd managed to patch things up. Somewhere inside, Jonny had an inkling that he was again doing the church's dirty work. Although

Jonny didn't see it at the time, Bethany knew that Jonny, no matter how charmingly he spoke, was coaxing a woman of color to be silent.

. . .

Bethany and I had met at a Love Feast several months earlier. She was standing by the inflatable birthing tub at Rachel's South Philly congregation, talking to a sopping-wet friend whom Bethany had recommended for baptism. When I approached to ask her about her experiences at Circle of Hope, she offered to meet me for lunch. Several weeks later, we met up for Indian food. She talked to me about why, as one of only a few dozen Black women at Circle, she loved these gentle weirdos so much, and how she saw herself as a "missionary to white people."

"I take my survival skills, particularly my ability to charm white people, and make them feel convicted for anti-racism," she said. Adept at crossing boundaries, she felt called to point out to her white church friends, with as much humor and grace as she could muster, how living the gospel required being honest about the role racial privilege played in their lives.

Since childhood, she'd grown accustomed to navigating white spaces, like tennis camp and dance. After homeschool, she attended public high school in Middletown, Delaware, where, inspired by a show she loved on MTV, Bethany entered a largely white world of cheerleading. She went on to captain the cheer squad at Delaware State University, a historically Black institution, where she also joined a Black sorority.

Above all, Bethany was a funny and preternaturally perceptive observer of human nature. As a pastor's kid, like so many others at Circle, and like me, she'd spent her formative years hanging out in liminal spaces, watching wild Christian rituals as a sometimes-reluctant participant observer. Our lenses were distinct. She'd watched Black women swoon in fine hats; I'd watched white ones dance around a labyrinth with roses clenched in their teeth in Chartres Cathedral.

Yet at Circle of Hope, we shared many of the same observations, agreeing on the craziness of following Jesus by not showering and on how it seemed a pretty extreme act of devotion to put your head underwater in the possibly toxic Delaware River, as Bethany had done. And yet there was an absolute kindness in this community, a living example of being "in the world but not of it." The depth of their devotion was inspiring, and offered a powerful alternative vision of some of the lesser-known forces shaping evangelicals. It seemed possible, at the moment, for this redolent crew to hold on, even amid tensions of which they weren't fully aware. And then the world banged its fist against the glass door.

PART II

5

JULIE

*"For I tell you that unless your righteousness surpasses that
of the Pharisees and the teachers of the law, you will certainly
not enter the kingdom of heaven."*

—MATTHEW 5:20

Between the demands of church and family—including her efforts to keep her kids healthy—Julie Hoke was spending days and nights in the unfinished basement of her and Steve's Germantown row house. After Zooming all day under the map of India and the bansuri flute, she and Steve returned to the basement after dinner for a family circuit-training workout they called Jump Around. They'd devised a makeshift boot camp with several stations, including a mini-trampoline, a set of hand weights, and a kid's punching bag Julie's mother had found at a yard sale in rural Pennsylvania. An app they'd downloaded beeped to alert them to shift stations. Jump Around wasn't just for the kids. In the stress of the pandemic and the conflict at the church, Julie guessed that she'd gained close to thirty-five pounds.

During the fall of 2020, she and the other pastors were setting goals for their annual map that were sharper and far more directed than usual. To make sure they were finally following through on their longstanding claims about being anti-racist, they'd set concrete aspirations "to amplify the voices of people of color, increase their presence on the leadership team, and commit to listening to their perspectives, *even if it causes discomfort"*—an italicized qualifier that Bethany Stewart insisted they add. Bethany, who was gifted with uncanny foresight, had anticipated how difficult fulfilling this goal might become. They also committed to hiring an anti-racism consultant who would help them root out the places where racism remained hidden in the church.

Then another wave of violence gripped Philadelphia. On October 26, two police officers responded to a 911 call from Cathy Wallace, who needed help with her mentally ill son, Walter Wallace Jr. When the officers arrived, twenty-seven-year-old Wallace was wandering in the street with a knife. From fifteen feet away, the officers fired a dozen rounds into the young man, killing him. When news of Wallace's murder broke, protests erupted once again in Philadelphia, and Circle of Hope began to argue vociferously about how as Christians they were called to respond.

Many believed it was time for the church to speak out more forcefully against police brutality. Three of Circle's compassion teams of activists circulated a statement calling for the dismantling of the Fraternal Order of the Police (FOP), the labor union that critics claimed protected even its most murderous members.

"We each have a personal responsibility to step up and pressure the powers that be to alter course," Circle Peacemakers wrote to the church's listserv. "The actions that bring that pressure can take many forms, but they are a necessary part of 'Loving your neighbor as yourself.'" The statement went on:

As Christians, we must engage in this work because dismantling these institutions provides us with blocks needed to build the Kingdom preached by our savior Jesus Christ. Additionally, we are called to see Jesus in the poor and oppressed. This seems easy in the case of Walter Wallace Jr., who was murdered by the state in front of his mother just as our savior was. Jesus died for our sins, Wallace died because of them: because of racism and the things that we allow to divide us. If we truly believe and want others to believe that "There is neither Jew nor Gentile, neither slave nor free, nor is there male and female, for you are all one in Christ Jesus," as Paul wrote, then we must work towards conditions which bring that spiritual reality into focus. If the material realities of people's daily lives tell them the exact opposite of this truth, then we appear to be hypocrites and liars.

Signing onto such a statement as a unified body would send a clear statement as to where Circle of Hope stood, the activists argued. Who could object? Yet Gwen White called for pause. "Our whole community as a church has not had time to come to an agreement," she responded. Instead of firing off a petition demanding political action, which Circle of Hope had never done, Gwen thought the community first needed to talk. "Dialogue," she added, "is our heartbeat." Gwen had no love for the FOP, and Rod called them the "devil," but pressing people into signing statements wasn't the Circle Way. Another longtime member echoed Gwen: "I have to speak to the manor [sic] and means our very simple and organic body of Christ is being led in the thread. Forming coalitions, drafting statements on behalf of the church, and consolidating internal power demonstrates a quasi-legislative approach to our public witness and leadership in our church. This has never been our way."

Jasmine Umana, the medical fellow who was a member of Julie's cell, was on her way to a shift at the hospital when Gwen's email dropped. Astonished by this reluctance to do something so anodyne as condemning police violence, she called Julie. "I need white leaders to speak up! I need you to speak up!" she urged. To be an ally, she explained, Julie needed to publicly push back against Gwen. This marked the second time that Jasmine had "called in" Julie. Several months earlier, when Jasmine became a cell coordinator, Julie wrote to the Germantown congregation, announcing Jasmine as a new "leader of color." Jasmine pointed out to Julie that emphasizing racial identity was tokenization. Julie took these lessons as gifts. She was grateful that Jasmine trusted her enough to make the effort at correction. "Calling in" was an act of love. Julie agreed with Jasmine that the confrontation around the FOP required a deft and public intervention, yet she needed a beat to figure out what to do next.

In the meantime, Jasmine circulated her own churchwide missive: "I am rather confused by the concern regarding making a statement. Isn't that what we do every year with our Map? Isn't that the point of our proverbs? To make a declaration of what we believe and stand for?"

Pete McDaniels, a corporate attorney and a relatively new member of color in Jonny's Fishtown congregation, followed suit. "If we are uncomfortable saying defund the police or dismantle the F.O.P., why does the website say, 'We will do what it takes to be anti-racist'?" he asked. Naming Circle's "hypocrisy," he quoted Martin Luther King Jr.'s "Letter from a Birmingham Jail": "I have almost reached the regrettable conclusion that the Negro's great stumbling block in his stride toward freedom is not the White Citizens' Counciler or the Ku Klux Klanner, but the white moderate . . . who constantly says: 'I agree with you in the goal you seek, but I cannot agree with your methods of direct action.'" Although Circle of Hope liked to call itself radical, maybe it was really a community made up of the kind of white moderates King decried.

Julie paced the back alley between her family's row house and their yard, which they'd opened to their neighbors for everyone to use. Julie and Steve had strung white lights through the trees and around a wooden trellis, installed a firepit, and hosted potluck dessert parties. Soon, as public health strictures eased, the Hokes installed basketball nets in their alley so that kids would have something to do. As long as kids complied with the limited numbers of players allowed, Julie and Steve were willing to endure the incessant and all-hours *pang pang* of the ball against concrete. When the nets broke, which they did often, they quietly bought and installed new ones. This kind of invisible service to her community was in keeping with Julie's vision of collective pastoring.

However, speaking up in the middle of racialized conflict required a different kind of leadership. Julie needed to put herself forward in a new way on behalf of Jasmine, and others, and for herself. She understood the competing ideals at play, and empathized with Gwen's call for discussion before the church took any kind of action. "Dialogue made us who we are," Julie said. "There's great integrity to this." Collective decision-making was the core of the Anabaptists' theology. Circle of Hope had always discerned where the Holy Spirit was leading them through reasoning things out together. People could disagree while still loving one another. Yet in these charged times, disagreement took on a new meaning.

To disagree with a call to sign a petition against police violence, or to call for a pause in taking collective action, risked ignoring the suffering of people of color in the church. Suddenly, Circle's old insistence on dialogue was hurting people. To follow Jesus, in 2020, required trusting the wisdom of those expressing hurt. Building the Kingdom of Heaven on Earth wasn't about tolerating or including people at the margins of society. It was about *being led* by them. Prostitutes, women, lepers, the poor, gentiles—all were reviled during the first century. Yet these outcasts were the first to recognize Jesus. That's why Jesus had said that "the last will be first."

On a lawn chair outside her parents' garage in Middletown, Delaware, Bethany skimmed the email chain in outrage. Gwen's call for more dialogue was a call to do nothing. For nine months, since Rod and Jonny had blocked her from writing Black History Month prayers on the church website, she'd mostly stepped out of leading at Circle of Hope. She'd been going through a bad breakup and focusing on her parents' health. But this discussion felt too outrageous for Bethany not to speak up. Gwen, along with the male pastors, rarely showed up at the anti-racism events Bethany led, and here she was calling for more of them. So Bethany waded into the email fray, writing to the whole church, but really to Gwen.

"If we're under the impression that the dialogue isn't happening then we actually need to be asking ourselves if we've been participating and listening to these voices because, if it's one thing we do, it's dialogue. A lot." To drive home her point, she listed dates and examples:

We had a book study and hosted the author of *Rethinking Incarceration* in 2018. We had a discussion on the school-to-prison pipeline in 2017, we've hosted a festival every year since 2017 that's about getting people out of prison, Participatory Defense hub since 2018, we've donated almost $20,000 to the Philadelphia Community Bail Fund which is an organization that seeks to abolish cash bail and pretrial incarceration, we hosted a "Defund the Police" event that was streamed to Facebook in June.

Trying to de-escalate, Gwen responded privately to Bethany. Gwen worried that the intent of Bethany's email was to divide the church. "I'm not against anyone and certainly not you," Gwen wrote. "But I also hear from people who are fearful about speaking to you and others about their journey and their questions. I am not saying that means we do not speak out against police violence."

"That's my plight in life as a Black woman," Bethany replied. "White people will always be afraid of me for one reason or another, I'm okay with that." She sounded resolute, but in truth Gwen's comments stung. Bethany had always loved the Whites. Ben, who'd been her cell leader, was still secretly her favorite pastor. Rod was the first to recognize Bethany's potential as a leader; he'd invited her to help him lead his cell, and then multiply her own. Most important to Bethany, Rod had called her "prophetic" in a Facebook post several years earlier. He celebrated her willingness to speak truth to power. But now that she was shining a light on the church, and the Whites, his support for her "prophetic" voice had vanished.

Feeling betrayed by the Whites and the church, Bethany reached out to close friends in her cell, a white couple who'd adopted two Black sons. For the past six months of the pandemic, Bethany had been taking weekly walks with the family to get outside and to support one another. They met up at Lemon Hill, on a bluff above the Schuylkill River. Below, scullers skirted along Boathouse Row. As Bethany shared how hurtful it was to have white people she loved and trusted refuse to condemn the murder of Black people, the couple counseled her to risk being vulnerable, and share how she was feeling with the rest of the church. Maybe if, instead of being clipped and angry, Bethany shared how hurt she was, people at Circle would feel less defensive, hear her better, and accept that they were failing their brothers and sisters in Christ. Bethany took their advice. When she got home from the walk, she wrote to the church, "It felt, for me as a Black woman, that my grief was met with talk of the legalities . . . We missed each other here. God is calling us to keep meeting each other and his son." For Bethany, anti-racism at Circle of Hope always came back to Jesus: What else were they doing together but following him?

. . .

Finally, after days of discussions with members of color in her cell and congregation, Julie knew what to do. She wrote to the church, reminding everyone of the 2020 map and reiterating their common goal: "We have committed ourselves to amplifying the voices of people of color among us and listening to their perspective *even if it causes discomfort.*" To rid themselves of sin, white people had to change. "We are the sick ones," she explained one morning to Rachel and Ben. "We're the problem." Although the Walter Wallace email exchange was difficult, and spoke to new divisions in the church, it also hinted to Julie a new liberation. The fact that Bethany, Jasmine, Pete, and other people of color were willing to share openly about how their white family was failing them marked a shift in power at Circle of Hope. "This never could've happened before," Julie said. "This was never allowed."

In other practical ways, Julie could see that Circle was embracing the goals of the map and following the Holy Spirit in a new direction. With Julie's encouragement, Jasmine's husband, Iboro, was starting a team called New Humanity, through which people of color could report microaggressions and other racialized grievances in the church. Jasmine and Bethany were also starting a new kind of cell, Black Girl Cell, gathering fifteen to twenty women on Friday nights for cocktails over Zoom. (Bethany had picked up mixology to pass the hours of isolation. She'd also learned to pick Dolly Parton's "Jolene" on the guitar, to bake peach cobbler, and to plant a garden in her backyard plot.) For Black Girl Cell, Bethany sent out a recipe in advance—for, say, Alabama Slammers—so that women could purchase vodka, Southern Comfort, and grenadine; then, together, they sipped on signature cocktails and talked about how Jesus was showing up in their lives.

"It's about a woman being met by Jesus in the exact same body you are," Bethany explained. Yet Black Girl Cell served another purpose. This, she knew, was how people of color had long coped with white spaces: finding one another; carving out a circle, even within a broader community; and quietly building freedom. At Black Girl Cell, they shared raised eyebrows at some of Circle's practices—including a drum circle of white women who sometimes mimicked African dance during worship. The cocktails and laughter provided catharsis.

"It's not just me being weird," one Black Girl Cell member, Anita Wood, said. "Like, no, they're weird." Anita, a single mom from Germantown, was relieved to see women of color from other congregations whom she didn't know existed. "I always felt a little different as a low-income person at church, because there aren't many of us here," she said. Black Girl Cell was the first of its kind: a cell based on exclusive identity, which had always been anathema at Circle of Hope.

Julie didn't know what went on at Black Girl Cell, and it wasn't her business. She knew enough about being an ally to respect the space and autonomy of people of color. And as she set out to learn more about race in America, she didn't impinge on Black friends to teach her. Instead, she turned to books, beginning with Drew G. I. Hart's prescient 2016 book, *Trouble I've Seen: Changing the Way the Church Views Racism*. A theology professor at Messiah University, Hart traced the complicated moral history of Anabaptists in America, who weren't permitted by their communities to hold slaves but did little to oppose either slavery or the Jim Crow era that followed. He'd spoken at Circle and coined the term "anablacktivism," calling fellow Christians to lives of "radical discipleship, public witness, and solidarity with oppressed people." Julie read on: Resmaa Menakem, Howard Thurman, Austin

Channing Brown, Osheta Moore, and many others. She began to share books with her flock as a form of pastoring—both with those who agreed with the need to make changes at Circle of Hope, and those who didn't.

At the same time, Julie could sense the strain between her and the other three pastors creeping into almost all of their conversations and decisions. The divisions seemed to be growing more entrenched. Whatever was happening clearly positioned her and Jonny on one side, and Ben and Rachel on the other. But the true nature of the conflict was difficult to discern. They needed to trace the trouble back to where it began. From the start, it revolved around how each related to Rod.

When the pastors decided to go online in March 2020, they bucked Circle's long-standing teaching that being the church required being in person. For a time, Ben and Jonny had forged common purpose. But, as the months wore on, Rod began to complain. He didn't like virtual baptisms. Nor did he think it was wise to lead the church-wide mapping process, discerning their goals for the year, if they couldn't meet together in person. But his greatest grievance by far was the pastors' decision, after the death of George Floyd, to examine Circle of Hope's white supremacy culture. As the church began to look within, and ask questions about the Whites' legacy, Rod's disdain for the pastors intensified.

It seemed to all four that the more power Rod lost in shaping the church, the more critical and undermining he became of them. But the pastors disagreed over how to handle this criticism, and how to lead the church forward in crisis. While the four pastors debated, Rod grew angrier at being ignored. His only recourse became threatening to quit from his position as the strategic and spiritual advisor he called "development pastor." Although he gave no official date for his departure, the fall of 2020 became his long goodbye.

Rod's months-long departure forced the pastors to ask questions. Was the community coming apart? Was this the end of a movement doomed to fail? Was their infighting a symptom of how the pandemic was killing communities? Was this a necessary but painful step toward a new beginning?

Julie hoped as much. To bridge the gap among the pastors, she bought Rachel, Ben, and Jonny each a maranta—a prayer plant—for Christmas in 2020. She delivered the gifts by hand. Ben lived farthest away. Driving across the Ben Franklin Bridge to New Jersey, she met a frazzled Ben in the doorway of his brick colonial twin in Haddon Township, flanked by his two sons, quiet Ollie, ten, and rambunctious Theo, seven. She looped through South Philly to drop off Rachel's and walk with her in FDR Park. Then Julie drove to North Philadelphia. As she left the maranta on Jonny's front stoop, he peered from the window, coming outside in a mask only when she was safely back in her car. Watching Jonny open the door, Julie felt her eyes fill at the sprightly humanness of her friend. The following week, on New Year's Eve, Rod resigned.

. . .

As the New Year began, Julie walked slow loops around Fernhill Park. Each day she passed the basketball court and onward half a mile until the sidewalk ended for no discernable reason, and then back again, ear to phone, listening for hours to the people in her cell, who were telling her of their personal crises, and to the Whites. Few knew that, privately, Rod and Gwen were going through a difficult time.

Over the past year, they'd decamped from the rambling twin they'd purchased in West Philadelphia for $89,000 and sold for $695,000. They wanted to downsize in retirement. So they bought a duplex condo, listed on Zillow for $320,000, that boasted a wraparound terrace and a panoramic view of the Philadelphia skyline. To renovate the condo, the Whites hired a ginger-bearded local contractor who belonged to Julie's Germantown congregation. The Whites paid him $52,000 of their $100,000 project budget to get started, but the contractor delayed, citing supply chain issues. When the contract expired, according to the Whites, the contractor flaked.

With their old home already sold, Rod and Gwen were forced to move their bed into a classroom above Circle Counseling. It was a pain, but the Whites weren't picky about their surroundings: they felt lucky to have a full bathroom and a microwave. Once it became clear that the contractor was never going to finish, the Whites tried to convince him to return their $52,000, or at least some building materials. When he didn't, the Whites hired a lawyer, debating whether to sue. Inside the church, the Whites said nothing about what was happening—not even to their son Ben—in order to avoid gossip. Yet the conflict with the contractor worsened from 2020 into 2021, and it was hard, and humbling, after so many years of guiding everything at the church, to feel powerless. Finally, the Whites turned to Rachel, who pastored them, and to Julie, who pastored the contractor.

"We turned to these people and tried to participate not as leaders but as hurt people trying to process through a conflict," Gwen said. For a time, Julie convinced the contractor not to work for anyone else in the church, which the Whites found reassuring but incomplete. It wasn't that they expected Rachel and Julie to get them their money back, nor did they want a public apology, but they wanted a kind of unspecified acknowledgment that they'd been wronged. Rod complained to Julie that he and Gwen weren't being "loved well." But Julie's understanding of how Rod wanted to be loved was to continue to be in control. When Gwen tried to express how they felt, Julie listened but offered little comfort. Gwen found Julie distant, even scolding; a pastor's role was to make sure that people in the church knew they were cared for, not to shame them. Julie knew she'd disappointed Gwen by not affirming her grievance. In the subtext, she heard Gwen saying, *You're not loving me in a way that feels good to me. You're not a good pastor.* Julie's idea of being a good pastor was shifting: she was no longer willing to placate those with power.

After their attempts to work things out with the contractor failed, Rod and Gwen were still seeking some kind of closure. So, in March 2021, they sent an email to the pastors, their sons, and the two-dozen volunteers who made up Circle of Hope's "leadership team." Claiming they'd forgiven the contractor they sent a lawyerly list of grievances, detailing the conflict, the hiring of attorneys, and how the contractor and his wife had consistently failed to do the right thing. "As you can see we make a good argument," they wrote.

"We have told them that not working this out will follow them in one way or another. But we can't make them deal with their fault, neither will we judge them. We are not even going to wait for something more to happen. If we are surprised one day by their change in direction, that will be a blessing. Until then, we want our leaders and friends to know the story we have been holding in case letting it go causes some damaging variant to arise."

Their email, which read like a small-claims complaint, dropped in the middle of Lent. The timing was especially bad. The pastors were trying to weather a second year of repentance and reflection in lockdown. Rod and Gwen disrupted the season. They explained that they wanted to warn others against working with the contractor and to protect their reputation against whispers in the church—"a damaging variant" of their story.

"WTF??!!!" Jacob, the perceptive outsider, wrote to his parents as soon as he read the email. He knew it played into the worst of the accusations against them: that they were stubbornly refusing to stop wielding their power.

This email was the first that I, along with most of the church leaders, had learned of Rod and Gwen's story of being fleeced. Feeling powerless, they had brought their complaint to the church for support, only to find themselves put on trial. The 2020 map compelled the church to interrogate problems around power. Once that effort began, every conversation, text, email, and proverb came under investigation as to whether it perpetuated whiteness. As the pastors began to argue over its implications, this Lenten email became the most critical piece of evidence against the Whites. Depending on where people stood, the Whites were either victims or perpetrators. Yet Rod and Gwen also became an emblem of how the culture wars were splintering not only conservative evangelicals, but also progressive Christians.

Upon reading the Whites' complaint, Jasmine phoned Julie right away. Here was more of the problematic culture of whiteness at Circle. To Jasmine, it didn't matter that the contractor was white. Rod and Gwen's email exemplified an abuse of power on the part of the founders. Julie was being called in once again to do things differently. So Julie called Rod to explain why this email—which was being received as a carefully worded tantrum of sorts—felt wrong. The conversation didn't go well. Soon after, Ben blew up at Julie, claiming she was violating church doctrine, the one derived from Matthew 18:15–17, which required that one believer go directly to another. Instead, by sending an email to leaders about Rod's behavior without including Rod, she was talking about Rod behind his back.

"You're spreading gossip!" Julie recalled Ben shouting.

"I'm responding as a pastor!" she shouted back.

In the new heat of this exchange, Julie could see that anti-racist pastoring required her to stand in the breach, absorbing white people's outbursts so that people of color at Circle, like Jasmine, didn't always have to. This also marked the first time she'd raised her voice to Ben.

"You're causing trouble!" Ben blustered, warning her. "You'd better hope that Rod doesn't find out."

It was a child's threat, and Julie understood it as such. What exactly did Ben think his dad had the power to do? Punish her? Rod's opinions still carried weight among the older members he'd pastored for nearly thirty years. But newer members, especially those of color attuned to reading power, like the Umanas, knew nothing about Rod. They were alarmed by his sense of ownership of Circle and the fact that he seemed to feel he could do whatever he wanted.

Jonny urged Julie and Rachel to join him in publicly condemning Rod's not-so-subtle grab at control. "What Rod did was a vote of no-confidence in the leaders," he said. "It's a move of desperation." It was also a major political misstep. "I usually make my choices with political acumen," Jonny observed later. "It wasn't the politically savvy thing to do." But Rachel read it as a childish outburst that shouldn't be rewarded with overreaction. "I don't understand this mistrust and need to flex back from Jonny and Julie," she said. "We don't need to be threatened." Rod and Gwen may have been trying to push the pastors into reaction, but they didn't have to take the bait, and get yanked into Rod's sideways demands for attention. "We already hold the positional power as pastors," Rachel told Jonny and Julie. Instead of strategizing how to fire back, she suggested they breathe together and pray. "Can we pause and hold this?" she asked.

As the pastors privately debated over how to handle Rod, some members of the leadership team, the defacto elders, grew alarmed at their silence. Weren't Jonny, Julie, Rachel, and Ben the actual leaders? Rod had resigned months earlier from any kind of leadership role in the church. Why was he still allowed to write the whole church and why weren't the pastors doing anything about it? Concerned, Jasmine wrote to the pastors, and the rest of the leadership team: "In neglecting to address this head on and transparently, we are effectively setting a precedent that this is an appropriate form of communication within our church."

The pastors' inability to issue a unified response revealed what Jonny called "a Grand Canyon of a chasm between us."

Without telling Julie, Rachel, or Ben, Jonny forwarded the Whites' email to five different pastors outside Circle. "It's a founding pastor nightmare," one responded. Jonny also forwarded it to Circle's bishop, Bryan Hoke, to whom he'd been speaking for months about the problems with the Whites' refusal to cede control of the church. Hoke was attempting to field these concerns while being transparent with everyone involved. So, on his own, Jonny prepared to strike back. He drafted a reply that he shared with the outsiders, but not with Julie, Rachel, or Ben.

"What an email!" Jonny wrote to Rod, cc'ing all two dozen of the church leaders and accusing his former boss of sounding "vindictive."

Rachel was taken aback by Jonny's email. She called it "an authoritative smackdown" and was surprised that he'd taken unilateral action, a move that felt unprecedented. Julie was also surprised that Jonny hadn't even let his colleagues know it was coming. Still, although she wouldn't have chosen Jonny's language, she was glad that he'd responded. She didn't have the nerve. "He spoke the truth in a way that I didn't feel willing or able to do," she said.

The following Monday morning, all four sleepy faces were constricted and glum at the 9:30 a.m. pastors' meeting. The weekly meeting, which was sacrosanct and lasted several hours, was a tradition that Rod had started, and Julie, Jonny, Rachel, and Ben assiduously continued. It began, as cells did, with John Wesley's question, "How is it with your soul?"

When Julie shared the state of her soul, she said, "I'm carrying an overwhelming sense of grief around the depths of division on our team over the letter from Rod, and Jonny's email in response." She worried about Jonny's role with the Whites, and feared that in his willingness to openly oppose them, he would be cast as a scapegoat. Sometimes he responded to confrontations with grace, while at other times his rage was visible, and barbed; at those times, Julie said, he was "lit up by the flame." But she didn't think it was fair that he paid the price for voicing the discomfort with Rod that so many people felt. "I'm uncomfortable with you taking the weight of that responsibility, Jonny," she told him, defending him in front of Rachel and Ben. Over the past few days, she'd already heard accusations that cast Jonny's pushing back against Rod as a "power grab" or a "slam dunk." When Julie heard Ben and Rachel, along with others, talk about Jonny's attempt to win power, or take over the church, it angered her. "I'm not interested in picking apart Jonny's motives. I'm going to pinpoint the best and go with it," she said. "I really think Jonny wants to create something new within Circle. He wants us to be the fullness of what we can be, and it is different, and it is beyond Rod."

But transforming Circle of Hope was about so much more: dismantling the hollow structures of whiteness and power that were destroying the planet. This had always been Circle's mission, distinguishing the world's wrong directions from the pull of the Holy Spirit, and moving with the Spirit. Julie saw the symbols of this necessary destruction everywhere. One evening during Holy Week, to practice "waiting in hope even through disaster," Julie sat at her computer in front of a series of images that the Fishtown congregation had cut together reflecting Jesus's teachings about the end of the world. Here were pain and ruin: news photographs of the raging mob wreaking havoc on the U.S. Capitol two months earlier, flames devouring the spires of Notre Dame. The final image was the famous nineteenth-century Thomas Cole painting *The Course of Empire: Destruction*, which shows a troubled sky above a scene of a classical city being ransacked.

"Everything is unraveling in the world," Julie wrote in her journal.

. . .

For the second Easter in a row, the four congregations weren't gathering for Circle of Hope's annual sunrise service at Lemon Hill Park along the Schuylkill River in West Philadelphia. In 2021, Jonny, Julie, Rachel, and Ben and their congregations were no longer aligned on whether it was safe to meet in person. This wasn't simply about public health; rather, the disagreement reflected a differing moral call on what some saw as following Jesus and others considered virtue signaling. Jonny's Fishtown congregation remained on Zoom, while Rachel's, Ben's, and Julie's congregations met locally and in person. "I just don't buy keeping up appearances," Ben said.

Julie's Germantown congregation planned to gather on a knoll in Fernhill Park, directly across the street from her home. To set up for sunrise, Anita Wood, from the Black Girl Cell, and Aubrey White, Jacob White's wife, did the planning. Everyone would be venturing into Fernhill in darkness, so they needed to light their plot in the park. On a trip to the local dollar store, Anita spied some tiki torches and texted a picture of them to Julie and Aubrey to ask what they thought. In response, Aubrey and Julie shared !!!, along with 🖤 🖤 🖤 and 🔥 🔥 🔥.

Despite the emojis, Julie hesitated. Tiki torches had been ruined by association with the racist mob who had brandished them four years earlier at the 2017 Unite the Right rally in Charlottesville, Virginia. In a previous time, Julie might have shared her nascent concerns with Aubrey, who used to be one of her best friends.

Aubrey, like Julie, centered her family and her professional life around following Jesus. Years earlier, as an undergraduate, she'd dropped out of Yale, fearing that in pursuing an Ivy League degree, she'd grown too invested in mammon—the material things of the world. Aubrey finished college at Penn State, and then moved to Philadelphia. She and Jacob, like Julie and Steve, were intentional in choosing to live in northwest Philadelphia, among people of different racial and class backgrounds. Aubrey and Julie had babies within a few months of each other. They both sent their kids to diverse schools, and went to work in organizations where questions about race frequently arose. For a time, in Circle's collective model of sharing childcare, Julie had watched Jacob and Aubrey's son three days a week, making a book that charted his growth, as she did with her plants.

Yet, recently, the scrutiny of Rod's legacy at the church had created a subtle distance between Julie and Aubrey. A committed member of the Germantown congregation, Aubrey wasn't really sure where she stood, or of the nature of charges that seemed to be mounting against her husband's family.

In the park's predawn darkness that Easter, Aubrey and Jacob White arrived to set up for church. The symbolism of the tiki torches hadn't escaped them, either. But Anita was the one who'd bought them, so they relied on her judgment. As worshippers began to arrive, Aubrey overheard one longtime attendee standing at the card table where they'd set up a temperature check and sign-in station voicing objections. So Aubrey held off on lighting them, and Julie went to speak to the man. Although he'd been coming to Circle of Hope for years, he had been raised in the Jewish faith. (At the Unite the Right rally in Charlottesville, the white supremacist mob had chanted, "Jews will not replace us.") Upon hearing him, Julie feared that he was right. The tikis ran the risk of alarming people in a majority Black neighborhood about a group of white people gathering before sunup.

Kids were running around with DayGlo sidewalk chalk drawing arrows on the paths with CIRCLE OF HOPE. While volunteers hid plastic Easter eggs, Julie and Aubrey were hitting an impasse, and interpreted the events that followed differently. Aubrey recalled their moment of restraint as a shared decision: a coming together for the sake of the community. Julie remembered cautioning Aubrey against the use of the torches, and Aubrey being saddened by ceding the symbol to the alt right, which struck Julie as tone-deaf and the wrong place to focus. Marking the moment as a rupture, Julie didn't mention her dismay to Aubrey. No outside observer spying the two women standing together on the grizzled slope, heads bent toward each other, would've sensed the disconnection. Yet the incident became another fray in their friendship.

Dawn broke as a disappointment. Julie couldn't see the horizon or the sunrise; the sky turned the color of gruel. Before her, the slope was more crowded with blankets and stadium chairs than she'd imagined, which offered a sliver of hope. Aubrey and Jacob sat with their kids near Ben's twin brother, Joel, and his wife, Kathy, who'd helped Julie plant the church five years earlier. There was an awkward sadness to the Whites' Easter presence, but Julie was glad they were there. With everyone masked and at least a dozen feet from one another, it was impossible for Julie to read their faces, or for anyone to read hers. When Jacob and Aubrey's son, a gifted violinist, stood on the hillside and played "Christ the Lord Is Risen Today," Julie hung on to its thin strand of joy. Aubrey felt self-conscious and worried that people might complain about one more member of the White family claiming the spotlight. No one did.

Afterward, when she learned about the tiki incident, Anita, who purchased the torches, found it a little overblown—an example of "trying to be righteous at the wrong time," she said. Anita could cite plenty of examples of racialized slights at Circle of Hope, including the fact that her teenage son was frequently ignored when he ran into Circle people on the street in Germantown. Anita guessed that they didn't recognize him because he was Black. But the tikis didn't strike her as a problem. "Come on," she said, chuckling. "You think I'm the one bringing racist torches?"

. . .

When the pastors met that Monday, the day after Easter, Julie shared the state of her soul. "It felt so good to be together, but disconnected, too," she said. "We can't hear each other singing, and singing behind a mask is so awkward. We're not going back to normal." There were many layers to Julie's comment; nothing was returning to what it had once been: the planet, the country, the church, the pastor—all had changed. "My growth requires little deaths," she wrote in her journal. "Reach out for Jesus's hand. The wrong needs to end."

To guide herself, Julie kept returning to the 2020 map. It was time to fulfill one of the goals listed there: "Hire an antiracist consultant to lead us in an extended process of exploration that results in concrete steps to name, confess and address our personal, organizational, and systemic racism." To find the right person, the church formed a search committee, and Julie joined as its pastor.

Despite the written goal, there was resistance to hiring a diversity, equity, and inclusion (DEI) consultant. As some of the boomers, including Rod, and Gen Xers saw it, hiring a professional consultant was a mistake for their anti-establishment church. "I didn't grow up with this stuff," Rod said. "I'm a flower child." No outsider could evaluate Circle's revolutionary DNA, Rod contended, and corporate consultants lived off the fat of capitalist empires. Other members agreed: "I'm not tithing my salary to pay for a DEI consultant; a church doesn't need a consultant," one said. Yet Julie and the other pastors agreed that Circle required an outsider's eye to name what needed to change. "Even if it causes discomfort," Julie said, repeating Bethany's phrase.

After several months, they found Nelson Hewitt, an organizational specialist from Ohio who, along with two other professionals, formed a team that had been doing racial justice and equity work for more than thirty years. Hewitt had a long history of working in churches. A former pastor, he had led four congregations of his own and had been deputized in Ohio by Protestant bishops in mainline churches to lead diversity forums for those who "kept diverse voices away," as he put it.

The crisis over race in white churches had become existential. As surely as 2020 had exposed the contradictions within secular organizations, which had, for decades, glossed over the racism inherent in their patterns of hiring and compensation, the newly resurgent crisis had laid bare the same problems in religious institutions. Black Protestants held views very different from white ones over the role that racial justice should play in the church. For instance, a 2020 Pew poll found that 62 percent of Black Protestants believed churches should "offer sermons that address political topics" like "race relations." In contrast, 42 percent of white Protestants felt discussions of race had no place in the church.

This opposition was strongest among white evangelicals. The largest Protestant denomination, the Southern Baptist Convention, founded in 1845 to defend the institution of slavery, was decrying all discussions of social justice and structural racism as a scourge of secularism. Some went as far as calling the legal framework of critical race theory "evil."

"I fear for the faith," Hewitt said. "I fear for the church writ large." He welcomed a chance to work with Circle, which looked, from its website, like the kind of progressive church where change was actually possible. After he flew to Philadelphia for a final interview, he and his team were hired. To get a feel for the racial and power dynamics at play, Hewitt suggested the pastors invite a small number of diverse leaders to join them for six exploratory Zoom sessions.

Julie startled awake on April 19, 2021, the day of their first session, at six o'clock. (When Julie woke up like this, she paid attention: to her, it usually meant that God had something to share.) She was envisioning the first Pentecost, when, as described in Acts 2, the Holy Spirit descended on the apostles, imbuing them with the gift of speaking in different languages and, by miracle, allowing the diverse group who gathered around them to understand them. At Circle, as in many white liberal churches, Pentecost was often cast as a celebration of multiculturalism. But Julie's vision revealed something else. At that first Pentecost, the apostle Peter called Jesus's followers to renounce their old lives: "Repent and be baptized," Peter told them. "Save yourselves from this corrupt generation." Rejecting the world, these new believers sold all their property and traveled from house to house in secret, hiding from the centurions. Eating together and relying on one another, these first Christians formed the early church. Celebrating Pentecost, and following Jesus, demanded much more than acknowledging difference: it required repenting, then challenging corrupt power.

Nelson Hewitt had cautioned that the exploratory sessions needed to be small so that every face fit on a single screen. But the pastors had tripled the suggested number, inviting all two dozen church leaders, along with every person of color at Circle willing to participate. As the sessions continued throughout May and into June, on every other Monday night, some thirty faces overfilled the screen. The too-high number of participants emerged as only one of myriad snags. Another issue arose after splitting the participants in each session into racial affinity groups: one for white members and one for members of color.

Hewitt's first goal was to assess if Circle had the necessary elements of a "learning environment": a willingness to listen without being defensive. Vulnerability required trust, and his intention was to bring both racial affinity groups together to begin to share specific stories of racialized harm at Circle. But Hewitt and his team found that week after week, the group for people of color expressed that they did not trust that the white group could listen to their truth "with an open mind and an open heart," as he put it.

In Hewitt's assessment, the white people refused to acknowledge their racial power, along with the inherent power dynamics established by the family that founded the church. Hewitt worried about what he experienced as "a flatness" in the white group. "There was no emotional investment," he said later. He'd seen such tensions many times in a variety of organizations, but he was puzzled at the lack of trust among people who shared cells and houses and lives. Didn't they share the same values? How could a church with members who'd woven their lives together so tightly for decades have so little confidence in one another?

The first inkling of trouble arose during the initial session, when Hewitt asked everyone to go around and identify themselves. Ben and some of the other white members insisted on calling themselves "so-called white." This seemed bizarre to Hewitt. But it also created a major block. If the white affinity group wasn't able to be honest about positional power, then Hewitt wasn't sure how they could proceed. Afterward, he talked to Ben about "owning your whiteness."

Every other week, following the session, Hewitt held a separate debrief with the pastors. "The organization can only grow as far as the leaders grow," Hewitt told them. He explained, gently, that the exploratory sessions weren't going well. "Racial justice is an advanced topic," he said later. "If we can't be safe, it's hard to be brave," he said.

By June, Circle had muddled through four largely unsuccessful sessions. For the fifth session, Julie was away on a vacation at the Hoke family cabin along Pine Creek, in Lycoming County. The modern home had large windows and air-conditioning but no cell phone signal, so Julie paid to log on to the satellite internet. Crouched and uncomfortable on the floor of a guest bedroom, Julie felt awful in her body. The room was dark, and her laptop illuminated her face with blue light. She kept shifting the device from her lap to a chair. The discussion was supposed to last ninety minutes.

Finally, in the last twenty minutes, Hewitt brought the two racial affinity groups together. Since the people of color still weren't ready to share their experiences, Hewitt pivoted, asking participants what kind of anti-racism work the church had already done. He knew nothing of Bethany's fundraisers, book groups, or any other of the dozens of events and trainings she had organized over the past six years.

To Bethany, Hewitt's ignorance of her work signaled to her how little value it had in the pastors' eyes. She knew, by sheer numbers of attendees, that her events were popular and that the work mattered to the larger church. She also knew that the male pastors almost never attended. Maybe that's why she'd been erased. "Wow," she thought. "You didn't even think to tokenize me. I really don't matter."

When the question turned to *who* had failed to inform Hewitt about the work that Circle had already done, Julie felt her body run cold. It had been her job to brief him. She knew she'd told him about one book group, in which they discussed Jemar Tisby's 2020 book, *The*

Color of Compromise. He'd forgotten. Hot and nervous, she wanted to correct Hewitt. She willed herself to pause and remain quiet. She'd learned this skill from the psychologist Resmaa Menakem, author of *My Grandmother's Hands*, who argued that the trauma of racism was not simply in people's heads but also in their bodies. To teach people how to heal, Menakem pioneered "somatic abolition," which he defined as "an individual and communal effort to free our bodies—and our country—from their long enslavement to white body supremacy and racialized trauma." After reading *My Grandmother's Hands*, Julie took a workshop with Menakem, forming a triad with two strangers to process incidents of racialized trauma. For months, she'd been learning to sit and hold her first reaction: the defensiveness that signaled "white fragility"—the term for white people's discomfort in discussions about race, coined by the author and educator Robin DiAngelo. Here, where it mattered, Julie found herself able to practice silence until the angry session closed. Then she went downstairs, quietly telling Steve that the session had ended abruptly and upset Bethany, and many other members of color.

Following the charged session, Nelson Hewitt and the pastors invited any people of color with concerns to join his debrief with the pastors several days later. In addition to Bethany Stewart, who dialed in, still furious, the Umanas and Pete McDaniels joined the call. Julie remained on vacation at the Hoke family cabin. As Hewitt explained that he felt it was "unsafe" to continue the work, it took her a minute to catch what he was saying. His team was accustomed to facing resistance, but they drew the line when people began to actively fight against their work. Without a high degree of willingness, it wasn't a great idea to ask people to open their most sensitive wounds: the risks of people hurting one another were too great. Confronting racism was sacred work, he said, "because we're working with people's souls and trying to get closer to God."

And Circle of Hope seemed unable to do it.

Julie listened as Hewitt started to talk about the contract that she had signed on behalf of Circle of Hope. "There's a clause in our contract that allows either party to terminate the training at any time," Hewitt said. "I'm invoking that clause."

Julie's mind spun. Was their anti-racism consultant *quitting?*

"This is such an indictment of us!" Pete McDaniels, the corporate attorney, exclaimed.

Hewitt tried to calm the situation. Julie didn't feel calm. Now they'd have to tell the rest of the church that their anti-racism consultant had actually quit. Pete was right. What an indictment of their church! In despair when the debriefing ended, she went down to Pine creek for a float. Plunking herself into the water, she rested her cheek on her inner tube as she waited for the current to catch and carry her gently downstream. Suddenly, it burst against her face, stinging mightily. As her feet found the rocky bottom, a strong wind rose out of nowhere. A massive tree crashed in front of her and into the stream. It occurred to Julie that whatever had been decaying inside the tree had been going on for so long that only a small breeze was enough to blow it down. That felt like what was happening at Circle. Waiting for the sting to ease, she balanced herself against the current, and felt Jesus speaking to her. "You have to stand still in the muddy water," he told her. "You have to wait." The church was stirred up, and racism was clouding the water.

"The truth is that I am guilty and it is much bigger than me," she said. "As surprising as this is and as sickening as this is, Nelson Hewitt is holding up a mirror." Yet no matter what that mirror forced her to see, Julie was willing to stare into it. "It is shocking when structures and systems that provide shade for me prove to be rotten inside," she wrote to her congregation. "But it is safer for everyone when they come down."

6

BEN

"All you need to say is simply 'Yes' or 'No';
anything beyond this comes from the evil one."
—MATTHEW 5:37

Outside his brick colonial twin in Haddon Township, New Jersey, Ben weeded his front yard, studded with clover. Clamping his cell phone to his ear with his shoulder, he listened to his dad complain. During the summer of 2020, Ben felt torn between his colleagues and his parents. He wasn't sure which side reflected the path the Holy Spirit was calling them to take. "Rod is in my ear all the time, irritating me, and me feeling impotent to execute on what he's telling me," Ben said. Rejection was hardening Rod, who ranted about Jonny's influence campaign to drive the Whites out of the church. Jonny kept claiming this was a structural critique, not a personal one. Rod found this argument mind-bending.

"They say that I'm a principle, something in the abstract," he said, puzzled. "I'm a smart guy, but I don't understand what that could possibly mean." Rod was a flesh-and-blood human who'd served as a father figure to nearly every member of the church, including Jonny. "Jonny is unrecognizable to me," Rod said. "He's gone off the edge and been consumed by the zeitgeist." Rod saw Jonny's narcissism driving him once again. "This isn't Jonny's church," Rod said. "It's Jesus's."

None of the pastors seemed strong—or willing—enough to challenge Jonny, not even Ben, who knew that his father's complaint about the pastors included a tacit criticism of him. "I don't need his fucking critique my whole life," Ben grumbled.

Rod didn't care about being liked or being famous. He cared about influencing people only as much as it led them toward Jesus. "I know I rub people the wrong way," he said. "I don't even care what you think of me. Say what you think and let Jesus decide." He was vying not for himself, but for Jesus, who was, and would always be, the true center of all things.

And although Ben got mad at him sometimes—one day, Ben had called Rod a "dickhead"—and felt dwarfed by his preternatural ability to bring people to Christ in unlikely places, such as record stores, he admired his dad: a visionary spiritual leader who'd planted the coolest church on the planet.

Rod was beginning his long goodbye. He announced, in the fall, that he was letting go of his last official paid position at the church; that of "development pastor." Since 2015, Rod had attempted to hand over Circle of Hope so many times without actually leaving, it was hard to know what his resignation entailed and how to honor him amid all the questions about the legacy he was leaving behind. Rod decided that Circle's 100th Love Feast, in October, would be his last.

For the Love Feast, it fell to Rachel to ask people to write letters celebrating him. She appealed to them as "seekers, lovers, cynics, artists, troublemakers (thank God many of you are still here!)—folks recovering from traditional church and wanting to do something new with Jesus." The letters stacked up.

"Such a powerful and healing impact you have made, and continue to make, on Philadelphia and the world," one read.

"I came to Circle as a pretty staunch Republican," read another, "and initially thought Circle was pretty weird."

A third called Rod "a real-life Mr. Rogers."

Rod's leaving dragged on; he gave his final talk as a pastor on November 15, 2020. Ben called it "a masterclass in saying goodbye." Up close in front of the camera in wire-rimmed glasses and a gray-and-white-striped button-down, Rod looked frail. The hardness of his hurt had vanished. His desire to remain among his flock, and to be cherished, was palpable:

> I'm not going to attempt a George Washington–style farewell speech here so that Lin-Manuel Miranda could make a rap out of it someday. I'm just changing. Still a member of the body, still want to write, offer my gifts, still love everybody, still be available. I just won't lead all the time. And you won't pay me anymore.
>
> I won't be in the Circle as your pastor, or as the development pastor. I'll still be me, and I'll still be pondering the gifts I've been given along the way. Gifts given by regular, flawed people just like you who showed me how ordinary people like us, following Jesus, create revolutionary outcomes.
>
> So let's go off to the margins after someone, and let's keep trying and experimenting with spiritual growth. Let's all love with our last breath. *I* want to love with my last breath . . . And when we do that we'll keep our lives, and we'll keep our church and God will use it all, even in this wild year and whatever comes next.

When Rod was finished speaking, Jonny, in a bright purple floral shirt, attempted to lead talkback up-tempo, but he found Rod's message troubling. When Rod wrote in a farewell note, "I'll always be your pastor," Jonny read Rod refusing to depart. "He wanted to make it clear that he was still going to be around," Jonny said.

Ben found this ridiculous. "Rod isn't trying to hold on to power," he said later. To tell people you'd "always be their pastor" was an offering of love and reassurance, not domination. "You don't know Jesus," Ben said, "and you don't know Rod." He still had trouble accepting that his dad was actually quitting. And when, on New Year's Eve, Rod sent his official letter of resignation, Ben was flattened.

Yet as 2021 began, with his dad's rants and disapprovals no longer descending on Ben, he expressed feelings of an almost vertiginous freedom. There had been moments early on in the pandemic when Ben had seen unexpected possibilities in leading a new Circle alongside Jonny. Sometimes he thought the two proved virtuosic together online. Quick with tech, they shared the Word with snappy repartee. Ben wondered if they should work on "pastor branding."

Julie and Rachel, however, couldn't "keep up," Ben said, and it was true that he and Jonny tended to "run away with it"—interrupting them. When the four recorded segments for virtual church, or midweek video missives, the two women needed extra takes and fumbled with editing software—which slowed the team down and frustrated Ben. In a nod to their mutual gifting, Ben sent Jonny a card quoting Isaiah 30:16: "We will ride off on swift horses!"

During one Monday meeting Ben recounted a curious dream to his colleagues. "I was swimming in a stream that had no bottom," he told them. "It was fathomless. I was swimming at great speed with purpose. The depth of me, the depth of God is without boundaries." For an instant, Ben's face broke open. Jonny looked bored, eyes darting around, multitasking; Rachel murmured affirming tones; and Julie said little. No one stopped to ask Ben what the dream might mean. Within a few minutes, they moved down the agenda to plan the end of Lent and Holy Week.

During Holy Week, to mark Jesus's final days, according to Circle tradition, all four congregations came together, traveling from neighborhood to neighborhood. This culminated in their Easter sunrise celebration at Lemon Hill, heralding Jesus's victory over death. In 2021, for the second year in a row, the pastors struggled to come up with creative ways to be one body while still forced to stay apart. On that Ash Wednesday, when many Christians have their foreheads marked with ashes as a reminder of mortality and the need for redemption, Jonny taught people to make their own by applying a lit match to a cork nub. Ben offered a DIY tutorial in at-home altars.

"Find something fragile because you know we're tending to these things that are fragile or broken or misused, or you know all the things that need to be seen," Ben instructed the small band viewing him in his living room. Behind him was the sewing machine Gwyneth used to make baby quilts for friends. On the living room's lintel, Ben and Gwyneth had placed small, starkly painted wooden icons of saints and other revered figures, including Martin Luther King Jr. and the radical Catholic activist Dorothy Day. On the wall hung a decorative scroll with a pacifist manifesto from Menno Simons, the sixteenth-century Anabaptist preacher for whom the Mennonite order is named:

> The regenerated do not go to war, or engage in strife. They are the children of peace, who have beaten their swords into plowshares and their spears into pruning hooks, and they know no war. Since we are conformed to the image of Christ, how then can we kill our enemies with the sword? Spears and swords made of iron we leave to those, alas, who consider human blood and swine's blood as having well nigh equal value.

As Ben continued, he lifted a pale shard before the camera. "My favorite piece is this fragile shell." He loved the delicate artistry of the altar he'd constructed, until his boys covered the altar with an offering of cardboard Pokémon counters. The pink and orange disks calculated how much damage a Pokémon character had suffered, and how close the character was to death. Yet Ben, grumbling about the ruined altar, was too distracted by his troubles to observe the parallel between the damage counters and his fragile shell.

He and Gwyneth wanted to get the boys outside to feel Lent in their bodies, so they took them on a bird-watching pilgrimage in Middle Creek, Pennsylvania, to see a hundred thousand snow geese lift off together, migrating north. Watching the birds rise in waves, at sunset, Ben took their squawking as a reminder that the geese were traveling north. The earth was thawing and life was returning. The time that marked Jesus's death on the cross was approaching, and although death was necessary, it wasn't final.

On his pastor's blog, Ben offered Lenten thoughts on the need to repent of racism: "Hey (!), White People (!), We Get to Repent!" He kept it general, not offering specifics:

> The thing I have to offer to what's happening as one who has spent some time learning to repent is to bring a non-anxious presence to the process of exposing my own internalized white supremacy. Yes, it hurts. I confess that I have been confused and uncomfortable often in the past few weeks. I haven't figured it all out, and I really like to figure it all out. The discomfort is real, but I am letting it burn rather than snuffing it out. It feels like it is the consuming fire of God.

He finally read *The Cross and the Lynching Tree*, by the Black liberation theologian James H. Cone, whom Jonny kept citing. The book's relevance was uncanny. Only two months earlier, during the January 6 insurrection, someone had hung a noose outside the U.S. Capitol. Ben wrote on his blog:

> This symbol of a lynching rope is impossible to separate from this legacy described so well by Cone. I am a white man who can forget about this stuff . . . When American Christians who are white look away from the cross and the lynching tree for too long, as I am confessing I could conceivably do, they lose their way and come up with terrible news for everyone instead of the Good News that Jesus offers us all.

Ben was aware that his audience included skeptics, like his dad, who thought that Circle of Hope was simply doing what was trendy— "consumed by the zeitgeist"—in their misguided effort to root out whiteness by hiring a DEI consultant. Although Rod opposed hiring Nelson Hewitt, Ben had broken with his dad and supported the call from members and his colleagues to hire an outsider to help Circle identify and reckon with its problems. This act of dissent marked a departure for Ben. For Anabaptists, the idea of subjecting the church to the whims of worldly culture was especially problematic. As the theologian Karl Barth said, the church needed to remain "an unreliable ally" to any and all political systems.

On his blog, Ben defended the pastors and the direction of the church, asking the questions he knew some others were afraid to voice: "Is it just popular to be anti-racist now and that is why we are doing this? Are we caving to philosophy that is not from Jesus? No! We were here first. Circle of Hope has had anti-racism written into our DNA since we began."

To Jonny and others, Ben's exegeses could feel callow, as if he were naïvely trying to lead others into places he really didn't understand. He wasn't faking anything; he was simply too trapped in his parents' belief that Circle of Hope was ahead of its time to realize they'd fallen behind.

Ben's enthusiasm for all things Jesus had always been a part of who he was. But as questions over race and power arose at Circle, he heard people telling him to be quieter, that as "a big white guy" he took up too much space. He knew they were right. "I'm developing my dimmer switch," he said.

Privately, in his journal, Ben asked searching questions: "How much of my comfort in Christ is really white supremacist culture?" The notion of individual confession was easier for him than a collective one implicating the Whites' utopian vision. Sure, Rod liked to have his fingers in everything: he was known for coming into church and rearranging the chairs just before worship, or creating a Monday-morning competition among the pastors, pitting one against the other to see who had the highest number of attendees and managed to cadge the most emails for the database. He didn't always take the time to lay his visionary ideas out to others, and grew angry when people didn't anticipate them. But what, Ben wondered, did any of this have to do with race?

. . .

Ben tried to hang on with the pastor team, but Jonny's ongoing observations about Rod's desire for power, and his disregard of Gwen's role at the church, soon became too much to bear. "You insulted my father and erased my mother, Jonny! You have to call them and repent!" Ben shouted and pleaded with Jonny. He'd heard his parents' psychological read on Jonny's character many times. Rod believed that he'd become a surrogate father to Jonny. Pushing Rod out of the church allowed Jonny to symbolically kill his own problematic dad. Rod also knew that Jonny loathed this kind of talk. "Jonny hates to be psychologized," Rod said. "He reads it as being shamed." As Ben saw it, Jonny was now attempting to shame Rod in public by calling him "vindictive," and calling into question Rod's intentions and his legacy.

"Honestly, I learned how to do that from *your* dad," Jonny told Ben. He was referring to a book that Rod had the pastors read called *A Failure of Nerve*, a leadership guide that explored the basic reason leaders fail: they lacked courage.

"Fuck off," Ben said.

To lead Palm Sunday together, the pastors divvied up roles to read aloud the story of Jesus's entering the gates of Jerusalem on a donkey's back. Rachel asked Ben to read the part of the Pharisees, legal scholars who were reviled in the early church for opposing Jesus and denying that he was the Messiah. All four pastors laughed gently.

"Okay," Ben said, dejected.

Jonny took the role of the Messiah, declaring, "I love being Jesus!"

Ben cast his eyes down and read, in a flattened tone, "Teacher, rebuke your disciples."

Afterward, he fumed. Jonny was shoving him into a box, along with his family, making them examples of the old way, the wrong way, *Pharisees*.

. . .

Despite the official resignation that Rod had tendered on New Year's Eve, he and Gwen lingered as members of Circle. They also kept seeing clients at Circle Counseling. To assess their ongoing influence, Jonny and other leaders decided to form a "discernment team" in the spring of 2021. They gathered members from all four congregations. Rachel was assigned to be the team's pastor. Jonny also insisted on joining. This was unprecedented: discussing anyone at Circle without them around violated Matthew 18:15–17, the teaching on church discipline. It was gossip. When the Whites heard about this team, they thought that Jonny was leading "secret meetings," which had never been a part of Circle's DNA.

Audrey Robinson, an outspoken leader from Ben's congregation at Marlton Pike, joined the discernment team. She assumed they were meeting to figure out how to get the Whites their $52,000 back from the contractor who had left the Whites high and dry. "Anyone who would take fifty-two thousand dollars is a bad person," she said. Audrey, a fifty-one-year-old Black woman with deep dimples and a chin-length bob, saw Rod as a straight shooter she'd known for more than two decades, since not long after she arrived from Nashville to work as a nanny during the 1990s. Audrey had landed first in Philadelphia at a Southern Baptist community church but migrated to Circle of Hope. Over the next two decades, she came and went from Circle as she moved around the city while working in the Ralph Lauren shop at Lord & Taylor. Eventually, Audrey married, moved to Camden, and became a foster mom to a baby she later adopted, Shadi. When she learned that Ben had become the pastor in Camden, she returned to Circle of Hope.

Audrey was always there on Sundays. Although she didn't drive, she found rides or took public transportation. She usually arrived laden with trays of chicken and other hot food, not just the cold cookies others sometimes brought. The physical plant of the church, and keeping the doors open, mattered to Audrey; when Marlton Pike needed money to pay the mortgage, it was Audrey who hustled, using her local connections to rent the space for quinceañeras and elaborate first-birthday parties. Over twenty years, Audrey had come to see the Whites, especially Ben, as her family. Ben picked up Shadi at day care when she needed him to, and babysat. Audrey relied on this kind of pastoral care, and she believed that this was, in part, the purpose of church—to share practical support through Jesus.

So, when Jonny asked people to declare their biases at the first discernment team meeting, Audrey grew suspicious. Did the fact that she liked Rod or had known him for twenty years disqualify people like her and Rachel from participating? Soon, others were dredging up old grievances with Rod. No one was talking about Rod's money. They were building a case against Rod, and Jonny seemed to be leading the charge. Jonny told a story about how Rod hadn't wanted him to fly a gay-pride flag. (Rod believed the flag was political and stereotyping of the queer community.) Although Audrey found the narrative hard to follow, the subtext came through loud and clear: Jonny was bad-mouthing Rod. She was starting to think that Jonny was duplicitous, and that he was dangerous. "He's a snake," she said.

Rod had never claimed to be anything he wasn't. "All pastors make mistakes," she said. "They're human." Instead of dissecting Rod in his absence, Audrey suggested the discernment team call him up and ask him questions directly. Why, she wondered, were these people so afraid of Rod? When team members tried to explain structural racism, she found it offensive and patronizing. "Please tell me what power you have?" she asked later. "If I walk into a room of white men it's just white men. You don't have any power. Who told you that? If you got hired at work above me, then that's white power, but once we walk out those doors, you have none."

At Circle, she noticed, there was a lot of talk about race and none about class. Some thought that people like her lived in Camden because they were poor. But Audrey Robinson and her husband owned their home. They lived in Camden because it was safer to raise Shadi in a neighborhood where no one looked twice at a Black boy in a hoodie, rather than in some of the nearby bedroom communities of white suburban New Jersey. And Audrey was increasingly bothered by Jonny's constant talking about suffering abuse as a person of color, which she felt was part of an endgame to disparage the Whites and take over the church. "As far as I can see, he's a doctor's son from the suburbs," she said. (Jonny, in response to Audrey's criticism, dropped a line by the Harlem Renaissance writer Zora Neale Hurston. "Skin folk ain't necessarily kinfolk," he paraphrased.) All this talk missed the basic point of the Whites' disputed loss of $52,000: "Whoever has the money has the power," Audrey kept repeating. After a few meetings of the discernment team, Audrey withdrew. Soon, she became Jonny's most vocal critic.

Yet Audrey wasn't opposed to Circle's anti-racism work; she joined the Black Girl Cell and got a kick out of Bethany Stewart. Supporting fellow Black women in the church, where they were scarce, was important to Audrey. As Circle began to examine its past, stories were surfacing that Audrey had never heard. She listened and respected the experiences of others without feeling that she had to declare other Black women right or wrong.

Some stories held abiding pain, beginning with that of Calenthia Dowdy, a chaplain at Messiah who taught cross-cultural and biblical studies. Rod and Gwen had met Calenthia when they arrived in Philadelphia in the 1990s, inviting her to join their effort to plant a diverse and beloved community. Calenthia became one of the first Black women to join Circle of Hope. Despite Rod's insistence that the church aimed to be diverse, Calenthia felt there really wasn't space to include traditions outside of white evangelicalism. When she'd attempted to bring Black men to the church, some had balked at the contemporary Christian music, which she actually liked. For Calenthia, feeling out of place was deeper than music. "I always felt like my voice was eclipsed even when I was invited to preach," she said. "After I offered my sermon, Rod would come up and reinterpret it."

Once, Rod invited her to lead a celebration of Kwanzaa. As Calenthia began the ceremony by pouring out libations and acknowledging ancestors, she could see Rod growing visibly uneasy. Eventually, he stepped forward to qualify the practice as an idolatrous one that didn't center Jesus. "You can't change a spiritual expression because you're uncomfortable with it," she said later. After several years, she gave up attempting to offer her opinions, and when she stopped coming to Circle, no one contacted her to ask where she'd gone.

"By the time I left, people thought I was just this angry Black woman, but, boy, I could've been angrier," she said. Without naming Circle, she wrote an article, "Why I Quit the White Church," which began with a quote from a friend: "When it comes to Black people, white Christians are the most dangerous people on the planet."

Other people of color had left the church, too, including four Black pastors over the past thirty years. In a church history time line Rod kept, he'd noted the personal reasons each of these partnerships had failed: "health problems," "poor relationships," "differences in philosophy," "did not work twenty hours a week," "codependent relationships," "needs of a family," and "not enough prayer," among others. When Circle of Hope began to interrogate itself, Jonny rewrote the time line, annotating each case through a lens of racialized harm. Rod called this "revisionist history" and noted that one Black pastor had stayed at Circle for seven years, when the average length of a pastor's life at any congregation is closer to three. The Whites still shared dinner and posts on Facebook with several of the Black pastors who'd departed, and felt that for Jonny to recast their history was manipulating and objectifying.

. . .

Almost no one in any of the four congregations knew about the deepening conflict among the pastors over the Whites. Ben said nothing to his flock. He didn't want to spread gossip about his fellow pastors or give his congregation more of a sense that they were estranged from the three others across the river. Ben also didn't want to share his parents' anger and hurt with the church, in order to protect both them and the future of Circle of Hope, which he still believed in. So he tried to keep his feelings inside, which wasn't working out too well.

At the Monday-morning pastors' meetings during the spring of

2021, Ben screamed at Jonny and Julie, or cut Julie off, as he defended his dad. He either hunched forward and glared at the screen or turned away from it completely to signal his disdain. He shut off his camera. He could seem menacing, a troubling look for an avowed pacifist, yet he was unable to stop the growing divide. He'd spent his whole life learning to lead this next generation, most of whom were now past thirty. Although many of the Gen Xers who remained, including some of the older millennials, like him, supported his parents, the younger ones wanted to go in a different direction, led by Jonny. "I have to keep reminding Jonny that I'm not a Southern Baptist. I'm Ben White," he said.

Ben tried to share with his fellow pastors how feeling so torn was wearing on him. "The overwhelming feeling for me is powerlessness," Ben told his former friends in a quiet moment that spring. Yet most of the time, his powerlessness rendered him angry, and he began to accuse Julie and Jonny of leading "a power bloc" within the church. Holding "secret meetings" and seeking private counsel outside the church were ways to broker power, he believed, not to follow Jesus. Ben's flip-outs were growing so bellicose and destructive that cell coordinators were joining the Monday-morning pastors' meetings on a regular basis to try to understand what was happening among all four, as well as to monitor Ben.

．　．　．

Beyond protecting his parents, Ben had worries of his own. His congregation kept shrinking. In 2020, Marlton Pike faced a net loss of twenty-one members: one out of every five. Eighty-seven remained on the roll, which seemed paltry to Ben, although it was also true that the vast majority of American congregations were a similar size: less than one hundred people. Churches all over America were contracting. "Satan threw a major wrench in the works with this pandemic," Ben said. His Marlton Pike congregation, which saw some of the public health measures of other congregations as virtue signaling, wanted to meet in person. "I have a higher percentage than anyone else of people who are like, 'I'm not doing your online thing,'" Ben said.

Ben arranged for them to meet outside during the summer in Camden County's Newton Lake Park, where people paddled along Newton Lake and arrived by kayak. Outdoor church proved hard to hear, and Ben had to chase away malicious geese that left behind land mines of "goose grease." Soon, a louder charismatic preacher, with more followers and a more powerful sound system, came along and co-opted his spot. The other preacher also had a permit. Ben didn't. So, for a time they merged worship meetings in the park.

The major pressure at Marlton Pike for Ben remained the opposition to the emphasis on anti-racism. "At least fifteen people are leaving because of our single-minded focus on race," Ben said one afternoon in the church office at his desk, where he kept a picture of Matthew Henson, a Black Arctic explorer, to remind him of adventure. Mustard-colored drapes hid the parking lot's cracked macadam. In white chalk, a blackboard read: WE MUST LOVE EACH OTHER. In this exodus, no one wanted to say openly why they were leaving, since objecting to anti-racism work risked painting them as racist. "I don't want to go to the church of Black Lives Matter," one said. "I want to go to church for Jesus. And if Christianity isn't what we're here to discuss then I'm really not interested." It wasn't that focusing on identity was wrong, or that structural racism and its wounds weren't real; it was that they weren't the purpose. "Go find what you need," the observer added, "but stop calling it church."

Marlton Pike focused on following Jesus locally by setting up a food bank in a utility closet, and running two hubs of South Jersey Mutual Aid out of the church. On Saturdays, volunteers met up to lay out piles of diapers, dog food, and maxi pads, along with pasta, rice, tuna, and vegetables from the Simple Way. Then, two by two, they paired up to load their vehicles and headed out to deliver food to local families, who were mostly Spanish-speaking and had called asking for help.

Ben was sharing his office at Marlton Pike with Marcus Biddle, a member who was a public radio reporter and worked with veterans at risk of homelessness. When Marcus had asked Ben if he could work in the church when no one was around, Ben handed him the keys to the building and told Marcus he was welcome to use the space as he needed. "It's a total game changer for me," Marcus said that afternoon. "I don't know if I'd be able to get my work done without it."

It wasn't just Marcus; when another member needed a place to stay, Ben gave her the keys so that she and her cat could spend several nights on a church couch. This was perhaps Ben's greatest pastoral gift; he shared Jesus's love by showing up, no matter what. "If I said, 'Hey, Ben, I'm trying to move a piano out of my house,' he'd be there in ten minutes," Marcus said, laughing gently. This impulse toward unbounded love had drawn Marcus into Circle of Hope. Raised a vegetarian in a Black Seventh-day Adventist Church, Marcus was no stranger to unconventional practice, and he'd fallen in love with the small-group experience of being in a cell. His first cell met on Wednesday nights at Bobby Ray's Pennsauken Tavern. Marcus didn't really drink, but at the bar the men talked about everything. Not all of them even believed in Jesus, which Marcus found wild and pretty wonderful. What mattered more was the rawness and honesty they shared and the trust bred from opening their lives to one another. Marcus had also been having a hard time with dating. "I had a lot of days where I called Ben and I was just like, 'Hey, man, like I don't know what to do with this situation. What do you think?' He was always kind of on point to take a phone call from me and just kind of, like, hear me out."

Marcus was close with some of the white people leaving Marlton Pike. He'd shared their frustrations when one member tried to ask questions about anti-racism, only to be told that as a white person, he shouldn't speak. Marcus didn't agree with that, and his friend left the church soon after. That didn't mean that Circle of Hope was exempt from problems, and Ben had some white-guy tics for sure. Marcus knew that Ben could be overbearing, and that he had messianic leanings. "Ben has a bit of a God complex," Marcus noted, "although Jonny's is worse." And Marcus had never had trouble speaking up when Ben's enthusiasm tipped into stridency or bullying. "He has a tendency to throw his weight around," Marcus said. "But there was never a time when I put my foot down that he didn't accept it, and dial it back."

Marcus was clear, however, that his defense of Ben didn't absolve the church of racism. In a city divided almost evenly between white people and Black people, the tiny fraction of the latter in the church remained an indictment.

"Something is wrong with our church, because it doesn't reflect the city," he said. "Our church has a problem with Blackness. It's not just a Circle of Hope problem; people are very uncomfortable with Blackness." Take Jonny for instance. Marcus didn't want to disparage him. He appreciated Jonny as an Egyptian ally, and his parents were immigrants, but Jonny's racial ambiguity didn't threaten white people as much as Blackness did. Jonny and others used the term "BIPOC"—for Black, Indigenous, People of Color—which Marcus didn't much like. Lumping all people of color as one bloc risked erasing important distinctions. In an effort to bring people together, the term "BIPOC" obscured the distinct disenfranchisement of Black Americans.

. . .

Despite Ben's defensiveness when it came to his parents or their legacy, he remained eager to examine himself. He looked forward to the sessions that Nelson Hewitt was leading in the spring of 2021. But when they began, and Hewitt asked people to identify themselves, Ben balked. That was why, instead of calling himself white, he—along with some of the other white leaders—hedged by saying he was "so-called white." After the session, Ben told Hewitt, "Of course there's work to do to uncover my racism. But I worry about essentializing whiteness in my identity." Hewitt explained to Ben that in America, the church wasn't simply a by-product of a racist system. "The white Church has been one of the leaders of racializing our society, and everyone knows that," Hewitt said. As far as evading racial essentialism, Hewitt replied gently, "People of color don't have that privilege. So I don't think you realize what happens to you unless you end up in a Black neighborhood where your rules do not apply and you might get a glimmer of that."

"Ben grew up in a Black neighborhood," Jonny said.

"Yeah, that gave me a glimmer," Ben added.

Although, week after week, Ben found the work that Hewitt was asking him and other white people to do difficult, he welcomed it. When Hewitt quit at the end of June, Ben tumbled. "I need to rely on Jesus, as I'm having a hard time," he told the other pastors. "I'm feeling like I might crash." Lost and trying to make sense of what had just happened, Ben sought out his dad, telling Rod about Hewitt's observation that the lack of trust between people of color and white members made the church feel "unsafe."

Ben never imagined that, within days, Rod would use Ben's private conversation to craft a blog post. Rod loved to stir things up in his posts.

On July 5, two weeks after Hewitt quit, Rod posted about the DEI consultant's departure on his website as well as on Facebook. He wasn't going to let his flock feel condemned by some outsider. Condemnation was the old, flawed way of church, which Rod had spent his life trying to undo. "He can't leave making you think you're condemnable," Rod argued. "Condemning oneself or others or absorbing condemnation will not solve the problem." Effective peacemakers, Rod wrote, are "not thinking of anti-racism as a battle." If Ben couldn't see his anger as a problem, then Rod also missed how his sniping blog posts defending the old way at Circle strengthened the accusations against him.

When she woke up several hours later, Bethany Stewart, who was still in the habit of reading Rod's blog, couldn't believe that Rod was taking aim at their sessions with Nelson Hewitt. Rod hadn't been in them. On Facebook, Bethany decided to stand up to Rod, calling his comments misleading. She went on: "I'm assuming it's hard to provide an accurate depiction when you haven't been in the room for the conversations and only get secondhand information."

"Great," Rod replied.

"You're tearing down this church stone by stone," another member responded to Rod in the comments.

When Ben read the post, he was hurt: Rod had put Ben in a terrible position. He looked like a spy.

Although Circle of Hope didn't celebrate the Fourth of July, that Monday the pastors were supposed to be taking a well-deserved holiday and break from one another and the church. But as news of Rod's blog spread, and members shared the post in group chats, they contacted the pastors, expressing concerns and asking how the pastors were going to respond. The pastors called an emergency meeting online to figure out how to respond once again to another of Rod's disruptions. This time, everyone could clearly see that the blog was divisive and that Rod's meddling undermined their authority as pastors.

At first, Ben admitted that he thought the blog was problematic. On the one hand, it seemed petty that a church could be at risk from internet sniping and hot takes. In the weeks that followed, Jonny used the blog as further evidence among the pastors and leaders that Rod was attempting to divide the church, which was just about the worst thing you could do as a Christian. It was, Jonny said, "problematic and sinful." Jonny reminded Ben that he'd already agreed the blog was a problem.

"I didn't say it was sinful," Ben replied. "He's an enigmatic motherfucker."

Still, Ben stood by Rod, who continued to maintain that he didn't care if people took aim at him on Facebook. "In our family, we call being mean on Facebook being tiny," Ben said. Somehow, Ben didn't see that Rod was being small, too, and Rod didn't seem to see that he'd started the virtual fight and that his family was defending him out of loyalty. Some members also called for an end to the pillorying of Rod on Facebook; they cautioned against a new strain of condemnation and legalism that seemed to have infected the church in its emerging generation. In earlier days at Circle of Hope, even when Gen Xers disagreed over deeply emotional theological differences, they'd hung on to the need to remain in community. That's what following Christ really required, working it out together, and some held that all Rod was doing was all that Rod had always done: disrupt bullshit—speaking prophetic truth that the church was off course. Rod kept making it worse by upping the ante, forcing his right to say whatever he wanted on his blog. He was no longer taking a paycheck from the church, though, so how could they stop him?

Not for Ben, but for Julie, Jonny, and Rachel, it was becoming clear that Rod's pattern of willful disruption was hurting the church and becoming an obstacle to their ability to lead together. Something was going to have to change.

As spring deepened to summer, Julie tried to explain to the other pastors what was emerging in the state of her soul. "I feel—" she began.

"I'm despondent," Jonny interrupted, as if no one else had been speaking, "I'm very worried about the church," he went on. All of these conflicts felt like a waste of time when their congregations were flagging. "Why am I dealing with this? I want to plant my congregation."

"I feel a lot the same way," Ben replied. "I've got to trust God that we can survive this mess."

It was the first sign of agreement among them in months.

"Maybe we just need a crisis," Jonny said.

Ben hesitated. "There is an opportunity here for transformation," he mused.

But Julie wasn't going to let this kind of empty rhetoric go. Ben kept saying that the only way for Rod to change was for the pastors to appeal to him. To Julie, this wasn't a solution. They shouldn't have to keep stroking Rod's ego by appeasing or appealing to him. Rod had a responsibility, too. "I feel like we're going to keep appealing to Rod unless Rod changes," she told Ben.

"What's the alternative, Julie?" Ben asked, his voice rising.

"Last time I said this to you, you turned your screen off," Julie answered.

"Don't say it again then," he warned her, glowering.

"We're just going to keep cleaning up problems every time people get hurt?" Julie asked in exasperation.

"I hope not," Ben said.

"I appreciate that you're willing to talk to him, Ben," Julie said, shifting tone and resetting. "I think he will listen to you."

"He won't," Ben answered. "I'm not in control of him. But it's the same thing that Jonny said: We have to trust Jesus, and people are going to have to change, and we are not powerful enough to change them."

"Well, Jesus better start doing something," Jonny added.

"Yes!" Ben said. He'd been using a breath prayer offered by Osheta Moore, whose book *Dear White Peacemakers* had sparked one of Rod's contentious blogs.

"Let's pause and have that prayer," Julie said.

"'Jesus faithful confidant'—that's the inhale," Ben said. "The exhale is 'Help me.'"

7

JONNY

"Watch out for false prophets. They come to you in sheep's clothing,
but inwardly they are ferocious wolves."

—MATTHEW 7:15

O ur commitment to anti-racism is like buying a gym membership on January 2nd," Jonny told me one afternoon in 2020.
He was filling quarantine hours tempering chocolate and preparing Peruvian ceviche, and posting his creations on Instagram under
the handle @foodpastor. Then, he drove his two small children to the
Japanese garden near the Please Touch Museum. The beaux arts building topped with a green dome was closed, but Jonny sat on the white
stone steps tracking the local and national BLM protests on his phone
and issuing pronouncements.

"Nonviolence is the way of Jesus," he tweeted during the protests.
"But when it comes to antiracist activism, calls for nonviolence should
come from people of color. Until white people are actively divesting of
their white power (and white violence) their calls for nonviolence are
still violent." Online, people were forming racial affinity groups. Despite the church's long-standing rejection of dividing people by identity, Jonny decided to form his own group, inviting Circle of Hope's
members of color to a meeting in June 2020.

"I want to know if you are up for this sort of thing. We don't have to do it," he ventured tentatively in the group invitation. "Doing this is a departure of the status quo. So we know it will stir up people's white fragility, and so we expect and welcome it." The point of the meeting was to surface long-buried experiences of racism at the church. "This is a project of uncovering and discovery; the racism that is all over the U.S. may be within us, too," Jonny explained. Within hours, he'd received more than a dozen yeses, and later that month some thirty Circle members of color from different congregations met for the first time on Zoom. Although this group would become an example the Whites used of Jonny's "secret meetings," it wasn't secret. It was simply closed to white people, which allowed for an entirely new kind of frankness, during which Jonny solicited experiences and opinions while another participant took notes to share with the rest of the church afterward.

There was a lot more to being anti-racist "than just protesting, having more diverse friends or a multiethnic congregation," one member commented. "It's building coalitions and creating safe places for persons of color to be." In such observations, Jonny heard how Circle had failed, over three decades, to connect to people of color in their communities, favoring instead young white transplants to the city. People began to share their discomfort with the tone-deafness of appropriation. Sometimes pastors removed the context of slavery from spirituals like "Wade in the Water," to make them into relatable tools for spiritual growth. As the discussion wore on, participants realized that these racialized moments, which they'd long assumed were awkward one-offs, reflected habits of whiteness and control.

Rod also kept a tight hold on the musical landscape, which was less about ethnicity and more about power. Continuing his metaphor of disease and infection, he "quarantined" songs, banning them from use. In Circle's online music database, banned songs were marked in a red font: "This song is quarantined." Anybody could suggest a quarantine, but usually Rod was the ultimate arbiter. He'd quarantined some songs with indigenous roots, including "River of Life," written by a Mohawk musician, and the song "Jesus" by the indie band Page France, in which Jesus emerges from death with "worms in his hair." The practice of quarantining felt to members like a not-so-tacit form of command, and one of the subtle ways that whiteness maintained its power in the name of protecting the church from "infectious" influences.

Although Circle claimed to practice collective decision-making and consensus, this wasn't always true. "Everybody gets listened to," one proverb read, "but people who make and nurture disciples and who make love happen get listened to more." Those who demonstrated they could grow the church earned the power to talk about it. In open discussions, Rod sometimes handled opinions he didn't agree with by simply not recording them in the notes. When he explained this process to Gerry West, a Germantown pastor during the 1990s, Gerry recalled telling Rod, "That's pretty deceitful, bro." Gerry left Circle in 1998 and became a taxi driver in Dallas, Texas.

As the meeting continued, the analysis sharpened and grew more structural and steeped in academic theory. One participant, a Chinese American cell leader at Fishtown, and a close friend of Jonny's, had recently graduated from Princeton Theological Seminary with a masters in divinity. Circle of Hope "can sound like the punch line of a joke," he offered. "A church so full of people who are so dedicated to being antiracist, yet still so stubbornly white in demographics. I think we need to begin measuring according to impact and outcome, not intention."

While at Princeton, he'd attended a guest lecture by Willie James Jennings, a Black liberation theologian at Yale who argued that the "spirit" of white supremacy culture "haunts all western institutions." Jennings had used the term "paterfamilias" to define this white-male dominated system, which had struck the seminarian as revealing and apt. The apostle Paul had used the term "paterfamilias" in Scripture to define the head of the patriarchal Roman family system. As Jennings described it, this was "a system set up to afford comfort and stability to the man at the center, at the top of the hierarchy, the man who's an expert and demonstrates control of his domain." The term stuck with the seminarian. He'd also grown up in the Global South and observed the "paterfamilias" dynamic in his own multiracial family. His dad, a white evangelical pastor of a megachurch, was awarded deference based in part on patriarchy and race. To undo this pattern wasn't easy. It took a commitment to do "the work," as the seminarian put it.

"Rod and the rest of the White family will have extra work to do," he said.

The note-taker recorded these comments alongside the term "paterfamilias" in the meeting's minutes. Jonny had planned to share these notes with the whole church, as part of feedback in planning their annual map. Reviewing the notes before clicking on the "share" button, Jonny felt anxious. Rod and Gwen were almost certain to read these comments and take umbrage, and that might blow back on Jonny. Still, Jonny decided that it was time for an honest assessment of the problems at Circle. Among them, according to Matthew 18:15–17, was a tacit understanding that no one was supposed to criticize the Whites, especially in public.

"The last thing I wanted to do is have a direct conflict with Rod and Gwen. If you crossed them, they're going to make your life as hard as they can," he said later. "You don't criticize Tony and Carmela Soprano."

When Gwen scanned the comments, and saw the word "paterfamilias," she was furious. "Paterfamilias" was a public insult. It was pure misogyny. She called Ben to explain that labeling Rod as a paterfamilias erased her role in building the church. She also pointed out Jonny's sideways manner of criticism: allowing a member to take a swipe at the Whites, while claiming it wasn't him. But Ben defended Jonny, trying to convince his mom that Jonny had only the best intentions. Gwen didn't buy it. In response, she wrote to Jonny, Julie, Rachel, and Ben: "Although Jonny strongly contends he sees these comments as 'not personal' and only 'organizational,' our feelings tell a very different story." She'd also decided to quit her longtime position as teaching pastor. "Gwen is stepping down from leadership," she wrote to the pastors and her family, referring to herself in the third person. Shortly after, Joel, Ben's introverted twin who'd voluntarily run the church's finances for six years, resigned from his position in protest.

. . .

Jonny didn't want to care what the Whites thought of him anymore, but he still feared that somehow they could take his job away. "Circle of Hope shaped my life and my direction, and I was very honored and proud to be a pastor," he'd said. "Losing that would be the height of failure and shame for me."

However, Jonny believed that to be a Christian required fighting for what was right. On Twitter, Jonny's voice of protest had grown more pronounced. He built his platform by subtweeting people he disagreed with. In an effort to protect marginalized people, he picked fights with those who had larger followings than he did. For example, the evangelical commentator David French and the author Tish Harrison Warren were fundamentalists passing as reasonable among the white liberals who read the op-ed pages of *The New York Times*. Jonny worried that they didn't recognize how dangerous their ideas were.

"I could ignore Tish, but I tweet about her. I do the TikToks about her when I feel like it," Jonny mused one afternoon as he scrolled through his Instagram. There were so many dog whistles of toxic theology that most white liberals weren't religiously literate enough to catch. Take those Jesus ads during the Superbowl, with the tagline "He gets us." The campaign, which featured Jesus as a refugee and women's rights activist, was tied to the Alliance Defending Freedom, a conservative Christian legal organization that had battled against LGBTQ rights. This was the kind of abusive religion hiding in plain sight that Jonny felt compelled to take on publicly. He also wanted to be heard. Jonny's audience had inched upward from a few hundred followers to nearly two thousand within several years. Yet his sister, who wrote mostly self-help books for Christian couples, had a much larger and enviable following.

On January 6, 2021, Jonny watched the Capitol riots unfold on-screen and tweeted commentary: "The White Nationalists surrounding the Capitol right now are much more aggressive than any of the protesters of police brutality this summer that sent Trump to his bunker."

For those who might miss its signifiers, he pointed out that the Capitol riot showcased a newly resurgent evil: "Christian Nationalism." This was the poisonous amalgam of racism and religion that had sought to destroy him and against which he'd been fighting since he was nineteen. The story was personal, he blogged: "My parents suffered oppression, as a result of hysteria around Islam fostered by Fox News pundits. It pains me to say they received their oppression, and accepted the lesser dignity that White and Christian Supremacists offered them, just so they wouldn't experience again what they did in Egypt."

Jonny's faith, and his belief in the need to fight against evil, was shaped in reaction to exactly these forces. "I definitely will not cede any territory to the Christian Nationalists. Not the term Christian, not even the term Evangelical, and *certainly* not my faith."

On February 22, 2021, an editor at the Christian publishing house Herald Press who followed Jonny on social media queried him, wondering if he might have an idea for a book. Excited, Jonny worked up a proposal for a theological polemic. "*Jesus Takes a Side* is for oppressed Christians and their allies who are frustrated by the neutrality and complicity of political quietists," he wrote. The proposal called to task white liberals and Anabaptists who used Jesus to avoid taking a political stand.

Still identifying strongly as an Anabaptist, Jonny was taking apart the third way, the central teaching that Jesus transcended binary conflicts between good and evil, and instead, through love, found a creative solution. Jonny argued that, too often, the third way allowed evil to thrive under the banner of coexistence. "When it comes to matters like anti racism, LGBTQIA dignity, there isn't a third way, or a compromised position that does not burden the most vulnerable first," Jonny blogged. Jesus, Jonny argued, was a fighter. He hadn't just let money changers and profiteers in the temple go about their immoral behavior; he'd flipped tables. Jesus certainly *did* come to overthrow the Roman Empire, and any Christian who didn't understand that wasn't really a Christian at all. The editor loved the idea, and Jonny began drafting the manuscript on Fridays from 9:00 a.m. to 4:00 p.m. at his standing desk, whizzing through a chapter a week. (Later, he came up with a proposal for a second book, to be titled *Fleeced*, a biblical double entendre, that remained unpublished.)

Living the gospel had material consequences, and the Circle proverbs that had once drawn Jonny in now felt hollow. Sayings like "We are one in Christ" allowed people to fool themselves into believing they'd already dismantled their prejudices. "In an effort to be one in Christ, we ignored the racism in our midst," Jonny wrote. "In the gospels Jesus takes a side—with the marginalized and oppressed—choosing truth, justice, and morality over moderation."

Jonny had made this choice himself, he blogged. He'd moved beyond the "moderate" view, which allowed him to tolerate homophobia in the church in the name of including different theological perspectives on sexuality. That kind of tolerance was a form of oppression, of which he was ready to repent. He went on:

When I was younger, I made choices I regret today, especially regarding inclusion of queer folk in Circle of Hope . . . I was held to account, in some sense, by my friends, by my colleagues, by the victims of my behavior, and I even got written up in a newspaper. As a result of this, people left our church, I lost friendships, and it significantly impacted my personal and professional life. At the time, I may have thought it was unfair, but in hindsight I believe it was a natural result of my actions and my defensiveness. I was hurt too, but my pain doesn't preclude my repentance. I wish I was more inclusive then, but I am glad people have stood aside me to be more inclusive now. Not everyone can walk beside me when I mess up, but I have people that do and I am grateful for them. We cannot burden everyone to have the power to demonstrate the grace that people did with me and with others that helped me grow.

There were many necessary correctives happening in the world around him, and Jonny was eager to help lead them. What others saw as "cancel culture," Jonny viewed as essential collective action. "We can expect that our sin will hurt and send people away," he blogged. "That's a consequence of our actions, that's not condemnation or cancellation."

· · ·

Jonny diagnosed the Whites' struggle to let go of power as "founder's syndrome," a problem in business when CEOs fail to adapt to organizational change. This led to abuses of power and laid ruin to companies. Jonny first read about founder's syndrome in secular organizations, but churches also suffered from it.

In his dissertation for his doctor of ministry degree from Asbury Theological Seminary, Steve Murrell, a church strategist and evangelical missionary to the Philippines, wrote, "Most ministry leaders not only have their identity tied to their ministry, they also have most of their friends connected to their ministry . . . How can a leader turn over the position to the next generation, yet still identify as a minister of the gospel, stay relationally connected with friends and colleagues, and do something with their time that matters?"

Jonny had observed founder's syndrome at Circle as early as 2008 in Rod's desire to control all aspects of the church. "I slowly brought it up with the other pastors, cautioning against it," Jonny said. But no one had paid much attention to Jonny's business analogy. "Circle didn't think that 'conventional wisdom' applied to them," he explained.

Circle of Hope, like most churches, had no human resources department or handbook to follow, but by almost any standard, Ben's behavior in the spring and summer of 2021—swearing, shouting, hanging up, hurling insults—was not acceptable. When Ben accused Jonny of "brokering power," Jonny argued that there was nothing wrong with doing so. He felt that his efforts to "amass power" by holding meetings, building consensus, and influencing leaders were means by which people of color fomented necessary change.

"If you want to make a change, you've got to collect power," Jonny said. Later, he reflected, "I think quite honestly I've learned to build power as a person of color. But as a white guy, Ben never had to—he always had the political power without realizing."

. . .

Hoping to make these racialized dynamics clear to everyone, Jonny welcomed the arrival of the DEI consultant Nelson Hewitt. When, during that first "exploratory" session, Jonny heard Ben and other white leasers refer to themselves as "so-called white," he felt irritated but also validated. "You guys can't even claim being white, let alone being racist," Jonny thought to himself. (Rod had also previously referred to himself as "so-called white," since, he argued, "white" was an oppressive concept.)

Jonny was reading *The Myth of Colorblind Christians: Evangelicals and White Supremacy in the Civil Rights Era*, a searing indictment of the limits of such progressives, by a Temple graduate and history professor, Jesse Curtis. Here was a problem of exceptionalism no one could deny. Fifteen years earlier, popular liberal teachings around race still favored being "colorblind." At Circle, one early anti-racism training was built around a 2003 PBS special called *Race: The Power of an Illusion*, which argued that race was a social construct. In the 2000s, Circle adopted this logic. But, Jonny felt, this absolved them of dismantling structural racism by adopting the delusion that they'd left it behind.

During the initial session when Hewitt had the Circle participants form the two racial affinity groups, Audrey Robinson, the New Jersey member skeptical of Jonny, asked Jonny about his experience of racism at Circle. She wanted to know what kind of evidence lay behind his accusations. At first, he was reluctant to share, given his fear of retribution by those loyal to the Whites. Asking that what he said be held in confidence, he offered his salary as empirical proof. He'd been a pastor at the church longer than Ben and Rachel, he told Audrey, and he held a master's in divinity from Palmer Theological Seminary at Eastern.

Circle had paid his full tuition at seminary—$8,200 a year—as part of his compensation. But now, years later, his salary was still the lowest among the four pastors.

"Ben was paid most because he was a white man and also Rod's son," Jonny had argued. "The women were paid less because of their husband's salaries." This sounded appalling to Audrey. Although she was already coming to distrust Jonny, she vowed to support him "one hundred percent" if these claims were true. In reality, the numbers were harder to parse.

Here's how they broke down: Jonny was paid $352.50 less than Julie, who held an advanced degree in social work, not in theology, but had been serving as a pastor five years less. At Circle of Hope in 2021, Jonny, with a tenure of eleven years, earned $54,011.22; Julie (six years) earned $54,363.72; Ben (eight years) earned $55,910.00; and Rachel (ten years) earned $56,330.00.

Jonny told Audrey the truth when he said that he was paid the least, which he felt was part of a larger lack of transparency and ethics. But what he didn't say was that when the other pastors wanted to correct the discrepancy in pay, he hadn't allowed the change, which he felt amounted to a cover-up.

When Audrey Robinson learned that Jonny had refused the increase, it hardened her distrust of his accounts of racism and abuse. "He's just trying to make people feel sorry for him," she said.

· · ·

During the five exploratory sessions, Jonny was reckoning with an internal conflict. In Hewitt's weekly debriefings with the pastors, Jonny confronted the role he'd played at Circle. "The consultants are surfacing what I've experienced and what I've been trying to hide," he confessed to Hewitt, Ben, Julie, and Rachel. "I've instituted racism and I suffer from it." He was coming to see himself as both a victim and perpetrator.

It had only been a little more than a year since Jonny, as Circle's company man, had summoned Bethany to his office, telling her that writing daily prayers for Black History Month was "divisive." "I deceived myself into thinking that I was doing work that was more impactful than what it was," he ventured. In such realizations, Jonny felt that the anti-racism work at Circle was making progress. He saw his role of making excuses for the church as a form of enabling, resulting in his own abuse.

"I get beaten by the alcoholic, but I stock the fridge with beer," he told the other pastors during a Monday-morning meeting. Jonny had developed a tendency to tailor versions of events for varying audiences. "It's better to tell people what they want to hear," he often said. This, he argued, was a form of self-protection. For instance, when Jonny had helped kick the queer social worker Andy Stahler out of the church, he'd apologized to Rod for allowing "infection," to spread, parroting Rod's language, although at the time Jonny remained deeply ambivalent about the decision. And in his office, while he was attempting to dissuade Bethany from writing Black History Month prayers, he'd confessed to her that the church needed to hire a DEI consultant, as if setting himself apart from the abusive pattern that he was perpetuating. Jonny called this conflicted messaging his version of "code-switching," which is typically defined as shifting language and behaviors in order to adapt to shifting cultural norms. Jonny, some church members observed, had a tendency to tell different people different things. It bothered Bethany that Jonny justified this doublespeak as code-switching. "It's lying," she'd said. Still, Jonny, who didn't consider it deceptive, defended the pattern as a necessary survival skill. "I know how to adapt in white environments," he said.

When Nelson Hewitt quit, Jonny burst into tears. Feeling utterly lost, he called Hewitt later to ask the consultant if he might continue to coach him one-on-one. Hewitt declined.

· · ·

As agonizing as it was, Nelson Hewitt's departure galvanized Jonny to take on the Whites in public, albeit rendering them anonymous. He began on Twitter, calling the church "unsafe." One tweet read: "Early on in my life, when I was barely in my twenties, a pastor misdiagnosed me as a narcissist, and I believed him. I'm finally awakening to that trauma."

The term "spiritual abuse" was first defined in 1991 by an evangelical pastor and an intervention counselor who observed pastors or others in positions of power misusing discipline and manipulating vulnerable people. The term came to be widely used in discussions of sexual abuse born out of #ChurchToo, a faith-based version of #MeToo launched in 2017 by the author Emily Joy Allison. The hashtag #ChurchToo provided a space for those who'd suffered from structural sexism embedded in many churches to speak about their experiences.

On May 27, 2021, the media organization Christianity Today began airing a podcast titled *The Rise and Fall of Mars Hill*, which told the story of the megachurch's charismatic pastor Mark Driscoll. Famous for being very smart but also foulmouthed and rabidly macho, Driscoll preached mostly to men about how they needed to stop whining and watching porn and start taking care of their families. After eighteen years of apparent success, Driscoll resigned from the fifteen-thousand-member church in 2014 amid allegations of bullying, misogyny, and mishandling of church funds.

No two men could appear to be more different than Mark Driscoll and Rod White. Rod couldn't tolerate Driscoll. Driscoll screamed his sermons of damnation; Rod almost whispered his talks on belovedness. Driscoll strode around a stage, thick-thighed in Carhartts, presenting himself as the manliest man on the planet; Rod nearly floated in shorts and sandals. One preached about the weapons of spiritual warfare; the other spoke only of peace at all costs. (Once, years earlier, at the suggestion of a friend enamored of the church-planting success of Mars Hill, Rod and Gwen visited it during a trip to the West Coast. The Whites were so appalled by Driscoll's misogyny that they left the service before it ended.)

When the podcast about Mars Hill launched, however, Jonny and some of his Fishtown flock started listening. In Driscoll's patterns of twisting people's weaknesses and making them doubt themselves—forms of manipulation that qualified as spiritual abuse—Jonny saw Rod. "Rod psychologized my criticism of the church as narcissism," he put it.

The common denominator was control. Both Rod White and Mark Driscoll held power absolutely and, when questioned, were swift to put down whoever dared oppose them. "The people that were favored were the ones who were loyal," Jonny explained. "When you're disloyal, you get dropped so quickly." Both Driscoll and Rod, he thought, preyed on people estranged from their families—"fatherless people," Jonny called them—like cult leaders did.

Jonny reviewed the popular podcast on Twitter, comparing it to his own experience. "The way the Mars Hill podcast describes the trauma from working on staff led by a narcissist is way too real," he tweeted. "For me it brought up some old trauma, honestly."

Jonny also compared his experience to that of Taylor Swift, who, in an intense legal battle, had lost the rights to her first six albums. So she rerecorded them. Her boldness in sharing her feelings on her own terms, inspired Jonny. "This encourages me to share my feelings of pain around racism in my life and in my faith and even in the church," Jonny wrote, on his pastor's blog. "When I do not tell my story, I let my oppressors continue to colonize my heart and my soul."

. . .

As Jonny's exploration of spiritual abuse deepened, he grew warier of Ben and Rachel. On a Monday morning in the summer of 2021, Jonny clipped on his faded brown fanny pack and rode his bike five miles from North Philly to Germantown, where the pastors were meeting on Julie's newly finished screen porch.

The porch, which extended off the Hokes' open-plan kitchen and overlooked their communal backyard, had become the pastor's outdoor office. It was just large enough for the four of them to fit, along with Julie's wooden potting bench, a swing chair suspended by a rope, and shelves of baby succulents, wisteria, hyacinth bean vine, sweet potato, mint, rosemary, scallions, oregano, and kalanchoe.

When Jonny arrived, he greeted Steve, who was still working from home at his desk in the kitchen. Steve had brewed the pastors a vat of supercharged coffee, then put in his headphones, so as not to hear them arguing again. Jonny continued through the house to flop into his seat in the corner. Julie stationed herself between Jonny and her potting bench. Rachel had adopted the Hokes' hanging chair, her bare feet tucked beneath her, the subtle musk of her perfume mingling in the close air with caramelized sugar from Julie's homemade blueberry cake. Ben, who came in last, squeezed awkwardly into a small wicker chair by the back door.

As the meeting began, Jonny dropped his easy, slangy manner, along with the usual banter about the week's culinary feats. He held himself taut as he informed the other pastors of changes afoot: people of color were finally meeting together regularly, finding solidarity, and charting a path forward for the larger church.

Ben thought this sounded wonderful. "I want to kindle that," he told Jonny. "I don't know if we can ever build a bridge, until we walk on it together," he waxed euphemistically. "As it's made, it will be a bit janky."

"I don't know if I want to keep building this bridge," Jonny replied, sounding as if he'd had enough of Ben's sunny and patronizing metaphors.

Being a go-between was exhausting Jonny. He resented having to defend the anti-racism work and his character from what felt to Jonny like a constant campaign of people maligning him. This included a small number of members of color. Recently, one person of color in Rachel's congregation had come to her voicing objections about the "elitism" of the church's anti-racism effort. To her congregant's thinking, Jonny and his divinity school friends had captured the conversation about racism by holding forth on intellectuals and theologians such as Willie James Jennings or James Cone. Those who couldn't cite such heady work, or didn't agree with Jonny and others, felt that they were being left behind.

"He's worried that the only people of color who are welcome are educated transplants to the city, not people from the neighborhood," Rachel told Jonny.

"It's a racist accusation to tell people of color you're just listening to the academics tell you who you are," Jonny replied. "And that is a

vile critique. It's a wicked critique that, frankly, should be repudiated."
If members couldn't embrace the anti-racist goals on the map, Jonny
argued, then they could leave Circle of Hope. Just because white people
hadn't heard these accounts of abuse didn't mean they didn't exist.
"There are many people who don't speak up because of what they've
experienced as racism in the church. Because they will get yelled at or
something bad will happen," he said. "They're called 'troublemakers.'"

After the meeting Jonny added a note to the minutes: "Jonny feels
despised."

· · ·

Fishtown was worshipping outside during the summer of 2021 at Hart
Lane Neighborhood Farm, three vacant lots of bee boxes and organic
kale beds in the middle of Kensington. Years earlier, Circle members
had bought the lots at a city auction, hoping to feed the neighborhood,
but no one had too much interest in the kale, so they'd taken to leaving bunches on people's porches. The dozen masked members of Fishtown gathered on blankets and in stadium chairs, including Jonny's
wife and children, patiently reading in the heat, as a man jittered past
pushing a shopping cart.

In the scant shade of a scraggly pear tree, Jonny preached parables
about abusers in the church, "wolves in sheep's clothing." He alluded to
undisclosed problems at Circle of Hope. "Jesus has plenty of parables
and stories about what to do with folks who are operating in bad faith,"
he began. For too long "wolfish" people had been allowed to prowl
around cells and congregations, Jonny went on, warning to "watch out
for false prophets."

Later, Jonny explained he was talking not about Rod, but about
a former member of Ben's congregation, a fan of the conservative
commentator Jordan Peterson. The following week, Jonny blogged: "A
church that strives to be safe for everyone but does not ask questions
around power is actually dangerous for the least of these, for the little

ones. And for those who make it dangerous for the little ones, it would be better for them to have a millstone hung around their neck and tossed into the Sea of Galilee than the judgment that awaits them."

In the kale garden, as elsewhere, anyone could see that Circle of Hope was contracting, as it had been since 2016 when the church hit a high of 720. After that, the exodus began. In 2017, Circle lost 27 regular attenders, bringing the total down to 693. In 2018, 35 more people left. In 2019, another 31. In 2020, 104 people left. Julie's congregation lost 1 out of every 5 members, amounting to 29 gone. Jonny's congregation lost 72, or about 40 percent. Over in South Jersey, Ben lost 21 members, about 20 percent of the congregation. Rachel's, however, managed to grow, adding 18 new people that year.

Both sides cast the other as the reason people were fleeing from Circle. Jonny explained the emptying out as a result of a legacy of whiteness and abuse; Rod and those aligned with the Whites saw people fed up with fighting, and with Jonny. But this pattern of declining numbers stretched far beyond Circle; it was a national trend. In churches, as elsewhere across the country, bonds of all kinds were fraying. Disillusioned by scandals and skeptical of institutions, people already were bored and sad and disconnected from church before the coronavirus pandemic. In comparison with overall church attendance in America, which, according to Gallup, fell by roughly 5 percent from 2019 to 2021, Fishtown, Germantown, and Marlton Pike were losing people at about four times that rate.

It cost money to maintain churches, and the fewer people who showed up to pray together, the less cash there was to fix a roof. Although Circle claimed the church was its people, not its buildings, there were still mortgages and staff to pay, including the pastors. In 2021, sixty-four more people left, about one-sixth of the remaining church. And the pastors still tallied their numbers of weekly worshippers in spreadsheets. When Jonny calculated summer attendees, he sometimes inflated them slightly by including the Hart Lane Farm volunteers who happened to be weeding during worship.

8

RACHEL

"For where your treasure is, there your heart will be also."
—MATTHEW 6:21

Afraid that Jonny was leading the church from a place of woundedness, Rachel tried to get him to back down and stop fighting with Ben. "If all of us are doing the work of the Spirit, there's everything to share and nothing to hoard," she explained to him. "We don't want to be a system that shames and coerces people. The only power in the church is spiritual power."

She also felt like Jonny was beginning to target her, since she wouldn't take a side with him against the Whites. He'd called Ben "loyal to the Whites and not the church," and by standing up to Jonny, she was leaving herself open to the same claim. Of course she felt allegiance to the Whites: Gwen had helped save her marriage; Rod had helped her find the courage to become a pastor, including when that courage required pushing back against him. Beneath any sense of personal loyalty, however, Rachel felt called to hold the church together, especially since Jonny seemed intent on pulling it apart.

And although it wasn't okay to say as much to him and Julie, Rachel could plainly see how the time and effort the pastors were spending arguing with one another took them away from the suffering in their communities outside of Circle of Hope. What had drawn her from the first to Circle was its devotion to serving their neighbors as Jesus did, not as white saviors, but in solidarity with those struggling with poverty, addiction, and all the other illnesses related to America's sick systems. Yes, there were problems inside the church, and she, more than anyone, knew that firsthand, since she'd been quietly struggling with Rod for more than a decade. But in a time of global crisis, with their city bleeding out, weren't they called to help heal the neighborhood?

Being the church had always required *doing* something. For Rachel, anti-racism wasn't simply analyzing structures; it was building relationships, and she measured her progress by these more human metrics. Take, for instance, when she'd gone out to march in West Philly with Jeff in October 2020 after the police shot and killed Walter Wallace Jr. In the oak-lined Malcolm X Memorial Park, she'd run into a Black covenant member, a woman from her cell whom she'd baptized in the inflatable birthing tub in December 2019. At the protest, this woman had introduced Rachel to her friends, saying simply, "This is my pastor." Rachel felt validated: showing up in person mattered. Being with people was also an essential part of her ministry. These brief moments of connection weren't enough, however, to keep Circle from dividing along hardening ideological lines.

Meanwhile, at South Broad, their neighbors were dying in the street. One Sunday, a man ODed outside of the church during worship. He died slumped against a parking meter in front of Starbucks. South Philly was also a little-known epicenter of the opioid crisis, where drugs hid behind closed doors: addiction retained a heavy stigma in the tight-knit Italian and Irish American community, as did queerness. "If your kid has a problem, keep it a secret and don't let anyone see them. If they're gay, put them in the priesthood instead of letting them live their life until the shame builds up so bad they start using," one sober addict said. He, like many, came to recovery meetings at Circle, and eventually ran a halfway house business out of the church basement, which he rented for $600 for a month. Rachel encouraged their new tenant to check out worship, but he demurred.

"I'm not too sure about the religious side of things," he told Rachel.

"That's the whole hope of the gospel," she replied. "That we're here to support each other in life."

Rachel's church was becoming a much-needed sanctuary for recovery, hosting Alcoholics Anonymous meetings three times a week thanks to her right-hand guy, Jimmy Weitzel. He was a shepherd in recovery to his own motley crew of struggling addicts. The meetings, in a neighborhood reluctant to admit its kids had a problem, grew so popular that people lined up outside to wait. Such liminal figures had always been common characters at Circle. At South Philly, however, recovering addicts were a more integral part of the congregation, and Rachel relied on them to help organize things. In addition to Jimmy, who ran tech, there were others who came to Circle, fresh-faced and hopeful. Many relapsed and vanished back into the streets of the neighborhood.

For a time, Circle had formed an Opioid Crisis Compassion Team, but the effort hadn't lasted. Lots of people at Circle of Hope in all four congregations worked on the front lines of the opioid crisis and its intertwined social problems of homelessness and struggles with mental health. Employed by a battery of nonprofits, some spent their days under Kensington's bridges, searching out clients who needed to be ferried to doctor and dentist appointments, making sure they had Narcan and something to eat. But sometimes there were problems with this approach: local activists saw how, in the name of altruism or Jesus, those coming to "help" were often seeking short-term solutions that perpetuated the crisis, like offering wound care in the streets. "If you're buying tents, and giving them out with food, socks, and clean needles, how is that helping them get to safety?" one longtime community activist and clinical psychologist in Kensington asked.

At South Broad, however, becoming a much-needed hub of recovery was the opposite. No one was giving out anything but love. One of Circle's proverbs read, "Generating justice and hope in our neighborhoods must be at the heart of us." If Rachel was building a church that brought justice and hope to her neighborhood, then including her neighbors required including addicts. She held fast to the beatitudes, which began the Sermon on the Mount, Circle's guiding Scripture: "Blessed are the poor in spirit . . . Blessed are the meek."

. . .

Rachel's commitment to serving the neighborhood kept the church close to all kinds of crises. Some at South Broad were also undocumented, and at risk of being deported. In 2016, Rachel had formed a compassion team, Solidarity Without Borders, in which volunteers appeared as character witnesses, accompanying undocumented people to Immigration and Customs Enforcement (ICE) interviews for support, writing letters that validated their marriages, preparing paperwork, or, when necessary, trying to protect them from deportation. The Solidarity Without Borders compassion team worked with the New Sanctuary Movement of Philadelphia to support people at risk of deportation who were living in churches and other places of worship as safe havens. The compassion team dropped off groceries for the Thompsons, a Jamaican family sheltering in a Unitarian church.

Oneita and Clive Thompson had been in the United States for decades. They owned a home in New Jersey and held steady jobs, but their legal status left them in jeopardy of being deported. Their teenage daughter, Christina, lived with them in the dank basement. Every morning, she left the church with her backpack to attend a local high school. Christina told no one about her living situation or her parents' case. She joined a teen cell led by Rachel's daughter, Cori, on Zoom, where for the first time Christina risked sharing her story with other kids. "Whenever I try to talk about it, I cry," she'd said. Soon, Oneita and Clive joined Rachel's cell, too, and one Sunday the Thompsons led online worship from their sanctuary in the church basement. To pay their legal fees and help secure the Thompsons' U.S. citizenship, Solidarity Without Borders hosted a virtual benefit that raised $18,000.

For Rachel, the story of the Thompsons was a rare victory. More often, through her congregation of social workers and teachers, Rachel witnessed the pandemic's most violent repercussions. People were falling through the cracks in the mental health system at an alarming rate. Domestic abuse and violence were surging. In Philadelphia, one hotline saw a 30 percent increase in calls in March 2020 alone.

Sometimes, these tales of despair, injustice, and murder touched her church. Rachel, as a former social worker, was accustomed to the mentally ill, and familiar with a delusional woman who'd been hanging around Circle before the pandemic. One evening, the woman appeared on a Circle couple's porch, asking them to take in her son for the night. It was late, and given the public health strictures, the couple said an awkward no. The woman left behind a shopping bag of her journals for "Pastor Rachel," then went home and murdered her son. Afterward, the Circle couple reeled in grief and in guilt. If they'd welcomed the boy, maybe he'd still be alive. Rachel, as their pastor, helped her friends wrestle with powerlessness over trauma.

· · ·

Some days she felt like she was failing her flock. To keep herself going and to see other humans, Rachel walked a four-mile loop, turning right out of her row house on Wolf Street and striding south to FDR Park. Its 348 acres, designed by the Olmsted brothers in 1913, had once been a sprawling urban refuge, until it was co-opted by street vendors and rowdy Eagles fans tailgating outside the stadium. Rachel strode past Marconi Plaza, where a statue of Christopher Columbus had recently been hidden inside a wooden box. The statue, like many others across the country, had become a flashpoint. When protesters assailed it in 2020 as a symbol of genocide, a group of white men with baseball bats and wrenches assaulted the protesters in the name of defending their Italian American heritage.

"I'm so mad at those idiots at Marconi," Rachel said. Yet this was her neighborhood and these were her people. "I have no idea how to help my Italian brothers understand what's really going on," she added. "As much as I love Italian culture, it's really fucked up." Along with racism, there was misogyny, which had left women like her grandmother struggling to feed her kids from a kitchen garden while her coal-miner husband drank his salary on Friday nights. The traditions that enabled men to swing their machismo around persisted.

Although to tourists South Philadelphia seemed a quaint throwback of cheesesteak joints and Italian coffee shops, it simmered amid the ongoing tensions between its longtime Italian and Irish residents and those they deemed outsiders. Rachel delved deeper into the neighborhood's history during the social unrest. Racialized violence had begun some two hundred years earlier, when Catholic immigrants competed with free Black people for jobs and arguments often descended into mob violence. As Irish Americans began to dominate the Philadelphia police force, they used their power against Black and Italian residents. Black people and their businesses were disproportionately targeted, and the white police force usually sided with the white mobs, arresting more Black suspects than white. Impunity and police brutality drove Black residents out of these neighborhoods, and working-class whites dug in. This history continued during the seventies and eighties in Philadelphia, where, for nearly a decade, police killed citizens at a rate of one a week, and the city claimed national infamy for the firebombing of MOVE, which left eleven people dead, including five children, and hundreds homeless.

In 2020, the "bat boys," as the white counterprotesters in Marconi were sometimes called, claimed to be protecting their property and managing public safety themselves, as their ancestors had done. Their real enemy, they maintained, wasn't their Black neighbors; it was the "woke" millennials and gentrifiers who were buying property, pushing up property taxes, and driving white working-class people out of their historic neighborhoods. When the newly arrived urbanites appeared in their streets, with cold brew coffee and progressive T-shirts, they became a physical target for the rage and frustration of young white men, many with a history of violence.

Months earlier, an unknown assailant had shattered the windows of Circle Thrift. No one knew why they'd attacked this store; maybe it was the flavor of the secondhand shop, which sometimes featured progressive symbols along the lines of rainbow stickers or the Holy Family in exile on a donkey, reading IMMIGRANTS ARE WELCOME HERE. Such slogans could become targets for those hostile to the arrival of millennials at the edges of their neighborhood. As talk of anti-racism and Black Lives Matter became the touchstone of their common life in the church, some of these neighborhood guys came to Rachel, asking her, in private, about "all lives." She posted the following at her blog on Circle's website:

> We must talk about racism and listen to the body in order to heal. The apostle Paul also gives a great response to the dismissive quip that "all lives matter" in Corinthians 12: "But God has put the body together, given greater honor to the parts that lacked it, so that there should be no division in the body, but that its parts should have equal concern for each other." Black lives have been denied the honor that is inherently theirs in this country; that calls Jesus-followers to show greater honor to our neglected parts now so that we can be whole. This is not paternalism or patronage; this is not charity from white people—this is God's idea of JUSTICE so that the Body can be restored! (Romans 8:31–39.)

. . .

As she welcomed AA into the church, she explored the relationship between recovery and faith. Rachel turned to Richard Rohr's 1989 book, *Breathing Under Water*, which explored AA's gospel principles. Rohr, like Rachel, didn't identify as an alcoholic, but he was also a pastor who'd grown fascinated with the Twelve Steps. For a time, Rohr had lived at a Catholic church that rented space for AA meetings. The members smoked outside his apartment window, so Rohr came to know them, attending open meetings, where all were welcome. Rohr saw in the Twelve Steps the ancient Christian tradition of confession. Rachel saw the same, which tracked with her love of the early followers of Jesus and with the Eleventh Step: "Sought through prayer and meditation to deepen our conscious contact with God, as we understood him." "People in recovery, people who are really working the steps have an awareness of themselves and their emotions, that really attracts me," she said. "And that's what I feel like the open arms of Christ offer, too."

Meanwhile, a strange plague was sickening some of the neighborhood guys who'd come to the church in and out of recovery. People were wandering the streets covered with lesions reminiscent of late-stage AIDS. One, sadly, was Danny P., the pale young man in the white plastic slides baptized the previous spring in the Wissahickon Creek. For a few months, he'd thrived: making friends in his halfway house, logging on to virtual church on Sundays, and joining Jimmy Weitzel's Saturday cell. Then, one morning he logged on, and in a dazed voice, shared the state of his soul. The previous evening, he'd discovered his roommate dead from an overdose on their bedroom floor. Danny P. skidded around after that, going to live with his dad, who was chronically ill, and then he relapsed and disappeared.

Since he'd stopped showing up at Jimmy's cell, I'd lost touch with Danny P. One day in April 2021, he DMed me on Facebook asking for help. His family had kicked him out of the house two weeks earlier, and he'd been sleeping in his old BMW until that morning, when he'd sold it for $300. Now he was squatting on a street corner in Kensington, a few blocks from McPherson Square, also known as Needle Park.

When Danny P.'s message arrived, I contacted Rachel. Rachel knew that Danny had been having a hard time staying clean since he'd discovered his roommate dead. She'd followed news of Danny's relapse through Jimmy. Together, we decided to go pick him up and deliver him to the emergency room. There was no guarantee that he'd stay clean or choose to remain in the hospital for more than a few hours. But he didn't have to promise so much: for the moment, he wanted to live, and that was enough.

Rachel and I drove to Kensington and waited for Danny P. outside Lewis Elkin Elementary School. In its brick entry painted with butterflies, custodial staff began at six every morning to pick up syringes, coaxing addicts out of the schoolyard. In the car, Rachel pushed play on the Johnny Cash version of "Ain't No Grave," a popular Appalachian hymn sung at tent revivals, and which they'd been singing recently at church. When the refrain played, she sang along:

There ain't no grave
Gonna hold my body down
When I hear that trumpet sound
I'm gonna rise up outta the ground.

When we spotted Danny P. shuffling down the street past the school with a wheelie bag, he was bone thin, his baby face bearded. Lesions were visible on his bandaged arms and legs. Lifting his wheelie bag into my open trunk, he climbed into the back seat, and asked if I could drive north to the emergency room at Einstein Medical Center, a hospital where he'd heard people talking about a ten-day detox. "I'm sorry," he said. He owed neither of us an apology. We were proxies for family and friends who'd shown up on other such street corners, offering previous journeys toward hope, only to have them end in disappointment. There was nothing to indicate this ride would be any different, but it was also a one-time shot, I told Danny P. If he left the hospital, I wouldn't be coming to pick him up again.

A sickly-sweet smell filled the car. Danny P.'s infected injection sites were killing him faster than the drugs were. He already knew that he had staph, he told us. "We're all getting these sores." He held up his hands. They were weeping through the gauze. "There's fentanyl on the street, but it's not mixed with heroin—it's mixed with this horse tranquilizer and it's given us these weird sores," he went on. "We don't really know what's in it."

Xylazine, an animal sedative also known as "tranq," was killing addicts all over the city. The disruption of supply chains due to the pandemic affected every market: heroin and fentanyl dealers were adding xylazine to their product to supplement it. Tranq was more dangerous than opioids, since it couldn't be reversed by Narcan.

Every few days, Danny P. was ducking into an ER for twelve hours of IV antibiotics. Then the withdrawal symptoms became impossible to bear, and he left. This time, he vowed, he would stay. Hard days lay ahead.

"For the past few months, I haven't been able to stop crying," he said from the back seat.

"That's because you want to live, Danny," Rachel replied. "You don't want to die."

"I can't pray," he said. "I'm sorry," he repeated. "I still have faith. I just feel like I've lost my relationship with God." On the streets in Kensington, where all kinds of missionaries wrestled for souls, a woman had recently preached to Danny P. from Ephesians. Taking the conversation as a sign, he strained to remember the passage. "It was something about armor," he said.

"'Put on the whole armor of God, that you may be able to stand . . . ,'" Rachel said, trailing off. She didn't finish the verse, which ends with "against the wiles of the devil."

Danny P. didn't need to talk of devils.

Rachel went on: "Ephesians 6:10, Danny. You've got to be able to stand. It means you've got to stay in the hospital no matter what." She hit "play" on Johnny Cash again.

There ain't no grave . . .

Twenty minutes later, we pulled into the hospital parking lot and followed the signs through the corridors for emergency medicine. Danny P. ducked inside a bathroom. "Danny you've got to keep talking to us so we know you're okay," Rachel called. When he emerged, we continued toward the metal detector that marked the entrance of the ER. Danny P. threw out four packets of dope and a needle, then opened his wheelie bag and placed it in the machine. Inside were his old slides, dirty tees, some family photos of his sick dad, and a pair of jumper cables from his trunk. The security guard didn't blink as the ghostly cables and clamps floated past on his screen. Maybe the guard had seen too many mysterious and tragic anatomies.

With his few possessions waiting for Danny P. on the far side of the machine, it was time for him to pass through. He lingered. Jimmy arrived, his brassy highlights growing out, looking sad and furious at the disease, at his relapsing friend who was likely to die. Danny P. emptied his pockets and handed Jimmy his lucky red lighter, along with a couple of crumpled dollars. Jimmy told him to get going inside. It was up to Danny P. now, and to God, the universe, or whatever power greater than himself he could find and hang onto. Jimmy and Rachel headed back down to South Philly together, and I continued north. On my way home, I passed the bend in the Wissahickon Creek where Danny P. was baptized in the foul, freezing water, and prayed aloud for him, for what it was worth.

In 2021, Philadelphia broke its own record, with 1,276 drug-related deaths. Danny P. was in the hospital a few days to disinfect his wounds, but he didn't stay. It would take another six months, and the loss of his left leg below the knee to infection, for him to get clean and stay that way.

After he had some time sober, he moved back in with his mom in the old coal town of Mount Carmel, and, three months later, his dad died. Danny P. was disappointed not to have his new leg yet at the funeral; he was in his wheelchair by the graveside with his family and their few close friends when someone tapped him on the shoulder. He turned around to find Jimmy and Rachel, a total surprise. Rachel and Jimmy were the only friends to show up. He hadn't been forgotten. When his new leg finally arrived, Danny P. sent Rachel an eleven-second video of his learning to walk again, and thanked her for not giving up on him. He sent me the video also. I watched him take his first steps on repeat.

. . .

Such glimpses of death could make pastor drama seem pretty pale. In the heat of the debates among the four pastors, it was difficult to step back from the pointed and personal to ask which fights were worth having and which weren't. Perhaps more than any of the other three pastors, Rachel found herself asking these questions, although she knew that to do so publicly ran the risk of undermining their unity as leaders. And unity was essential for two reasons: first, it underscored that the problems they were called as pastors to address were real, but just as important, leading together in love was the Spirit of Jesus.

Rachel had no doubt there were structural problems at Circle. But she didn't see them as solely related to race. Gender was also an issue. Although it wasn't popular to admit it, there was an undeniable aspect of alpha-male power struggle in Jonny's and Ben's wrestling over dominance. She hated the way the conflict set the two men against each other, with Rachel and Julie cast in supporting roles. She knew how it looked to many younger members: to follow Jonny (and Julie) was to embrace a radical future; to stick with Ben (and Rachel) was to cling to a reactive past. This interpretation was not only wrong but also misogynistic. In this shifting era, in which speaking up was a necessary precursor to any legitimate change, Rachel's way of doing things sometimes betrayed her by being too subtle for people to see. They assumed that in avoiding public confrontation she was carrying on all of Rod's traditions.

"People see me as under Rod's thumb, and there's sexism there and I don't know how to address it," she said. "It's not that I don't think it's a problem—it's the kind of problem that we're made for." This was the gift of dialogue at Circle, where, in the past, they'd been able to surface the world's problems when they invaded their community. Still, to call attention to this as a white woman in the midst of a racialized conflict felt distasteful to Rachel, so she kept it to herself. People rarely understood how much work Rachel had done to set herself apart from Rod. Her easy smile and relaxed manner, which were her coping strategies against patriarchy, had proven effective for most of her life by allowing her to actually change the system without fighting endlessly about it. It was a lesson she'd learned as a child with her military father: open rebellion was bloody, costly, and usually unsuccessful, but if you moved quietly, you could make your own way. She tried to be still and hold conflicting points of view.

When others thought she was hesitating or avoiding action, Rachel was waiting because she truly trusted that Jesus would reveal the next right step. Along with Jonny, Julie, and Ben, she had wholeheartedly supported their decision to hire an outside anti-racism consultant. Rachel had looked forward to Nelson Hewitt's sessions, and to exposing the patterns that kept Circle so white. Then the sessions, like everything else at Circle, devolved into argument.

To draw closer to Jesus, she spent early hours in contemplative prayer on her cozy living room couch, where she wrapped herself in a red chenille blanket and dived into her soul. She saw Jesus the mother on the cross, arms outstretched, forced open by nails through his palms, welcoming everyone and every trouble. A river flowed from the hole pierced in his side. He didn't speak to her exactly, but she knew he was asking her to stay open, even when it hurt, to welcome skeptics to come and see, as they moved together in the common effort to name how the sin of racism had co-opted the body of the church.

In their pastors' meetings, Jonny's habit of talking over the two women bothered Rachel more than it seemed to bother Julie, although he did it to both of them. The pattern went beyond interrupting. When she and Julie were speaking in a meeting, laying out a thought on process or theology, Jonny would launch into a new idea over them. It wasn't in response or rebuttal; it was as if he didn't hear their voices. When she attempted to point this out to Jonny, he dismissed her claims about patriarchy as more deflection of racism, saying later, "That's what white women do."

The only time Rachel felt that Jonny really listened to her was when he wanted her support on the latest perceived infraction by Ben or the Whites. For the past year, he'd been calling and texting, demanding she add her voice to any situation in which there was a *for* and an *against*.

On Slack, Jonny, and soon Bethany Stewart, attempted to pin Rachel down, tagging her in chats and directing her to reply in writing to their criticism of Rod. Rachel answered only sparsely. She felt hounded, but knew that if she said so, her words would be used against her as examples of her white fragility. She put her fears aside to follow through on what she'd committed to do: to be led by people of color even if some of their directives caused discomfort.

Rachel believed that Jesus would intervene if they made space for him, so she tried to slow down as messages pinged at her. Finally, after several days of silence late in the summer of 2021, she replied to Bethany, Jonny, and the rest of their newly formed anti-racism team: "I feel so much tension and misjudgment in these conversations that I withdraw, and I am sorry for that."

Still, she struggled to balance her participation with her deepening unease about Jonny. She didn't fully trust his motivations, and she disliked his tactics, which seemed the antithesis of the pacifism at the core of their Anabaptist faith.

. . .

At one pastors' meeting, Ben thanked Jonny for his patience in their slow work of anti-racism and for, as Ben put it, "staying in the boat with us."

"Right now, we're four boats and an arsenal headed in the same direction," Jonny replied.

"An arsenal?" Rachel questioned. The militarism and grandiosity disturbed her. They weren't at war.

"It's spiritual warfare," Jonny snapped back at her.

It made Rachel uneasy to watch Jonny poke at Ben until Ben exploded time and again. One day, when Jonny suggested that Ben reduce his role at the church, Ben turned off his screen and hung up. In the stunned pause that followed, Rachel decided it was finally time to ask Jonny about his intentions directly. Any observer could see he was an expert in goading Ben, and then when Ben blew, she watched Jonny carefully note down, in the minutes of their meeting, the nature of Ben's violent response. Ben seemed oblivious, but Rachel wasn't. Jonny was making a paper trail, and using it to chart a path that pushed Ben out of the church.

"I'm just trying to help," Jonny said.

"You sound predatory," Rachel replied.

PART III

9

BETHANY

"It is better for you to lose one part of your body than
for your whole body to go into hell."

—MATTHEW 5:30

W hen Bethany Stewart went looking for a house to purchase
in 2019, she drove to the North Philadelphia neighborhood of Strawberry Mansion. She'd never imagined buying
her first home alone, but here she was twenty-nine and single again.
Growing up in Philadelphia, Bethany had heard of Strawberry Mansion
but never visited the neighborhood. She'd imagined a place of stately
streets lined in huge homes surrounded by strawberry bushes. Instead,
Strawberry Mansion was a working-class neighborhood, which had
fallen into disrepair. On West Gordon Street, she passed a black-and-
white mural celebrating the Black cowboys who'd tended neighborhood
horses for more than a century. Halfway down the block, she found an
updated three-bedroom redbrick row house for sale, for which she paid
$108,000. Her Circle of Hope cell helped her paint the walls bluish gray
and rip out the wall-to-wall carpet; her uncle installed a hardwood floor.
She painted one accent wall in her living room with blackboard paint,
inviting visitors to leave #homeowner goals. She changed her welcome
mat seasonally; fall's read HELLO, PUMPKIN! Her cozy home felt thick-
walled and safe in a neighborhood that soon proved otherwise.

"Gunshots are my white noise," she said after moving in. Out her back door, past a washer and dryer, was an overgrown plot where she dreamed of planting a garden. She came from a family of gardeners. Her grandparents had kept a large vegetable patch in Western Pennsylvania. Her mother grew flowers. She'd allowed Bethany to pick out spiky pink cleomes, which Bethany watched burst into bloom like fireworks. Yet growing things in her new backyard was more difficult than she'd imagined. By the end of summer 2020, she'd killed everything but a pot of cherry tomatoes. Still, Bethany remained determined to coax life from the ground. When winter came, she sought out and befriended Black women gardeners online. She also returned to the blog she'd been keeping since 2015. At first, she had about thirty readers, mostly sorority sisters and their moms, but when she began writing about gardening, hundreds of people started to read.

"Tending the earth feels like conspiring with God," she wrote. Gardening could be a source of healing for Black women who'd been severed from the earth through the violence of slavery. Planting and tilling restored "an intrinsic truth that we too can be rooted to the toiled soil, and grow," she wrote.

She tried her hand at gardening again in the spring of 2021. This time she used better quality soil. An organizer friend from the Philadelphia Community Bail Fund brought Bethany some four-by-eight wooden planks, and together they built raised garden beds, filling them with bags of Lowe's loam. Bethany planted cucumber and tomato seedlings. Daily, she sank her fingers into the fertile dirt, tugging out cucumber tendrils like spaghetti strands and weaving them through the holes in the chain-link fence she shared with her neighbors, whose backyard was overgrown with weeds. Two plots down, two ferocious-sounding dogs barked wildly at Bethany while she worked, but she paid little attention.

The garden remained her five square feet of peace. She took breaks between teaching a class she called Nonprofit 101 for Girls Inc., an organization supporting the holistic development of girls to be "strong, smart, and bold." She also took a part-time job at Roots of Justice, an

Anabaptist collective of anti-racism trainers. First formed in 1995 as Damascus Road, the nonprofit had provided diversity training for decades to secular and religious institutions, including Circle. At Roots of Justice, Bethany had grown into a popular trainer, relying on her high emotional quotient and her sense of humor to lead hard conversations.

The same could not be said of Nelson Hewitt's anti-racism sessions. During the final one, in June, she'd lost her temper over her work being erased by the pastors and chewed Hewitt out. When he'd announced he was quitting, she wasn't surprised. "There has been a problem of faith groups accepting African American members," Hewitt had explained. "Underlying all these conversations is power." That sounded right to her.

In his parting words, he'd cautioned against simply hiring another consultant and starting again. Instead, he'd suggested they form an eight-person steering committee, with the four pastors and four leaders of color who were on his final call. After he hung up, Jasmine Umana suggested Bethany lead it. She had the necessary professional skills. And after so many years of unpaid labor leading volunteer book groups and organizing fundraisers, Bethany would be paid. Jasmine's suggestion caught her off guard, and Bethany wasn't sure what to say.

"If you'd just come to me first, I would've offered this to you for free," Bethany joked acerbically on the call. Even if she took on this role, she wasn't sure that she should accept payment. She feared being judged by white members for charging $250 an hour for consulting; her fee for the year would amount to between $15,000 and $20,000. She also suspected that some would think it too messy for an insider to be hired as an objective observer, and in some ways she agreed. "It might be clunky and a conflict of interest," she said. Still, given her experience at Circle, she saw what few others could see. "I can name the nuances it would take an outsider years to observe," she explained. And Circle of Hope's sense of exceptionalism often made it impossible for the leaders to accept outside critique. But Bethany loved the church and knew she was loved in return. She hoped that this quality of love might make it possible for her friends to accept difficult truths. Before she accepted, however, she had three questions.

"To the white pastors," she began, "are you willing to listen if someone tells you the way that you're responding is white supremacy culture? Are you all willing to consider that everything that you've known and all that you've been taught about how to pastor is white supremacy culture? Would you be willing to not respond but to sit with that for two or three days?"

"That scares me, but I want to say yes," Ben replied. "How can I respond better?"

Ben's hesitancy felt genuine to Bethany; at least he was being honest, and this marked a shift from the white culture of posturing and politeness and concern with saying the right thing. "You have to trust me that I love Jesus even though I'm a spicy-ass Black girl," she told him. The warmth of her teasing reflected their decade of friendship.

Jonny asked, "Do you honestly think that we're ready to do this?" His voice quavered. "That everything's on the table? I want to take you at your word when you say it."

"If we can't do this, then how can we expect the church to do it?" Rachel asked.

Jasmine broke in to point out that Rachel and Julie still hadn't answered Bethany directly. "I want to call in Julie and Rachel. Can you answer Bethany's questions?"

"Yes," Rachel said.

"Yes," Julie added. "I'm ready to submit to BIPOC leaders."

Still, Jonny was nervous about hiring Bethany. "I may be projecting that Bethany needs to be protected," he ventured. "But I've experienced so much racism in Circle of Hope."

Bethany didn't need his protection. She felt the Holy Spirit guiding her. "You have to be willing to navigate some of the beauty and some of the ugliness that Rod and Gwen left behind," she continued. "Are we willing to focus on the ugliness?"

Although she didn't list them, she had her own examples of this ugliness. Once in 2014, when she was twenty-three and new to Circle, she'd asked Ben why there weren't more Black people at such a progressive church. In response to her question, she recalled his asking,

"Why don't your Black friends come?" At the time, his reply hadn't struck her as offensive. Instead, Bethany took his question seriously, beginning an effort to alter the complexion and consciousness of Circle of Hope, in which she was far from alone.

In 2016, she took over leading the Circle's Mobilizing Because Black Lives Matter compassion team from Candace McKinley, the daughter of a Pentecostal pastor and a young Black attorney who'd completed her undergraduate degree at Yale and attended the University of Chicago Law School. After moving to Philadelphia to practice corporate law, Candace joined Circle of Hope. In an effort to put Circle's anti-racist proverbs into practical action, she led a cell that read books together. However, when she invited an author who wrote about racism in Christianity to her cell, church leaders mysteriously dissolved it. Candace had gone to Rachel, her pastor and friend, for support and answers, but found neither, and Candace left soon after.

Bethany already knew Candace's story, since the women were friends, but she assumed that her experience at Circle of Hope would be different. "That's the naïveté of youth and not knowing whiteness that well," Bethany said later.

Soon, Bethany teamed up with Andrew Yang, the Taiwanese American attorney and gifted musician. Andrew, a friend of Candace's, was devastated by her departure. Fearing that the church discounted Black women, he decided to do all he could to make Circle a place where women of color would want to belong. A visionary with a reserved mien, Andrew had grown up in Allentown immersed in evangelicalism: his dad pastored a network of house churches, and his mom translated Rick Warren's *The Purpose Driven Life* into Mandarin. As a boy, he'd watched his dad implement church growth strategies for house churches as if they were fast-food franchises and factories churning out the American dream.

Andrew was already distancing himself from these ideas about church growth when he arrived at Circle in 2008. He was also committed to following Jesus, and what he found at Circle of Hope had changed his life.

"What stuck out to me about Circle wasn't the political activism or the fact that it was in a cool neighborhood," he said. "These people were creative artists creating art together, and that felt authentic to me in a way I hadn't experienced before." Members were expected to share their gifts, and Andrew's musical talent had grown up trapped in the sounds of contemporary Christian music. At his Circle congregation, which Jonny was leading, the music didn't have to be classified as Christian to be considered good, and his favorite church activity was playing along to the 1922 silent horror film *Nosferatu*. Tooling around for fun, they'd drawn a large neighborhood crowd. "There was just this feeling that we could do anything," he said. That didn't mean that Circle was flawless. Andrew recognized some of Circle's problematic practices before others did.

Even Jonny wasn't immune to making racial mistakes. Early on, Andrew brought along his friend Amy to church. She was also Asian American and would later become his wife. Jonny asked whether they were siblings or romantic partners. "It was a racist thing to say," Andrew said, but he took the microaggression in stride. Other things bothered him. To demonstrate that Circle was transracial and transnational, for instance, they often sang about Jesus in Mandarin, Swahili, and Xhosa, among other languages most members didn't know. As a native Mandarin speaker, Andrew noted the garbled pronunciations, and while it might not have risen to the level of cultural appropriation, there was something tone-deaf about it.

Then there was his brush with Rod. When Andrew graduated from law school and was looking for a job, Rod suggested that Andrew contact David Oh, a Republican member of the Philadelphia City Council. Andrew was puzzled. He and Oh had nothing in common politically, until he realized that Oh was Korean American and Rod was assuming they were from the same country since both were Asian. After that, Andrew stayed away from Rod, focusing his attention at Fishtown and dreaming up funny and subversive influence campaigns to wake his white friends up as to how despite their progressive positions, they weren't free of racism.

Of all these efforts, Bethany was most proud of Turn Up to Bail Out, the music festival she'd dreamed up in 2017 to raise money for the city's nascent community bail fund. She hosted the event at the second-floor loft space that the church had been renting for Sunday worship services since 2005. With high ceilings and a view of William Penn atop city hall, the attractive loft was also one of Rod's smart business moves, allowing Circle to make money by renting it out for weddings for non-Circle members. (For Circle people, the space was free.) Bethany, who managed the space, earned $300 to $400 per event.

For the first couple of years of Turn Up, when Bethany looked down from the control booth to the dance floor, she couldn't help but notice that most attendees were her white church friends. For a time, that was good enough, since Turn Up was geared toward wealth redistribution and sharing white resources, like money and the free loft, with the Black community. Although in some ways the event was also designed to help bring Black people to Circle, it was more about Circle living its principles: finding an alternative way to be the church and learning about its complicity in racism.

"If you're coming here for a concert to get the singing, you're going to learn the rates of incarceration for Black women as well," Bethany explained. Led by Black artists and performances by Philadelphia natives like Bethlehem Roberson, who'd coined the term "vocussionist" and danced in character shoes on a wooden box, Turn Up celebrated Black joy, which Bethany believed was a Jesus thing. "Jesus is present in joy," Bethany said.

Surveying the dance floor in 2019, she realized it had changed. "It was Black as hell, and that felt good," she said. "This must be what heaven feels like sometimes." A youth activist offered testimony about being sent to an adult prison on a $520,000 bail. The Philly bail fund had probably saved his life, he explained. Bethany, who was emceeing, wasn't a singer, but she joined in on "Before I Let Go" by Beyoncé. Unbeknownst to Bethany, one of her sisters from Sigma Gamma Rho snapped her photo. Toward the end of the evening, in the bathroom, the sorority sister asked Bethany if she could show her the picture. It had been only a few months since the photo trouble with Rachel. But Bethany had lost forty pounds and broken up with her difficult boyfriend, so she risked taking a look at herself. Here she was at the mike in her neon-yellow cropped sweatshirt and black leggings, with silvered green eyelids, chunky hoop earrings, and eyelashes curled for the ages. This Black joy was hers.

Bethany and Andrew also started *Color Correction*, which they, along with a white friend, billed as "a Jesus-y podcast about race and faith." The podcast was Andrew's brainchild. They met up at Fishtown's studio and recorded their riffs on provocative topics; episode titles included "Surprise Racism / Oh Sh*t, That's Racist" and "Cultural Appropriation / This Racism Is Delicious!" Bethany liked to joke, at first, that *Color Correction* was in competition with the pastors' podcast, *Resist and Restore*. But when she saw on SoundCloud that *Color Correction* garnered hundreds, and sometimes thousands, more listens per episode than the pastors' podcast did, she stopped making the joke.

The death of George Floyd really changed things at Circle, and she realized that white people were beginning to listen to her at the church. "I started Black Girl Cell just to help take care of other Black women at Circle who didn't know one another," she said. "I didn't realize that by doing that, or by hosting events with my friends on different compassion teams that I was helping forge new alliances." This increased sense of authority carried with it a responsibility to stand up for herself and for other people of color when conflicts arose.

A couple in their sixties who'd recently moved from Kansas to Philadelphia had joined Bethany's cell in 2019. Jill Schellenberg was a retired professor of criminology and restorative justice; her husband, Tim, a retired pastor and hospice chaplain. Knowing no one in the city other than Rod and Gwen, whom they'd met through Mennonite organizations, they decided to check out Circle. Gwen had tried to warn them away, saying they might feel out of place. And they did. They flinched when people swore and were taken aback when someone suggested they find friends by hanging out in the lobby of a local senior center.

One evening a few months before the 2020 presidential election, Bethany's cell members were sitting around on a porch in West Philadelphia mimicking Trump. Bethany was typically great at impressions but this one eluded her. "I've always had trouble doing Trump," she said.

"That's because you have to get the Black out of your voice," Tim Schellenberg offered.

Others laughed, but Tim knew immediately he'd said the wrong thing. "I wanted to sink into the concrete," he said later. "I was horrified." He claimed to have offered an apology right away. He tried to explain that as a missionary learning German, he'd been told, "You have to get the American out of your voice."

Bethany didn't hear any apology. "I didn't hear it because he didn't say it," she said later.

For the next few minutes, Bethany attempted to lead the cell onward; then she decided to try to call Tim in: "You know, Tim, it's hard enough to be the only Black woman in the white spaces of this church," she said. "But comments like yours make it alienating."

Tim felt singled out and embarrassed. "I thought you were proud to be Black!" he exclaimed.

His defensive reaction made it worse, Bethany told him.

After cell ended that evening, Bethany couldn't let the incident go. It was too emblematic of how people of color got hurt in white churches, but particularly at Circle of Hope.

Cells were intended to be intimate places where people supported one another, and nourished their souls through sharing their love of Jesus. They also required a high level of vulnerability, and what critics were calling "emotional labor." Bethany loved her cell, and she had no problem with being open, but to feel "slapped like that," as a Black woman, clarified to Bethany a pattern that needed to change. It wasn't the racial misstep that bothered Bethany. Those she could stand. It was what she experienced of Tim's reactivity, and his unwillingness to own his mistake. Tim wrote Bethany an apology letter, which Rachel, their pastor, delivered. Bethany refused to accept it, and Rachel stood by her, defending Bethany's right to handle the situation however she saw fit. For Bethany, this marked a shift in Rachel's ability to be an ally. "If this happened a few years ago, I don't think Rachel would've stood by me," Bethany said. But Rachel was showing a new willingness to support Black women, even if it cost church members. Tim didn't know what else to do. "What more can I say than 'I'm sorry, please forgive me'?" he asked. Several months after the incident, without using their names, Bethany blogged about their encounter under the title "Everyone Wants to Be Anti-Racist Until My Black Ass Tells You How":

> Anti-racism is about way more than individual acts that satiate your need for moral superiority. In its true form, it is some of the hardest work and the toughest journey that a white person can ever take on because it does in fact require that you both question and relinquish everything that you consider to be normal and reality. We are brothers and sisters in Christ, if I tell you as a brother or sister that you have sinned against me, that you have violated me, simply change the behavior. Our goal is to be the new creation God is calling us to, not to condemn you for an eternity.

. . .

When Tim read the Facebook post, he sent Bethany a private message. The Bible called believers to correct one another "with gentleness," he wrote. "Evidently you did not accept my apology and are using it to portray yourself as morally superior. You did not follow Scripture by correcting me in private. You tried to humiliate me and refused to hear any apologies. From your statement, I assume we are not welcome at cell."

Bethany replied that he should "grow up in Christ." Then she told him never to contact her again, and blocked him.

The Schellenbergs went back to Rachel for guidance. She suggested that they reach out to Bethany directly, but how could they do that, they wondered, since Bethany had told them never to contact her again?

But Bethany didn't budge.

Tim and Jill had no choice but to leave Circle, feeling shunned. Bethany didn't feel she'd shunned anyone. Anti-racism *required* discomfort, and so did Anabaptism. "If you're not willing to be uncomfortable, then you're not living into the Anabaptist tradition," she said. To stand by their commitment to nonviolence, Anabaptists had once been willing to die.

The Schellenbergs, who'd spent their lives following Anabaptist tenets of forgiveness, found this difficult to hear, and profoundly unfair. Bethany knew their story: after their disabled daughter was raped, Tim and Jill had worked with high-risk sex offenders, piloting a Kansas-based reentry program that functioned a bit like a Circle cell. Research indicated that surrounding offenders with love and care reduced rates of recidivism, but this required a willingness to offer their own hearts, and forgiveness, even when they didn't want to.

Bethany, however, contended that the incident on the porch was fundamentally different. Tim wasn't in the one-up position of *offering* forgiveness; instead, he was in the one-down position of having to *ask* for it. She'd seen this so many times at Circle: as much as people were willing to talk about the sin of racism in the abstract, they were unwilling to own personal ways they'd committed it. Bethany never spoke to the family again, but it didn't matter. She'd won.

Her shifting influence kept surprising her. As a joke, she reposted a satirical headline on her Facebook page: "Celebrate Juneteenth by Venmoing All Your Black Friends $50." When a white friend took the satire seriously and sent $50, Bethany wasn't quite sure what to do with the money, but she kept it. Andrew encouraged her to share the story on their podcast, which led to listeners at church suggesting that Bethany lead a reparations campaign. White members of Circle could give money directly to Black members. To Bethany and Andrew and others, the plan seemed radical and kind of hilarious. So Bethany sent around an email to the two dozen Black covenant members, asking if they'd like to be recipients. Almost everyone opted in. Not everyone found the subversive idea very funny, however. "Older Circlers had a big problem with it," she said. Much like asking people to sign a statement, it put members on the spot to ask them for money, they contended. Circle already redistributed wealth through sharing money with organizations and holding events like the baby-goods exchange. Member to member felt trickier.

Despite these criticisms, Bethany went forward, setting a 2021 goal to raise $20,000. The "Venmo Your Black Friend $50" campaign was just getting started as Nelson Hewitt's anti-racism sessions began in April. When Hewitt quit, contributions poured in. "We boomed past our goal," Bethany said. She surmised that his departure had revealed to people how problematic the church culture actually was. Finally, they wanted to do more to address the sins of the past. "The church was worked up, and when we had to face ourselves, everybody started to give." By the end of July, they'd raised $30,000. Although Bethany hadn't planned to take any of the money herself, friends explained that her refusal was actually fear of how she'd appear. Breaking a culture of white supremacy required ending white notions of shame, even if it caused her discomfort. In the end, however, she donated $450 of the $500 she received to the bail fund.

Hewitt's departure carried other unintended benefits. In July, following Jasmine's initial suggestion that Bethany become Circle's new anti-racism consultant, Bethany submitted a proposal as to how she'd take on the role. Circle of Hope was stuck, she wrote, diagnosing the problem as "an internal theological crisis point." She went on: "Some members firmly believe that anti-racism is inseparable from following Christ. While others believe that our present approach to anti-racism alienates the majority of Circle of Hope's membership, white people." Bethany didn't say so explicitly, but she believed that Circle of Hope needed to split in two. For months, she'd been telling the pastors they couldn't remain a single body, since the difference in visions between old ways and new was too great.

Ben had confessed to Bethany that he was afraid of creating an "us versus them" church.

"There's definitely a lot of white people who are afraid of being alienated and left behind," she'd told him. "If people don't want to follow Jesus, then let them go."

But the pastors had consistently rejected the idea of splitting. A schism would mean they'd failed.

Bethany believed she'd foreseen the end of Circle of Hope. Since childhood, she'd carried an unwieldy spiritual gift, a glimpse of the prophetic: images of the future came to her in black-and-white stopped time, like Polaroids. While she was kneeling in her garden's raised beds, one such snapshot flashed before her. Ben was in the front pew of a church she didn't recognize. Rod and Gwen, along with a half dozen tow-headed grandkids, filled the rows behind him. There were other familiar faces in that unknown church, belonging to some of the oddballs she loved most. Blinking the image away, Bethany surmised that Circle of Hope was going to divide whether the pastors liked it or not.

Bethany, however, didn't foresee that she would be an agent of this change. She sailed through the church's unanimous affirmation to hire her by the end of summer in 2021. Following Nelson Hewitt's parting recommendation, she formed the Anti-Racism Steering Committee. Leading the group was more volatile than she'd thought it would be. One evening in September, she'd tried to ask Ben specific questions about how exactly Rod kept learning about Circle's inner workings.

Angrily, he cut her off. "You are trying to make me a smoking gun against my father!" he growled.

Although Jonny had told her to expect this kind of behavior from Ben, she'd never experienced his acting out and certainly never directed at her. Bethany was determined to call Ben to account for his actions, and in writing. Using emails and Slack conversations, she compiled a report analyzing the role that Ben, and sometimes Rachel, played in upholding structural racism. She never intended for the whole church to see it; she meant it only for the pastors and the members of the committee who'd witnessed this behavior firsthand. Only later, when the controversy worsened, did she share it more widely, but Bethany knew her report had the potential to explode. It might cost her the friendships of people so close she considered them chosen family. But a white pastor couldn't keep raging like this against his church. It was time to push Ben to see the consequences of his behavior, and for him to decide, once and for all, to repent and submit to being led in this new direction by people of color, including her. Or he could leave.

Bethany thought and wrote best at night when, in her garden, time seemed suspended. Around ten o'clock on a warm evening in mid-October, she settled into her wicker couch. A miniature forest was growing of velvety, variegated greens: a kale overstory fell into arugula lowlands. She typed without stopping until two in the morning, filling eleven pages with her analysis of how racism stubbornly survived at Circle of Hope:

> White exceptionalism—Because team members are unable to be honest with themselves and the structure of Circle of Hope as an institution.

She added:

> This elitist idea that the organization has already arrived at a place of anti-racism keeps Circle of Hope from being able to more deeply examine and question historical documents, practices and theological frameworks within the organization that are deeply racist.
>
> Fear of Open Conflict—There is also a consistent fear of open conflict. There is an over-emphasis on resolving uncomfortable conflicts in "private"; however, these private conflict resolutions protect those with the privilege of Whiteness and leave BIPOC persons vulnerable to further harm . . .
>
> Defensiveness—This is the primary symptom of White supremacy that appears throughout all levels of leadership and church membership. This defensiveness shows up as dishonesty, shutting down and refusing to fully participate in sessions. It also shows up as white leaders pathologizing BIPOC individuals after they've raised concerns of experiencing racialized harm from leadership. Language such as "that's because of your depression," "those are your issues with your mother" and other statements

such as the above have been used to delegitimize the experience
of racialized harm for BIPOC within this institution. Most consistently, defensiveness shows up as blaming BIPOC for raising
the issue of racialized harm experienced. BIPOC are told they
are being divisive.

For the next two weeks, she worked on the draft when she could.
Her mom was battling cancer, and she spent hours shuttling back and
forth between Philadelphia and Delaware for doctors' appointments.

In her report, she cited "Pastor Ben White" for lying to protect his
dad, and "bullying" Jonny. She singled out Rachel for her lack of participation on the steering committee channel on Slack. Using these examples as "exhibits," as if this were a legal brief, Bethany drew damning
conclusions: "Glaring levels of dishonesty" were "abusive in the way
that it leads to gaslighting of BIPOC . . . and manipulation." These
kinds of patterns, she concluded, defined the main reasons why Circle
of Hope remained roughly 85 percent white.

To be certain her observations were solely her own, and not influenced by anyone else, she shared what she'd written with no one, not
even her friend Andrew. But finally, she pushed "send" on a draft to the
pastors and committee members who were scheduled to meet the next
evening, which was Halloween. For the next twenty-four hours, her
mind spun catastrophic fantasies. What if her mom passed and everyone
at church turned against her? By Sunday afternoon, she was so plagued
by projected fears, she couldn't leave her bed. She called Julie, whom
she had come to trust the most of all the other pastors. Bethany asked
Julie not to tell anyone about her anxiety attack; she was afraid they'd
dismiss her analysis on the basis of "mental health issues," a criticism
leveled in the past against Black women at Circle.

At Bethany's request, Julie canceled the evening meeting.

10

BEN

"Each day has enough trouble of its own."
—MATTHEW 6:34

This is theater of the absurd," Gwen said. It was July 2021, and she and Rod had just received "an invitation" from the five cell coordinators asking them to cease all writing and speaking about the church, surrender their circleofhope.net email addresses, and refrain from offering members spiritual direction. It was the cell coordinators' first attempt to limit the Whites' ability to lead and influence the church by inviting them into a conversation about boundaries. Although the cell coordinators hadn't yet asked Rod and Gwen to stop coming to Circle—that would happen several months later—the Whites received the "invitation" as a severance, and they had no interest in discussing any such terms.

"We're not employees," Gwen said. She and Rod were finally being cast out. To find some quiet so that she could listen to God's will and not simply react, Gwen decamped from the city and drove one hundred miles northwest to Hallowood Acres, the Poconos subdivision of large gray colonials where the Whites had purchased a lake house with money from Gwen's family trust. She spent the next few days cooling off. Gwen, who remained a preternatural swimmer, was at home in the amber water. Her wet gray hair slicked back, she floated on a raft in Hallowood Lake, a twenty-nine-acre reservoir trimmed in red spruce and tamarack. Bobbing around in a rage, she prayed for acceptance. "I keep begging God to give me the power to forgive," she said one evening from the Poconos. "They can actually throw me out, but it bothers me that they've hurt my kids."

As much as Rod and Gwen had planted Circle of Hope for a lost generation of Jesus followers, they'd also created the church for their four sons, and their children after them. "I wanted to give this to my kids—a community of Christ, people really seeking Jesus—a living body and not an institution," she said. No other community offered radical love and commitment to Jesus, as she believed that Circle did. That vision was in ashes, and Gwen held Jonny responsible for destroying the church in an effort to further his ego. "He's locked in a battle to gain power and notoriety through Circle of Hope," she said. And many of the church's leaders who'd come out of evangelical backgrounds were following him, bringing their dangerous patterns of black-and-white thinking. "They're making it back into the old church," she went on. "The rules, the casting out of sinners—it has an overlay of justice, but it's rules."

So be it. They would leave. She could let almost everything go, but not, however, the name. "Circle of Hope" belonged to the Whites. It didn't simply represent their life's work; it was divinely inspired. Landing on her tongue on her first drive with Rod to Philadelphia in 1995, the name embodied the concept of the beloved community. For the past twenty-six years, Circle of Hope had lived and breathed organically, in Love Feasts, mother blessings, thrift stores, mutual aid, debt annihilation, marches against America's misadventures in Iraq and Afghanistan— these were the fruits of love now riven by "principalities and powers." To Gwen, this felt like the presence of evil. "The devil got a foothold and is having a heyday in the midst of a beautiful thing," she said.

. . .

With Gwen away at their lake house, Rod puttered around the twenty-first floor of their penthouse condo in a fading high-rise above

Fairmount Park. They'd finally found another contractor to finish the renovations, installing a backsplash of cerulean tile and painting its textured walls a glittering white, which bounced brilliant sunlight back onto a wraparound terrace high above the city, its skyline shimmering through July's heat. Their neighbors, Rod noted one afternoon, were almost all Black, which was part of why they wanted to live here and one reason Rod found it particularly ridiculous that Circle's new guard would claim that he and Gwen were white supremacists.

"They've decided I'm a privileged asshole, which is massively insulting and irritating," he said. To sweat out calories and feelings of betrayal, Rod rode his bike fourteen miles a day around Philadelphia. At sixty-seven, heat, hurt, and worry had hollowed him out. One afternoon, he climbed off his bike to rest on a concrete bench next to Fairmount Park's tennis courts. "I represent white supremacy," Rod snorted. "That's the stereotype." He stared across the empty street at a ropes course still closed due to the pandemic. Rod had a complicated relationship with being told what to do. "Stop. Just leave me alone," he told his invisible critics. "I'm not accountable to you."

Yes, Rod held influence—lots of it—to which he'd openly admitted. "Obviously, I have tons of power in the system. It would be disingenuous to say that wasn't true." But he wasn't hiding or manipulating that power. "No one thought I was a puppet master, and I don't think there's much evidence that I was creating a hierarchy at the top." More troubling to Rod than these accusations were Jonny's intentions. "If you want to get power as the world gets power and you want to exercise power as the world exercises power, well, then you're an Antichrist," he said. And Rod had always stood up to those looking to exercise the world's power, especially when it threatened his church. "You wanna be evil, I will lay down in front of your train. You'll have to run me over. 'Cause I think that's what I'm supposed to do, especially as a pastor."

Why was that wrong? It was so uncreative to view him as the old white guy, the paterfamilias, and to think this would solve society's problems. It was a colossal waste of time. Jonny and his supporters could have used their passion for justice to help heal Philadelphia, instead of fighting among themselves. Disagreement wasn't new to the church. Among such a rebellious and unruly bunch, conversations about where the Holy Spirit was leading them often grew contentious. "Expect conflict," one proverb read. However, this kind of intractable infighting was unprecedented, and Circle had another proverb warning against it: "Jesus is living the greatest mutiny ever—we should not waste our rebellion on each other."

To watch Circle of Hope squander its energies in this manner depressed Rod. "After George Floyd, in the most divided city in the world, they could've done something," he said. Instead, the church had gone to war over Rod. Yet Jesus delivered an irrefutable teaching as to how to handle enemies. "We just have to love them," he said. "Damning them is useless."

The rejection felt generational as well as personal. He was a boomer, after all, and the young people taking over Circle didn't see the value inherent in his years of experience. "Sticking around and being available, I was supposed to be like a blanket. You don't have to use me, but I'm here if you need me. I'm the benign old guy," he said. "We need old people. When I started Circle, I would've died to have one of me. I'm a little golden treasure."

. . .

When Gwen returned from the Poconos, she called for a family meeting to speak with Rod and their boys about how, as a family, they should relate to Circle of Hope. She wondered if, together, the Whites should find a new church. Jacob, the perceptive outsider, remained the only one of the four who'd never joined Circle, and he had little interest in the new plan. Still, Jacob felt for his father, who'd lost his life's work, and even more so for Ben, who still didn't seem to fully understand what he'd followed Rod into. He wished Ben had taken another path.

"Churches used to be places where people actively built communities together," Jacob said. It wasn't just Circle: churches across America were in trouble. Social and political polarization had fractured many of them: sitting in pews with like-minded people was more important than coming together to worship. "All churches have to offer now is intellectual affinity, and these kinds of affinities die," he said. He cited as evidence a 2021 Gallup poll he'd recently read, which, for the first time since Gallup had begun polling, found that less than half of Americans belonged to churches. The following year, Pew would predict that Christians would shrink from 64 percent of Americans to as low as 35 percent in 2070.

"I don't know if it's possible to have emotional resonance with a poll," he said, wryly. "But I do."

Other factors were also polarizing progressives. They could behave terribly on-screen. Jacob had a term for those who dropped bombs in virtual spaces: "internet brave." In many cases, exacerbated by isolation, white progressives were destroying their communities and organizations by fighting over linguistic puritanism.

At the public high school where Jacob taught, he'd witnessed the stakes of these arguments. The insults students sometimes threw at one another on Instagram spilled over into real-world violence; kids had been victims of gun violence for less than the silly scrapping over circleofhope.net.

Nonetheless, to support their family, Jacob and his wife, Aubrey, hosted a potluck supper on their cramped back porch in Germantown, clustered among the neighborhood's busy backyards. The kids stayed inside watching movies so that the adults could hold a conversation over Gwen's fried chicken, accompanied by black bean and corn salad, rolls, grapes, brownies, and Jell-O. When they'd gathered around the table, Gwen did most of the talking.

"One of the reasons we made this church was for you," she told their sons. "We didn't know where else you could be Christians." When the talk turned to the other pastors, Ben, surprisingly, stood up for his colleagues. Despite his private fears that they were turning against him, Ben remained adamant against slipping into gossip. He refused to speak against Rachel, Julie, and even Jonny, who, he argued, were simply seeking to do what was right for the church. They were, he kept repeating, "trying to work things out and find their own way."

Listening to Ben, Jacob and Aubrey were struck by his courage and his conviction to speak ill of no one. Of the boys, reserved Joel was the angriest that evening. He couldn't believe that decades of his family's selfless service to Jesus and to their community was being called a power move. On Jacob's porch, Rod said little, quietly admiring how articulate his sons had become about the gospel. He noted the change in Joel, who had always been the more restrained of the twins. "He's not taking bullshit like he has his whole life," Rod observed. But that didn't mean that Joel, or Ben, would remain at Circle of Hope. "I don't know if they're going to get their church," Rod mused with his signature dispassion, as if he'd washed his hands and was no longer involved, when, in fact, his choices had helped to strand Ben.

. . .

Ben backed his Prius hard into a parked car in front of his New Jersey colonial three days after his parents received the "invitation." The metal twisted so loudly that a neighbor came out to eyeball the crash. *What a rookie move*, he berated himself, *hitting a stationary car.* Ben knew he'd been distraught and distracted by Jonny's campaign to "box out" the Whites. Although the other cell coordinators tried to reassure Ben that Jonny had nothing to do with the new guidelines limiting Rod and Gwen at Circle, Ben didn't buy it. Maybe he should quit, too.

Leaving, however, was the last thing he wanted. He kept imploring the other pastors to convince him that all of this pain in the name of anti-racism was necessary. "Please help me," he begged one late-summer morning on Julie's porch. His parents had just been dismissed. "If you cannot convince me that there is love in this, how will you convince the church?"

Jonny, Julie, and Rachel were tired of Ben demanding to be convinced, which required so much of their time and energy at meetings that they were rarely able to address the necessary items, so they disregarded him and pushed on, which he found enraging.

"Dear Team," he wrote in an email after the meeting, "I am very upset, and I don't know what to do with you all. The relentless loveless, antisceptic [*sic*] adjudication for the ostensible sake of our antiracist efforts will grind me to a pulp. The lens is power and not love."

Later, during another summer skirmish, he spat at Jonny, "You won."

But Jonny refused to accept blame. "Your parents did something terrible to the church," he insisted.

"Talk to them," Ben pleaded, oblivious to the fact that it was far too late. "Talk to them." At Circle, talking—relating—had always been the solution to everything.

"No," Jonny said. "If they have a problem with me, they should talk to me."

. . .

Ben insisted that there must be a way to move forward together with the Spirit. When Ben tried to back down and be vulnerable, telling Jonny how his family was hurting, Jonny refused to concede that they had a right to feel injured. "What I'm hearing is that everyone has to organize around Rod and Gwen, and that's white supremacy," Jonny told Ben.

"Your lack of empathy is infuriating to me," Ben said. "It's flip. It's political. It makes me think you are as calculating as you seem."

Ben stopped pleading. He knew that his anger was a problem, but he wasn't sure what to do about it. "Any communication of my feelings is an abuse of my power," he lamented. And the role race played was complicated. "If I call you foolish then it's a white person distrusting a brown person," he told Jonny. But people were people. He was still Ben! "I need a creative solution and I need God to provide one, or I'm going to quit," he threatened in a rage.

"Yeah, I'd quit, too," Jonny replied.

Ben asked the cell coordinators and leadership core team for their help in mediating. They suggested that both men find therapists. Ben was incensed. Who were these people to mandate that he needed emotional and psychological help? He viewed Jonny's desire for power and fame as proof of the fact that Jonny was using Circle as a stepping stone in his career and driving out all who opposed him under the cover of racism. In contrast, Ben saw his own counterattacks as protective of the church and his family, especially his dad. He didn't understand, until too late, that his outbursts and tantrums were creating a problem of his own making.

· · ·

Poetry had always been Ben's chosen form of prayer. As the outside world seemed to set itself against him, he turned inward, losing himself in the collections he kept in his Marlton Pike office. There were the usual suspects for a literary-minded pastor: Gerard Manley Hopkins's *Collected Works*; a volume containing John Donne's sonnet "Batter my heart, three-person'd God"; and another with contemporary poems by Malcolm Guite, an Anglican priest. Guite's *Sounding the Seasons: Seventy Sonnets for the Christian Year* was essential reading for both Ben and Gwen, who used the poems to write prayers for Circle. And there were others less overtly pious: Li-Young Lee's *The City in Which I Love You* and Todd Davis's *In the Kingdom of the Ditch*. Their thin spines on his shelf served as daily reminders to Ben of the Kingdom beyond this mess unfolding around him.

Ben was at his large desk on Halloween when Bethany's unanticipated report dropped into his mailbox. He read and reread these oddly dispassionate, pseudo-lawyerly, and damning observations of "Pastor Ben." She'd used his words against him as "exhibits." He had no idea what the implications of these accusations were. Was he going to be fired? He'd lost the desire to defend himself. He just wanted to understand what the Spirit wanted him to do next. As he waited for their Sunday-evening discussion, he received a message from Julie saying Bethany was sick. The discussion was canceled. Ben endured two more disorienting days of limbo. On the morning of November 2, he drove from New Jersey to Rachel's South Philly row house for their regular pastors' meeting.

Slumped at Rachel's IKEA dining room table, Ben caved in on himself. To his right sat Rachel, and to his left Julie, along with a cell coordinator from Germantown. She was there to make sure the pastors didn't go at one another—namely, that Ben didn't attack Jonny or Julie. This was part of the new process by which the volunteer leaders tasked with managing the pastors sat in on meetings that might blow up. At the opposite end of the table, Jonny took a seat facing Ben. A plate of untouched blueberry muffins sat between them, and hanging on the wall above was a Nativity scene with a brown Mary, Joseph, and Jesus in a pink stable. Nearby, a woodcut showed St. Francis stripping himself naked and becoming one with a tree, a crown of branches and fruit growing from his head. Around Francis was an inscription in Italian: *Togliere tutto ció che ostacola portare frutto* (Take away everything that gets in the way of bearing fruit).

"I'm part of the problem," Ben admitted. He placed a black notebook from Target on the table in front of him. Following his "smoking gun" tirade, he'd adopted a new practice to rid his speech of violent metaphors. (Circle of Hope had already shifted from using "bullet points" to using "pearl points," thanks to Gwen White and the Mennonites.) The poet Wendell Berry, one of his heroes, had practiced something similar.

"I'm not usually scared like this in my body," he said. Ben lifted his hand, which was holding a pen, to show them it was trembling. But the gesture fell flat—what did it matter if a big white guy felt afraid in his body? He wanted to talk about Bethany's report. "I was really looking forward to talking about it last night," he said. But it wasn't on the agenda, and the silence that followed indicated reluctance to wade into what threatened to be yet another round with Ben in the ring. Around the blond wood table, gazes lowered. "Please don't ignore me," he implored. "I believe in anti-racism. I believe I am a racist, white person. I'm a rare ally in the world, at least in that I actually want to do this work. And you're wasting me. I feel like I'm dead and we're not going to get anywhere."

Couldn't they see that Ben, this dude who bore every form of privilege, was willing to examine himself and help lead others to repent of racism, and that was "fucking radical for a white person"? Circle would fail if they put forward purity tests that even someone like Ben couldn't pass. He'd been raised in a Black neighborhood and brought up in a church that, for nearly thirty years, had attempted to welcome people of color. Did none of this matter? "Don't make a report of what I'm saying," he added. "Please, like, let's talk."

Rachel lifted her gaze and sat back in her chair, glancing around the table. "Just trying to push the White family out of the church is small for our anti-racist goals, I think."

Jonny said nothing to Rachel and turned against Ben. "I know more than anybody that the white supremacy in our church is a demon that we can't seem to exorcise," he said. "Ben, I don't experience you as a rare ally. I experience you as a white man." So much of their shared life at Circle of Hope was predicated on the myth of being exceptional, superior, different, but when it came to everyday racism, the church was plagued with the same American problem. "It just seems like an ordinary evangelical place," Jonny added. This double-barreled condemnation landed on the table with a thud. Circle of Hope strove to be everything other than ordinary or, worse, evangelical, and yet that's what the church really was.

Ben didn't argue. He turned to the cell coordinator. "What's your plan for me?" he asked.

They had no answer for him yet, she replied.

"This is punctilious and vague as hell," he spat back at her. "I don't know how to—I don't know how to receive this information."

Julie wasn't going to allow their meeting to devolve into consoling Ben. This was one of the many reasons they were stuck. By disrupting their meetings to take care of him, they kept centering whiteness. She insisted they move on with the pearl points on the agenda, and the pastors pushed through a discussion about their two new proverbs that, once accepted by the whole church in the coming months, would finally render Circle officially queer-affirming.

The pastors' meeting always ended with a prayer, and that week it fell to Ben to pray for them, but he couldn't. "I don't feel able to pray," he managed. "Will someone else pray for us?"

Rachel bowed her head over her dining room table. "Jesus," she asked, as if calling to a friend from across the room. "We need your open arms extended to help us, on our team, on all of our teams across the church, help us to see you, help us to know you and give us understanding and wisdom even beyond what we have now in this moment. Thank you for the gift of each other in Jesus's name. *Amen.*"

Ben was the first to leave. He made his way down Rachel's block and around the corner to where he'd parked his red Toyota Prius. Before pulling away from the curb, he sat in the driver's seat and screamed.

. . .

After twenty-five years as a son of Circle of Hope, and six as its pastor, Ben had no desire to leave. He'd spent his life being groomed to lead the church, and peacemaking was the core of his Anabaptist faith, but he couldn't see how to stay without going to war. What kind of peace church would Circle be if Ben rallied troops against Jonny? The only way forward for the church, and for Ben, was for him to quit. To deliver the news to their flock and their friends, he and Gwyneth spent Saturday, November 20, driving from house to house with Ollie and Theo, sitting on porches and in living rooms to explain why Ben was abandoning his dream of pastoring Circle of Hope.

On Sunday, November 21, Ben sprayed water on the firehouse's vinyl floor before people arrived for 10:00 a.m. worship. Most Sunday mornings Ben re-mopped the church; it never seemed clean enough. It was cold for November in the drafty garage, yet the edges of Ben's sandy hair darkened with sweat. Although he grumbled about the mess and the mopping, Ben liked the devotion, which he'd been practicing for eighteen years—since he was a twenty-year-old missionary sweeping the driveway of a Mennonite church in Mexico City, using the rhythm of the strokes to fix the Sermon on the Mount in his mind: "Blessed are the poor in spirit"—swish—"for theirs is the kingdom of heaven"—swoosh.

His friend and advisor John Londres, one of Marlton Pike's most long-standing members, wandered in. John was in his sixties and older than most folks at Circle. He was devoted to the place, and to offering Ben considered advice. Ben was the only pastor of the many he'd known whose practical generosity demonstrated real love, and Londres was saddened to see Ben go. Unlike those of his contemporaries who regarded Rod as infallible, Londres had a more nuanced take. He saw the problematic systems that Ben had inherited from his dad, right down to micromanaging where the chairs went, and re-mopping a clean floor, and for years had been gently guiding him toward a softer way.

. . .

"Circle has better things to do than fight about me," Ben told John. "The only other way is to stay and fight and gather people to my side. I don't want to do that. I consistently haven't done that," he added. He didn't claim to be a martyr, and he wasn't one. He'd bullied people and thrown tantrums. Thinking the conflict was his to manage and shoulder alone, he'd kept too much to himself. That, also, was a problem. There had been too much secrecy. Even this morning he'd planned to say nothing about his departure during the service. But Ben was rethinking this.

"Do you think I should say anything this morning?" Ben asked John.

"I think it might feel weird to get that email tomorrow and find out you already knew today," Londres offered.

Ben put down the mop and went to brew coffee in the firehouse kitchenette, where he could call Gwyneth in private. She was still on her way with the boys, and he needed her counsel. Although he didn't want to stop being a pastor at Circle, he could already feel relief in his body from letting go of the rope. While Ben was on the phone with Gwyneth, talking quietly into his hand, Audrey Robinson arrived, carrying a red designer purse in the crook of her arm and a tray of chicken covered in tinfoil, and still warm from her oven. By the time Ben had finished his call, a dozen members had trickled in and filled the small circle of black folding chairs that Ben had set up exactly how he liked them. In their center, on a coffee-table altar, sat a tin pail full of fake fall leaves and a red Jesus candle, which every pastor lit during every service to signify that Jesus was in their midst.

Gwyneth slipped in a few minutes late, wearing black-and-white polka-dotted sunglasses pushed up on her head. She took the empty seat next to Ben, keeping her eyes fixed on the candle flame. He was reading from the parables of Matthew: "The kingdom of heaven is like a mustard seed that someone took and sowed in his field." Ben came up with an unusual take. The parable was confusing, but parables were meant to be so, he explained. "They're unintelligible to the intellect." Ben had spent so much of his life in his intellect, he added, and sometimes the brain needed to be confounded. The seed wasn't bad in the Bible; its smallness was an allusion to the beginnings of faith, or the Kingdom of Heaven on Earth, but Ben spun the passage differently, because that's what a pastor was free to do at Circle of Hope, and that's what the day's troubles required. "Even bad things can be transformed into good things," he said, by way of segue. "I resigned as a pastor yesterday." Ben glanced around at the two dozen faces of his sparse flock. Only a few registered surprise.

"This past year I've been involved in a power struggle against my family," he went on. "It started as a righteous fight against racism. I've been trying to submit, but the knife keeps going deeper and it gets more personal." Ben had long feared that if he left, Marlton Pike would shut its doors; he'd misunderstood that he was the one holding the congregation together. "Me quitting doesn't mean this congregation is done," he said.

He felt so much remorse. "I regret many things I've done and that have contributed to the problem," he went on. In his pain, he wasn't sure he saw the situation clearly yet. "I might have to repent more." He already regretted that he'd kept secrets for so long. He just didn't know how to share what was happening. "I've done much to conceal this problem from you," he said. "I've been keeping this a secret because I haven't wanted to sink the ship, not sink you guys."

When Ben paused, questions sprang up from around the circle.

"Ben, are you staying in the covenant?" one woman asked.

"Gwyneth and I would really like to keep the covenant, but we're going to take a six-month break," Ben said. "Even when Circle of Hope is behaving badly, it's still the best church around."

"Are there things you need from us?" asked another.

"Don't isolate us," he said, almost pleading. "I want to forgive them like this guy," he said, looking down at the Bible in his hand. He was referring to Jesus. "But I don't think I can lead and stay in this entrenched power struggle with leadership."

"When you say leadership, who is that?" another asked.

Ben was quiet for a minute. "I'm pausing because it's not an individual thing," he said. "Me and my family got abstracted and treated like institutional bygones that needed to be replaced." He took another breath. "I've had a deep conflict with Jonny Rashid, but it's a two-way street."

One woman apologized to Ben. "I know I said some things about anti-racism that rubbed salt in the wound, like 'You're a big white guy, so don't talk so much.'"

"That's the confounding part," Ben said. "I believe that big white guys have to change, but not this way." Other than leaving for a while, he was out of ideas. "I don't know what I could've done," he admitted. "I don't know why it's so personal."

"Not every single thing is racist!" Audrey Robinson called out. She'd had it with the Whites being maligned, and now, as she saw it, Jonny and Co. had succeeded in breaking up her spiritual family. "These people want power!" She shook her head from her seat, poised to let loose a stream of invective, but Ben shut this down, saying, "Change is hard."

Much of Marlton Pike felt excluded from the conversations about power and race that seemed to be held elsewhere at Circle and by a small number of leaders. "It's a fundamental shift in our church," one said. To some, it seemed that only those who held the right views were welcome to participate; others were shut out as backward. Asking questions had become synonymous with dissent, and dissent, by definition, was anti-change and anti-progress, since it slowed pushing forward toward righteousness. "I didn't join a church for righteousness," another member said.

When Ben said nothing, Gwyneth began to share haltingly. She rarely put herself forward in church. "I didn't hear the call to come here," she admitted. She'd never wanted to move to New Jersey. She'd broken into tears when Rod had made the announcement, she reminded their flock. Gwyneth had relented, she added, because that's what it meant to be commissioned by God and by the body of the church. God's will was revealed in the collective will, and she'd trusted the community and followed the direction of the Holy Spirit. Over the past year and a half, she'd felt that the very same people, the body that had commissioned her and Ben to move their boys and give up the home they loved in West Philadelphia, had withdrawn that commission. It was hard to trust the direction of the Spirit when they felt so abandoned. That didn't mean that there weren't issues of structural power to address at Circle, but she and Ben just weren't sure these issues could be addressed if they stayed.

"We don't know how to do this anymore," she confessed. "We feel like we're standing in the way. I don't know what's going to happen next. This past year has felt like death by one thousand cuts. Ben and I have a lot of peace about him moving out of this role." But they still didn't think that they had to leave Circle.

"I'm not quitting the church," Ben added. He didn't want anyone else to break up the body, either. "I would ask you all to stay."

Then he began to sing "Seek Ye First," and others followed, breaking into voices of twos and threes, which braided themselves around the firehouse.

Later, Ben sat down after lunch and pushed "send" on his email to the entire church: "Our collective inquiry into the racism in our church has taken a very personal path," he wrote. "I have been enduring pointed, bad-faith scrutiny of me and my family, and I just can't continue in this hostile environment. Forgive me. I know that discomfort is unavoidable in anti-racism work, especially for white men like me. I accept that, but I do not think it has to be like this. Circle of Hope ought to do much more than fight with me, so I am not fighting anymore . . . Peace, Ben." Soon, to Ben's dismay, his own congregation chimed in, forming an angry chorus.

Within twenty minutes, Jonny replied to say that he shared their "fury, heartbrokenness, disgust, and confusion." He added, "I am sorry about what is happening. This entire circumstance fills me with deep regret and is tearing me apart. I will keep listening as I am able."

Audrey Robinson hit the caps-lock key:

SHUT UP JOHNNY! YOUR ONE OF THE REASONS WE ARE LOSING PASTOR FRIENDS AND BROTHER. YOU DONT GIVE A DAMN ABOUT US! IT SEEMS ALL U DO IS SIT IN FRONT OF YOUR COMPUTER AND WAIT FOR SOMEONE EMAIL SO U CAN FEEL POWERFUL! YOU THINK U KNOW EVERYTHING BUT WHAT U DONT KNOW WE DONT NEED A POWER TRIPPING FOOL IN OUR LIVES KEEP IT MOVING LEAVE ALONE! AND THATS ON 100 IS THAT BLACK ENOUGH FOR YOU!

JULIE

"By their fruit you will recognize them."
—MATTHEW 7:16

J ulie was the only pastor Jonny invited to his thirty-sixth birthday
party. He was cooking chicken tinga tacos and pumpkin cheese-
cake for some fifty-odd guests at a friend's white stucco home in
the suburban neighborhood of Roxborough. Taking a break from the
kitchen, Jonny was in a second-floor bathroom when an email arrived
from Ben with the subject line "my resignation." Coming out of the
bathroom, Jonny skimmed the message, which read, "I just can't continue in this hostile environment." Ben went on: "I do not understand
the consistent antagonism, the callousness, or the disrespect." Jonny
fell to his knees, sobbing, then headed downstairs and made his way
around the party, sharing his phone so that guests could read Ben's
resignation for themselves.

Julie, who hadn't yet arrived at the party, was still at home alone in
Germantown, futzing with her next-day's sermon on Christ the King.
Reading Ben's email, she dissolved on the floor of her sunroom into
a microburst of tears, which surprised her with their hold. When she
finally came up for air, she didn't know how much time had passed.
The rug was littered with crumpled Kleenex. She texted Steve, who'd
taken the kids to Lancaster to see her parents for the night. "Ben quit,"

she wrote. Then she managed to type a one-sentence reply to Ben: "I am heartbroken and I have no words." She looked out the bay window over the darkening park until a message came in from Jonny.

"You still coming tonight?" There was no need to mention Ben's email.

"Trying to pull myself together," she replied.

It was after eight by the time Julie reached Roxborough. Only five miles from Germantown, the predominantly white community with its close-clipped lawns and ornamental wreaths seemed a world away. When she walked in, one of Jonny's best friends spotted her, and tugged Julie through the crowd to find Jonny, who fell into her arms as she gripped him in a tight hug. She wandered between the firepit and the deck, not really talking to anyone, and a bit taken aback by the fact that people she didn't know very well from Jonny's congregation kept embracing her. Finally, emotionally exhausted, she climbed into her maroon jalopy of a 2007 Ford Fusion and left the white neighborhood. As she crossed back into Germantown, the potholes worsened.

On her way home, her head swam with questions as to how Ben's quitting would affect Circle of Hope. At the party, Jonny kept calling Ben's resignation "mean." The note and its timing were "an extraordinary display of white supremacy," as Jonny saw it. "It centered Ben as the one making the sacrifice." By putting his version of events out there first, Ben was attempting to steal the role of victim.

Julie didn't think, at first, that Ben was trying to be malicious or to damage the church. "I think he was trying to be honest," she said. "He's telling what he believes to be the truth." Instead, Julie felt that she and the pastors had failed: "I'm a wreck because we failed to make a partner of him, and he's our partner." If the sin of racism was collective, then so, too, was the act of repentance. Ben's leaving marked his unwillingness to repent, and that failure reflected on all of them.

The next day however, when Ben sent his resignation churchwide, and the online fracas ensued, Julie could see that Jonny was right. By claiming to be the victim, Ben was hijacking the narrative. At home at her basement desk, she tried to interrupt the vitriolic email chain by asking those on the listserv to stop for a minute with the complaints, rants, and screeds so that white people didn't consume all of the emotional space. But it was Audrey Robinson who launched the all-caps smackdown. And some others didn't take well to Julie's calls for restraint, writing back to her that "hushing" people wasn't "a good look."

Julie shrugged off the personal attacks accusing her and Jonny of ousting the Whites and driving out Ben in secret. Instead, she tried to keep focus on her professional role as an anti-racist leader. Yes, the church leaders were trying to maintain safety in public forums, especially for people of color. "Do not mistake intentionality and care for secrecy," she said.

. . .

Rumors about Ben's leaving spun out of control. The pastors spent hours triaging the concerns of those not privy to the past year's worth of problems. To so many, this departure seemed mystifying and alarming. If tensions at Circle had been high over previous months, now discord was climbing toward its apogee. In an attempt at de-escalation, Julie, Jonny, and Rachel decided to call an all-church emergency meeting the next week, on November 29, "to process Ben's resignation and to listen to God and each other for what's next."

The whole church would gather at Marlton Pike, and those who couldn't make it were invited to join online. However, the pastors didn't intend to lead an open discussion; instead, the three would share their version of Ben's resignation, which differed from his. To prepare, the pastors spent hours that week working through language and compromising on a narrative. But they didn't agree on who would stand up before the church and tell the story. Jonny insisted it should be him; Julie and Rachel thought otherwise.

So did Bethany, who coached the pastors on the morning of the high-stakes meeting. It was only nine days since Ben had resigned and people were worked up. Trying to convince Jonny to let one of the other pastors take the lead, she explained that Julie or Rachel could project an image of solidarity. This would help dispel the notion that Jonny was waging some kind of coup. But Jonny dismissed her concerns.

"Despite the racist stereotypes about me, I'm not an anti-racist activist trying to get white people out of the church," he told Bethany. He needed to confront the rumors the Whites had spun about him, and he wasn't afraid to be in "a hostile environment," he added. "How do you think I've survived in Circle of Hope?"

Bethany wanted to avoid a situation that evening where people of color might get hurt. By scapegoating Jonny, she explained to the pastors, Ben had caused racialized harm. They needed to be prepared for more to follow from "the old heads," who bought into the Whites' version of events.

But Jonny stuck fast to his position. Bethany didn't want to fight with Jonny in front of the two white pastors. It was essential to avoid creating any kind of narrative that people of color were divided. That's how white supremacy often perpetuated itself: setting people of color against one another to undermine the authority of their claims. So Bethany decided to let it go for the moment and call Jonny again in a few hours when she was alone to try to make him understand that if something went wrong, every person of color in that room would pay for it.

Julie also felt frustrated with Jonny, which was rare. Over the past several months, when negative comments about Jonny's personality began to surface, Julie had universally defended him: he was her friend and her brother in Christ. She wasn't going to let whiteness do what it always did at Circle: slip into a "pattern of deflection"—in which a person of color's personality was picked apart in a tacit effort to dismiss their call for change. Julie knew that people were criticizing her for seeming to follow Jonny unquestioningly, but this simply wasn't accurate. Rooting out racism at Circle of Hope was about much more than protecting Jonny. If someone attacked or criticized him this evening at Marlton Pike, that act of harm would damage the whole church. That's how collective sin worked: it injured everyone. But Jonny didn't seem to get what Julie and Bethany were saying. Instead, he kept repeating that he could handle the blowback.

"My question isn't whether you can handle the conversation," Julie told him. "But this moment calls for something different." The best way to end the false narrative of a tug-of-war between Ben and Jonny required Jonny letting go. "People already think I'm the asshole," Jonny replied. "It's good to know who hates me." The call ended unresolved.

Within hours, another spark flared. When Julie learned that Ben was planning to show up that evening, she picked up her phone once again. "What's your plan tonight?" she asked Ben with a forthrightness unusual at Circle, and a part of her new style.

Ben told her he was coming. There'd been too much talking *about* his family and not enough talking *to* them. So if a meeting was being held about his departure, he'd be there to speak for himself.

Julie said no. By resigning, she explained, Ben had forfeited his right to talk about the future of Circle.

Ben was furious, yet he remained calm and agreed to stay home. Julie could hear Gwyneth cursing Julie out in the background. "She speaks my mind," Ben said flatly.

After a terse goodbye, they hung up.

Late that afternoon, before Bethany left Strawberry Hill to drive to New Jersey, she had one hard call left to make. From her living room, she rang Jonny. She was no longer diplomatic. In the absence of the two white women, she demanded that he not put himself in the middle of the conflict. This would perpetuate the racialized distortion that the problem at Circle really amounted to a personal fight between the two men. Let the white pastors stand up and recount the complicated story, she told him, so that people could see all three were unified. Visual records made powerful tools. Still, Jonny refused. If he allowed someone else to share their narrative, the white people would've won by silencing him. By the end of the call, they still didn't agree. But there was no convincing Jonny.

. . .

230

Praying as she drove south from Germantown, Julie got caught in the crawl of Monday night traffic. Commuters were leaving Center City and returning to the New Jersey bedroom communities across the Walt Whitman Bridge. When she finally arrived around 7:30 p.m., the repurposed garage was filling with over one hundred current members, as well as some who hadn't shown up in a while: blue-jeaned and bearded Gen Xers greeting one another with big, back-clapping hugs and clustering on battered couches and machinist stools. Everyone was masked. Two aisles split the room into three sections. To the left sat many of Marlton Pike's members. In the middle of the room, four rows back, sat Joel, Ben's twin and the only White who'd come that evening in person. He kept his shaggy head down; from behind, overspilling the chair and clad in a plaid flannel shirt, he looked exactly like Ben. Audrey Robinson sat in the same row as Joel and a handful of the Whites' closest friends, who were also among Circle's oldest members. To the right of the room and up front gathered a group from Jonny's Fishtown congregation.

Julie made her way to the front row's folding chairs, where she, Rachel, and Jonny were going to sit next to one another. All three looked nervous. A large screen at the front of the room resembled the 1970s game show *Hollywood Squares*, with expectant faces staring into their cameras as if peering into the room. In an awkward reversal born of Zoom, the two dozen virtual participants were far larger and more prominent than those in the actual room. Several squares were blacked out with only a name; some participants, driving, were all nostril and streetlight hurtling past; others were cooking dinner bathed in glare.

When Rachel stood to open the evening in prayer, Julie could feel the room's anxious chill seep into her chest. "Many of us are coming in tonight with intense feelings," began Rachel, her tone as calm as a meditation app. No one, including Julie, knew how much pressure she was under from boomers and Gen Xers who'd been screaming at her for the past week over what the hell was happening at church. "We are all friends of Jesus," she went on, "and it's in that spirit we can meet each other and hopefully see and hear each other, even in new ways."

When the room had finished praying together, Julie stepped forward to offer ground rules for the evening's discussion. Her voice, tightened against interruption, marked an abrupt shift from Rachel's. "If you're feeling reactive or defensive at any point tonight, hold that in prayer. God is listening," she directed fiercely. "Let's start by agreeing together that we will consider power dynamics and we will listen to marginalized voices. When talking about race or racism or white supremacy, let's agree together to listen—to believe and to defer to the voices and the feelings of BIPOC members." If anyone was feeling triggered or overwhelmed, they could leave the room. Don't lash out or interrupt the meeting.

Once Julie had finished listing the guardrails, Jonny rose and began to recount the story of Ben's departure with a profound gentleness. He returned the audience to the summer of 2020, when, after the death of George Floyd, in May, the church first moved in "a decidedly anti-racist direction." He reminded them of their collective map. "We said things like, 'We're committing to amplifying the voices of color, increasing the investments on our leadership team, and committing to listen to their perspectives.' *Even when it caused us discomfort*," he emphasized. Bethany's italics now seemed prophetic. "We also agreed to hire an anti-racist consultant to lead us in an extended process of exploration that results in concrete steps—to name and confess and address personal, organizational, and systemic racism." He went on: "When you pull up the roots of white supremacy from our organization, it's hard work to do, especially for people that are very invested in the community. Ben agreed that how we relate to the White family was central to the work, so our work invariably related to Ben's family as it would to any founding family. Ultimately, we asked hard questions that put him in a difficult position." Having to choose between his job and his family posed an enormous strain for Ben, Jonny added. "We weren't able to relieve the tension for him. So he decided to get out of the way. He was done fighting. Ben hadn't wanted Circle of Hope to keep fighting, either. So we don't want to fight tonight."

Much of Ben's congregation thought this careful rendition wasn't fair and were baffled by the rules against participation. Why weren't they allowed to speak? A white woman from Marlton Pike called out in defiance from the left side of the room, "Gwyneth White is part of this, too! Gwyneth came to all of our houses with her children, the four of them, because they are a family unit and they were involved in this all year together!" The woman went on: "So I just want to point that out and include her because the ladies count!"

Scattered clapping washed over the room.

Soon, on Zoom, another Marlton Pike member, who was homebound, had something to say. (Limited by physical challenges, the member led an all-online cell and was helping leaders think through Circle's ableism.) On-screen, in his darkened room, he appeared as a pair of glowing glasses. "Well, I thank everyone for coming out to Marlton Pike. It's a wonderful place that over the past seven years Ben played a major role in helping build," he offered before venturing into more sensitive terrain. "Everyone knew that there was trouble between Ben and Jonny. I wish Jonny had not been the one to do the presentation."

Around her, Julie felt a collective intake of breath. Bethany Stewart, who was sitting to the left in front of Ben's congregation, stood up. "I just want to name the harm that Jonny must experience being called out as the only brown person on the team," Bethany said, turning to Jonny. "The assertion that you're the one person that he shouldn't hear from is wrong." This was how white supremacy worked. "It seeks to assert its influence in every opportunity, even in the most minute ways, and nobody was going to name it. I'm certain that he wasn't trying to be racially offensive," Bethany added, "but calling out the one brown person *is* a mistake."

From the corner of her eye, Bethany caught sight of someone standing up. She realized that it was a dear friend of hers. He was a member of her cell and had formed her pandemic pod, walking with her each week during lockdowns. But he was also close with the Whites. She watched him grab his metal folding chair and march out the back. Bethany couldn't believe how dismissive a gesture it was. But her friend contended that he was following the ground rules: if you feel triggered, step out of the room. Outside, he hung around, waiting for his wife.

Back inside, Marcus Biddle, the public radio reporter and Marlton Pike member who shared Ben's office, wasn't sure that the comment by the homebound member constituted white supremacy. But he didn't dare contradict Bethany, whom he respected. He also didn't want to disrupt the evening or put himself at the center of this fight, but he was growing more uncomfortable with what felt to him and others from Marlton Pike like the meeting was taking on a "mob mentality," with insiders from Philly dictating terms to outsiders in New Jersey. A lot of lines are being drawn, he thought to himself, yet he said nothing.

Next, the Chinese American seminarian from Fishtown drew himself up, adopting, for a moment, a posture familiar to the son of a megachurch pastor. He raised his index finger and pointed around the room. "How Bethany's comment made you feel was a pure and holy moment!" he intoned. "Ask yourself why she said it and you didn't!" Watching, Marcus wondered, Since when did people at Circle of Hope shake their fingers at one another? No way was he going to say anything. "People are afraid to speak up since any kind of confrontation will be conflated with white supremacy," he said later.

Soon, the meeting split into breakout groups of four and five. Marcus retreated to the hallway with friends from Marlton Pike. "Before this evening, Circle of Hope felt open, but the tenor has changed. It makes me concerned that there are certain loyalties you have to have before you are allowed to do the work or have a conversation," he said. "Jonny has completely hijacked the narrative himself about what anti-racism work actually looks like." Jonny, the Fishtown seminarian, and other well-educated members of color were claiming the right to speak for BIPOC. "You have to understand that when we talk about anti-racism, the conversation starts and ends with the oppression of Black people in this country," Marcus explained. As a Black man with a dissenting point of view, he felt silenced, and that freaked him out.

In another breakout group, Joel's wife, Kathy White, and Jacob's wife, Aubrey White, who'd joined online, confessed to their small group that they were afraid that anything they said would be used against them. The next day, on Twitter, another church member mocked them for their white fragility. Around the garage, the breakout groups murmured with other questions: Was Jonny trying to take over the church? Was white supremacy shutting him down?

By the time the pastors called the breakout groups back into one conversation, Julie could tell that some people were losing patience with the guardrails. She'd tried to temper the unruly bunch. For those accustomed to holding forth, this kind of Potemkin conversation, which silenced participants out of fear of hurting one another, was confusing and alienating. Several were no longer willing to hold back their opinions.

"We have to talk about the mission!" one white man stood up and preached. Their role as Christians was to evangelize, he went on, adding, "Which is multiplying cells and spreading the Word!"

Julie wasn't surprised. She'd heard this time and again from disgruntled members, and from Rachel. Circle's "true work" should be growing and planting new churches, not bickering over power and identity. Julie considered this line of argument, which seemed to prioritize numbers and church growth over anti-racism, to be another way in which white supremacy kept rearing its head.

Then one of Rod's friends who'd been at Circle since the Tower Records days pressed Jonny on this issue of lies and secrecy. Why, if the stories of racial harm and abuse were so prevalent at Circle, did so few people know what they were?

The answer to that was easy, Jonny replied. When members of color spoke out they were insulted and abused, so they kept such stories to themselves. "We're trying to build a church where it's safe!" Jonny said.

Listening to what he called Jonny's "stupid, sad pantomime," Joel White felt seized by a powerful fury. "This is the most bullshit thing I've ever experienced at Circle of Hope," he thought, rising and storming down the aisle. As he disappeared through the doorway, there was a loud crash. Heads craned: Had Joel fallen? Had part of the building come down on his head? Whispers rustled around the rear of the room from those who'd seen what happened. Joel, the pacifist, had punched the steel door frame. "What if I had seared my hand off on the lintel?" he wrote the next day on Facebook. Joel wondered, if he had seriously hurt himself, would anyone care?

When Bethany discovered the post, she had another interpretation: "No, Joel, you aren't sacrificing your body like Jesus did. You are just a raging white man protecting your whiteness." Incredible to her was the fact that the Whites weren't simply pacifists because they were Anabaptists. The Whites were some of the kindest people she'd ever met; to watch them rage against their loss of power perplexed her. "When I say, 'Be nice to Jonny,' Joel punches a wall?"

In the folding chairs behind her, Bethany could hear the sniffling of white women. "This is white fragility hell," she thought. As much as she wanted to leave, Bethany was determined to stay in her front-row seat, even if more white people stormed out. Julie, who sat ten chairs to the right of Bethany, kept her eyes cast on the concrete floor.

"I think we're going to have to do this again, and the pastors need to let it be messy," one member offered. "Messy" meant no guardrails, an open forum, as Circle used to be.

To Julie, this old-school "messiness" involved white people shoving their feelings into the spotlight and taking potshots at Jonny. She reproached herself for failing as an ally; people of color, she thought, shouldn't have had to defend themselves. Instead, once again, it had fallen to Bethany to interrupt harm.

It had been nearly two and a half hours, and all three of the pastors stood before the gathering to draw the meeting to a close.

Next to Joel White's now-empty folding chair, Audrey Robinson reached her hand into the air and soon rose to her feet. "None of you came to ask the three Black people here if we felt we were being harmed! We weren't!" she shouted. Ben, her pastor and friend, was part of her family. How was dismantling her spiritual family fighting racism? "Leave my family alone!" she cried, sitting back down, her mask slipping off her face. When the meeting ended soon after, Audrey was weeping, holding her head in her hands.

From across the room, Marcus wished he'd spoken up for Audrey.

Her opinions were essential, even though their language and delivery didn't sound like that of a graduate theology seminar. "As a church overall, we passive-aggressively reduce her to the 'loud Black woman' stereotype," he added later. "She is the type of person we need to hear from, but our church isn't ready for her."

Jonny's Fishtown crew filed out of the building. About a dozen were meeting up in Philly at Juno, a Mexican restaurant and bar not far from the Rodin Museum, to debrief over frozen cocktails.

Bethany was joining them. Walking out of the firehouse church alone, however, felt dangerous: it was as if she were exposing her body to a hostility that recalled centuries of violence against Black people. She didn't think anyone was going to physically attack her, but her body was telling her that she was in the middle of ancestral trauma. She approached a white man who was one of her close friends. "Just to be sure these Mennonites don't lynch me, will you walk me to my car?" she asked, only half in jest. For her, the evening had proven a disaster, and it was thick with grief. She'd warned Jonny against centering himself, but because he'd gone ahead, she'd had to make an impossible choice. Standing up for him as a fellow person of color, she'd lost friends for life.

Arriving at Juno, she ordered a margarita on the rocks, and watched Jonny smirk over how badly some of the white people had behaved. Unnerved by his excitement, she heard him retell the story of what they'd all just witnessed. "Oh, this was fun for you," she thought. For her it was devastating.

Jonny said that it was painful for him, too, yet he'd also felt vindicated that finally, people couldn't deny that they'd witnessed "racism at work" at Circle of Hope. "I wouldn't categorically call it a victory," Jonny said later. "There were successful moments."

What Jonny saw as "successful moments" registered profound loss for Bethany, and it disgusted her that Jonny saw the evening as a victory, however qualified.

. . .

For more than a week following the Marlton Pike meeting, Julie couldn't get Rachel on the phone. When Julie tried to call, Rachel texted back saying she was swamped with people who wanted to "process" one-on-one and who needed personal pastoral care. (Rachel didn't share that she'd spent a sleepless night stopping the cell coordinators from rejecting Ben's resignation in order to fire him, which felt punitive to her.) Instead, Rachel's radio silence alarmed Julie, who didn't know if Rachel was avoiding conflict or if she was once again centering white pain to keep people in the church. Finally, after ten days of ghosting, Rachel joined their regularly scheduled pastors' meeting.

"It felt really hard for me to have you have time to process with other people but not with us," Julie told Rachel, sharing the state of her soul.

Rachel responded by echoing the frustrations she'd been fielding all week about what went down at Marlton Pike. "I was frustrated with us, too," Rachel said. No one could really talk openly or ask questions about why Ben was leaving. She'd also seen comments on Slack about Audrey's mask slipping, which felt unkind. "Where is the Spirit in this work?" Rachel asked.

Julie was having none of this. Rachel was letting herself be dragged around by white fragility. "As pastors, we tend to what is growing! We don't convince the plant to grow into this or that!" Julie snapped, almost shouting. "That's terrible leading! I'm worried for you!" Julie loved Rachel, and she badly wanted to help her friend see her complicity in upholding the status quo, which was racism.

There was silence for a moment as Rachel paused. "This isn't what I'm trying to do, create a safe space for white people to be assholes," she said calmly. "I am trying to create a safe space for everyone, and that does create a pushback on white people, but I also do have these old heads that I love dearly and I'm trying to bring them along."

What Rachel called "bringing along," Julie saw as dangerous appeasement. "When we counter white people's anger in the church, we can't just personally pastor them," she reasoned with Rachel.

In the midst of this teachable moment, Jonny broke in. "We're not making room for people of color in our church!" he said.

"That's not true," Rachel replied.

"I can't even speak in a meeting without people defaming and demeaning me," he went on. "If we're serious about disrupting white supremacy in our church, we have to disrupt the power families."

But Julie wrested the conversation away from power families and returned it to faith. She reminded Rachel of "the Great Reversal," the Christian teaching that Jesus came to turn the world upside down, inverting power and society, and rendering the poor blessed and the meek powerful. "The Great Reversal" also applied to racism. "We have to listen to people of color in the church, even above our own pastoral instincts," she told Rachel. "I think you and I as white pastors have to humbly submit to what Jonny is saying."

Rachel bristled. Julie knew that Rachel thought she was ignoring Jonny's misogyny. "I refuse to bond with her over it," Julie said later. "If I bring it up in the moment, Rachel just uses it against Jonny and digs her heels in about being right. Dominance and superiority in the moment becomes a battle of victimhood."

What Rachel perceived as sticking up for herself and for women by questioning Jonny's motives and his methods, Julie saw as singling out an individual of color and enumerating their faults to undermine their power, a pattern that had a long history at Circle. There had to be a better way to dismantle these issues than to compete over them. Sexism and racism didn't need to be pitted against each other.

. . .

In the months following Ben's departure, Circle of Hope kept winnowing out. After Ben left, even South Broad, which had been holding steady, began losing members. The pastors weren't sure who still considered themselves a part of Circle of Hope, so they undertook the difficult task of updating the covenant list, which would require more excruciating conversations. To avoid unnecessary pain, Jonny suggested that Julie send absent people personal notes, and then go ahead and delete their names from the covenant list. But Julie didn't want to write anyone off, so she trudged through a process of contacting those who were missing one by one.

Being a covenant member of Circle wasn't a matter of keeping your name on a list. It required actively engaging in the community. "A covenant isn't like a status or a membership or a voting right," Julie said. "It's a process of living and relating in love." Turning back to re-read what Circle had once said about covenants, she was struck by this teaching on conflict: "A covenant is refined and comes to fullness when it endures conflict. It needs conflict like certain pine forests need fire to rejuvenate." The words of the covenant hadn't lost their meaning because they were irrelevant or untrue, as Julie saw it. "They've lost their meaning because so many of us didn't live into it when the fires came."

Circle of Hope needed to ask a new question: "Who has this love and mutuality not worked for? Who has been left out?" For months, Julie spent hours walking with people along the Wissahickon Creek and in Fernhill Park, fielding phone calls about the crisis. Julie wasn't indulging their grievances or convincing anyone to stay. She was pointing out, time and again, how their sense of injury was rooted in their whiteness. She took no pleasure in leaving old friends behind; it ran counter to her every fiber not to offer solace, but she held the line against old habits, no matter how cold and distant it felt.

"I'm not going to engage anymore in the kind of personal relationships that give cover to racism," she said. Among these relationships was her friendship with Joel and Kathy White, who'd hived off with Julie to help her plant the Germantown Circle. Joel and Kathy had stopped coming to worship with Germantown when Rod and Gwen were asked to stop influencing Circle and surrender their church emails the previous summer. Not long after that, a member of Germantown tried to bring Kathy a pie, but Kathy declined. The days of sharing baked goods were over. "I rejected the guilt-ridden pie," she told Gwen. Kathy wasn't sure where she stood at Germantown. She felt that she was being shunned by proxy because her last name was White. Julie wrote to ask Kathy if she still considered herself part of the covenant. The email was accidentally ill-timed. Julie didn't know that Kathy's dad was in hospice, which Kathy had posted on Facebook.

Kathy didn't reply: How could her pastor and close friend have missed such a huge thing?

When Julie emailed Joel to ask his thoughts about his covenant, he wrote back, "I haven't made a decision yet." Since smacking the lintel, he was trying to practice restraint. "I want to stop acting out of my trauma," he said. "I don't want to be invited back into it."

As much as Joel and Kathy felt they were being ushered out of the church they'd helped build, they were also refusing to participate. If the pastors wanted to cast Joel out, then he wasn't going to make it easy. "They need to just kick me out," he said. "I'm not leaving of my own accord: the refugee doesn't choose." Several months later, during the week her dad died, Kathy realized that she'd been removed from the covenant list. She felt that she'd lost both her families. "These people are terminators," Joel added.

. . .

When Julie heard comments that she was "dismissing" people from Circle, they cut her deeply. She knew they weren't true, and had agonized over her decision. The community had other pressing concerns that demanded her care and attention. Circle of Hope had decided, at last, to leave their denomination. This posed a risk. Since the Brethren in Christ claimed the right to seize the church's assets over Circle's decision to welcome and affirm queer people, they had to be willing to sacrifice to stand by the principle that Jesus's love included everyone. This decision might cost the church its existence. By the end of 2021, Circle had drafted two new proverbs: "Our church honors and affirms LGBTQ folks as beloved siblings—in covenant, in marriage, and leadership." And: "Our LGBTQ siblings offer us a special gift by challenging assumptions about gender and relationships. We seek to be a community where each person can express their authentic selves in Christ. We are enriched as a community when each of us can be open about who we are." Julie celebrated the new proverbs, which she and the pastors had helped draft with the guidance of queer members of Circle.

Approving these proverbs was a form of repentance for Circle's homophobic past, and it involved other tangible actions. Jonny and Rachel would have to surrender their licenses. (Julie had continued to avoid the denomination's accreditation process, so she wouldn't have to lie about where she stood on same-sex affirmation. As a result, she still didn't have a BIC license.) The matter came to a head just before Christmas when a disgruntled covenant member called Julie's brother-in-law, Bishop Bryan Hoke, to tell him about the pastors' decision to welcome homosexuality. The Hokes, however, were a family of pastors with a long history of navigating theological differences. Bryan Hoke called Julie's husband, Steve. "Let's not let this ruin Christmas," he told his brother. And it didn't. Julie and her brother-in-law stuck to their policy of not talking church business at family events, so she said nothing about affirmation, and he didn't ask.

Soon, however, Circle's decision to affirm queer people took an even more personal turn. As 2022 began, and Circle started to discern its yearly map, the pastors determined to do something new. To make "being led by the margins" mean something substantive, Circle had formed listening circles of LGBTQ members, members of color, and those who were disabled across all four congregations to come up with a vision of building the Kingdom of Heaven on Earth. Eventually, the pastors would join, but only to listen.

Julie, Jonny, and Rachel were slated to join the LGBTQ listening circle one evening in February. Jonny called Julie. He needed to share something intimate, he confessed. His voice sparked with nervousness as he began. He'd come to trust Julie with everything. She was the closest pastor to him on the face of the planet, and Jonny often reminded Julie that she was the reason he was still at Circle of Hope. "If it was just me doing this shit with the Whites, I'd be out of here," he'd said.

"I'm demi-bisexual!" he told Julie, recounting his realization in his therapist's office. It was less a realization than a declaration of what he'd already known to be true.

"I'm not surprised," Julie said.

The shared intimacy brought the two even closer. She couldn't believe what he'd endured in the past year. He'd borne so much ire as a pastor of color disrupting racism. Coming forward as queer, he was putting his body on the line to lead people to follow Jesus. Julie wasn't blindly following Jonny, but he was a teacher. "He really disciples me," she said.

When Holy Week began in March, Jonny and Julie met on Maundy Thursday at Rachel's white-brick church on South Broad for foot washing. This marked the night of the Last Supper, when, in a gesture of love, honor, and mutuality, Jesus washed his disciples' feet. Rachel had set up foot-washing stations along the right side of the room so that people could sit in the chairs two by two, with a basin between them. Jonny approached Julie. "Can I wash your feet?" he asked.

Fighting tears, she followed him to two chairs and pulled off her shoes and socks. He knelt, dipping her winter toes into the water and toweling them dry. Julie felt like she should be washing his feet for all he'd put himself through leading the church that year. And now, he was washing *hers*? When her feet were dry, not trusting herself to speak, she gestured to him to take off his shoes, and knelt before him, washing his feet in return.

· · ·

Together with Rachel, they worked on their new map: a stunning theological statement. "After two difficult years in a global pandemic, we are hearing a call to new rest and liberation through Jesus," the pastors wrote by way of introduction. "We are listening to the voices of the marginalized for ways we need to repent, heal, and grow. Their experience is the lens through which we are discerning the Spirit." Circle would discard all of its proverbs, to rid themselves of inherited teachings, and start again in order to authentically repent and reform. Their new goals were visionary but specific. They were also the work of a lifetime. Here were a few:

- Grow in solidarity with the marginalized in a posture of repentance.
- Recognize and confess the harm in our history; tell the story of where we were and where we are going.
- Repent of racist, transphobic, homophobic, and ableist oppression.
- Begin the ongoing work of divesting from religious institutions that further oppression, and partner with ones that further liberation.
- Ask the Mennonite Central Committee to hire LGBTQ people, and in the meantime, suspend our contributions (both the church and the thrift stores), and contribute money to another international aid organization.
- Gracefully leave the Brethren in Christ, and discern a partnership with an Anabaptist, LGBTQ-affirming denomination or conference.

Circle of Hope was extending a more radical welcome: "Laboring for justice, we hope our new posture makes us more hospitable and welcoming to people in our region who are moved by the Spirit to join the movement." This sounded right and real—it was humble and reflected the new spirit.

Easter 2022 offered glimmers of reconciliation. It was still dark at 4:00 a.m. when Julie drove to Lemon Hill. For the first time in three years, it was safe enough for the four congregations to meet together in person. In the past, the Whites' Easter sunrise service had drawn as many as seven hundred worshippers. It was so much a Circle tradition that some members of Julie's congregation decided to skip it, in order to break with the fraught past. Julie understood; she had her own struggles over which traditions to carry forward and which to leave behind. Consider the cross cookies. For Easter each year, in a nod to the disciples, twelve women baked batches of sugar cookies, iced with a red cross. The cookies recalled traditional hot cross buns, over which Gwen had toiled until they'd proven to be too much work—"unreasonable for three hundred and fifty people," Gwen put it—and not that delicious. At dawn, kids and grown-ups broke and ate the cross cookies together to symbolize Jesus's victory over death. To some, the cookies also represented the screwed-up role of women at Circle, who were supposed to be revolutionaries but were, in practical fact, more bound to motherhood and to baking than to being pastors. Tentatively, Julie had broached the subject with Rachel several weeks earlier and, to her relief, Rachel had her own misgivings.

"We can use store-bought dough," Rachel said.

It was the smallest of shifts, yet Julie felt relief in Rachel's willingness to embrace rest, ease, and change. To let perfection die. As morning crested the brow of the hill, Julie was relieved not to be stuck in the shallow gulley of Fernhill Park. Instead, as she looked around, she counted nearly two hundred people, many under blankets with puffy-eyed children in their laps. It was their largest gathering in three years, and almost twice the size of the terrible meeting at Marlton Pike after Ben quit. More people were showing up to celebrate than to fight. Although Julie believed that numbers didn't really matter, the crowd was an indication that people were willing to move with Circle into this new way of following Jesus.

"Everyone take a cookie, but don't eat it right away," Julie said. "We want to enjoy it together as evidence of God's sweetness for us in the power of death being broken." Julie watched Rachel snap the cookie in two. They were going to be okay.

12

RACHEL

*"And if anyone wants to sue you and take your shirt,
hand over your coat as well."*
—MATTHEW 5:40

In the weeks after Ben quit, although no one other than her husband knew, Rachel was also thinking of leaving. So much of her life
and leadership—her character—felt under investigation. She didn't
know how to talk anymore; even the word "love" had become contentious. For Rachel, love was the most basic building block of their community; for Julie and Jonny and many others, "love" had become code
for accommodationist politics. "I'm a shepherd and I'm trying to keep
this community together," Rachel said. "And I think that's what we're all
called to do as pastors: care for the flock."

Yet Julie and Jonny didn't seem to mind that people were fleeing
from Circle of Hope. "This bleeding out is a bleeding out of white
people," Julie told Rachel at the first pastors' meeting following the
debacle at Marlton Pike.

Jonny tried to reassure Rachel that the fury of those departing was
a sign that she was "leading well" and "no longer playing ball with the
Whites." Good leaders were required to take a side, which could be
divisive, he said, invoking Jesus's flipping tables again. "People being
upset with you is a good thing," he added. This was the theological ar-

gument he was developing in his book: following Jesus required fighting for good and disrupting those who, in the name of love and tolerance, upheld abusive structures. "If we don't lose anyone, what are we doing?" Jonny asked. "Unless they change, they need to leave."

Yet this kind of theology felt punitive to Rachel.

In her silences, Jonny intuited dissent. "I need her agreement," he said, "and I am willing to do whatever it takes to get it." If Rachel left Circle alongside Ben, the narrative would shift from the wrongdoing of the Whites to a story of a church's breakup, and that, he felt, wasn't accurate. "Someone said to me the most compassionate thing is for the church to split," Jonny said. "No, because this is like an abusive marriage splitting and people getting shared custody." To Rachel, he explained, "Churches don't peaceably split." There was no way to divide without a fight, and that would let the racists win by claiming there were two legitimate points of view. "When the pastors are united, we give people a choice," he told her. "Move with us or make a choice to leave."

Despite Jonny's argument, this us-versus-them theology still didn't track with Rachel. A church was made of people. You couldn't simply annihilate them in favor of principles. "I'm losing people from my congregation and you guys keep saying it's about you, and it affects me most," Rachel told Julie and Jonny. Their arguments about necessary losses felt patronizing to her, as if they thought she didn't understand what anti-racism required. "This is heartbreaking for me. These are people I've prayed their kids into existence and discipled dearly as friends."

"I hear that, Rach," Julie responded.

Rachel was also trying to shepherd people through grief, which took time. "Julie, how could we not acknowledge this pain when the Whites are such a large part of our community?" she asked. "They have been part of our community for over twenty years, personally, not just part of institutional structure and leadership. It's sad and hard on a human personal level."

"Yes, it is," Julie said.

"It's hard because I love these people," Rachel said.

"I do, too! You can't hear me say I love them?"

"I hear that they're more casualties of change," Rachel replied.

Then there were numbers. Rachel's congregation, which had been stable over the past several years while the three others dwindled, was suddenly hemorrhaging. After Ben announced his resignation, and the terrible meeting at Marlton Pike ensued, at least twenty people had come to Rachel threatening to leave. By going along with Jonny and Julie, she was failing her community and, by extension, Jesus. Unless she broke with Julie and Jonny, she stood to lose roughly one out of every ten members, and she felt powerless to stop them. This carried financial ramifications. Although many churches in America were still seeing sharp downturns in attendance after the pandemic, most were recovering economically. In 2021, nearly 75 percent of churches saw giving that matched or exceeded their 2020 offerings. Not Circle of Hope. For years, as much as $20,000 of the $50,000 of monthly "sharing" had come from the Whites and their friends who tithed. (These were some of the people Jonny referred to as "power families.") Once Ben resigned, many began to hold their money back as they deliberated over staying or going. As Circle's coffers emptied, South Broad's $7,000 monthly mortgage payment was becoming a strain. Rachel, however, wasn't concerned about losing the building. "If we didn't have the building we'd be fine," she said. She trusted that they could shed their assets if necessary. The early church had done this, giving all away and deliberately starting with nothing. A church was its people.

. . .

Rachel loved celebrating Christmas, with all its family traditions. Most years after midnight on Christmas Eve, she'd lead Cori and Zach around their house, placing baby Jesuses in the waiting mangers of crèches she'd collected from around the world. Rachel cherished the differing depictions of the Holy Family, with their varying contexts and interpretations. In their front window in South Philly was a glittery set of Italian figurines, a gift from Rachel's family. Her kids had colored all over the crèche with markers to complicate the lily-white Nativity. The more historically accurate depiction was the brown Mary, Joseph, and baby Jesus set against a pink stable, which a queer member of Rachel's flock had made for her.

On Christmas Eve of 2021, however, her head was so befogged by viral load that she forgot about the empty mangers. She was sick again for the second time that year with coronavirus—so ill she wasn't attending the Christmas Eve vigil, which was unprecedented. That night, she drafted a letter of resignation. When she called to tell Jimmy about her decision, he asked her to hold off. "Give it a month," Jimmy suggested. It was sober advice. The AA slogan went "Don't just do something, wait." But it was also the book of Matthew, which laid out a similar practice of "resting in Christ." Rachel did as her friend suggested, slouching through the holiday week in her socks, practicing divine pause, and asking God for a specific direction—to stay or to leave Circle. Again and again, she heard the word "stay."

Rachel's despair reflected a larger trend of pastor burnout. In a 2021 study published by Barna Group, a leading Christian market-research company, 46 percent of pastors under the age of forty-five reported that they were considering quitting full-time ministry. The rates were especially high among women, many of whom cited the same pressures that Rachel was under: "stress, loneliness, and political division."

By New Year's Eve, the viral fog had lifted a bit. Her wild little sister, Rebecca, texted from New Jersey to ask if she could spend the night. Rachel knew that Rebecca's marriage was failing, and careening rapidly toward a divorce. Rachel assumed that Rebecca, who partied hard, especially on New Year's, had somewhere to go in Philly and needed a place to crash. However, when Rebecca arrived in South Philly early that evening, Rachel answered the door to find her sister crying on her concrete steps.

"It's twenty-one years today," Rebecca told her, reminding her of the baby she had given up for adoption.

Rachel hadn't reflected on the significance of New Year's Eve for Rebecca; the sisters had never spoken of what the holiday actually marked. She brought her sister inside and sat her down at the dinner table. Despite Rebecca's protests that she was avoiding carbs, Rachel fed her pasta she'd made for the kids. After dinner, they sat on Rachel's cozy couch, ate gummy bears, and watched *A Bad Moms Christmas*. For the first time, they talked about the ordeal of giving up the baby and how it had shaped Rebecca's life. Rebecca had been raised to believe that by placing her son up for adoption, she was "redeeming herself." At many crisis pregnancy centers, including their mom's, counselors taught women about the supposed psychological damage caused by abortion, a pseudoscientific condition called post-abortion stress syndrome. Yet few, if any, talked about the wounds that adoption could leave. In losing her son, Rebecca told Rachel, she'd lost the tenuous grip she had on herself. For years, she'd distracted herself from the pain by drinking and chasing an ideal of beauty with surgery and injectables. Her new therapist wanted her to look in the mirror and say "I am loved," but Rebecca was having trouble repeating the affirmation. She'd felt like a fuck-up for most of her life. She knew that their parents measured her against Rachel and found her lacking. She felt empty and lost. Rachel shared the fact that she hadn't had a drink in two years, and she talked to Rebecca about how bad things were at Circle of Hope, how she felt like she was failing sometimes as a pastor. But mostly, Rachel listened. She'd known that her sister was struggling, but not how desperately.

"What was it like to have me as your older sister?" Rachel asked.

"It was hard," Rebecca gulped.

Rachel reached for her phone to search for a passage she'd come across recently from Margery Williams's classic book *The Velveteen Rabbit*. It wasn't Jesus or Julian of Norwich; it was a parable intended for children about a stuffed rabbit yearning to be real:

> You become. It takes a long time. That's why it doesn't happen often to people who break easily, or have sharp edges, or who have to be carefully kept. Generally, by the time you are Real, most of your hair has been loved off, and your eyes drop out and you get loose in the joints and very shabby. But these things

don't matter at all, because once you are Real, you can't be ugly except to people who don't understand.

As girls, they'd learned to avoid, or hide, everything ugly: family tensions, teen pregnancy, drinking—the list went on. Yet, as they risked sharing these stories with one another, they were coming to realize that honesty wasn't ugly; it was the key to the locked door of their true selves. At midnight Rachel and Rebecca went outside on the stoop with the rest of South Philly to ring in the New Year. People were banging pots and pans to ward off evil spirits. There was no use trying to sleep. Fireworks cracked and spattered against the macadam until two in the morning. In a few hours, in their spangled masquerade costumes and headdresses, the Mummers would be out on the streets for their annual parade. Rachel invited Rebecca to stay in the basement, but Rebecca wanted her own bed and went on her way.

New Year's Eve changed their dynamic. Rachel was no longer perfect; Rebecca was no longer the one who needed to be saved. Rebecca joined Jimmy's cell, with some members in recovery. Rebecca didn't feel ready for any of that, and Rachel didn't push it. She could see her little sister's spirit opening in a way she'd been praying for most of Rebecca's life. But it wasn't one-sided. Rachel needed Rebecca, too. Her church was in trouble, and there were few people she could trust. To support Rachel, Rebecca began to make the one-hour drive from her home down the Jersey Shore to South Broad nearly every Sunday. Their parents, who remained uncertain about some aspects of Circle, weren't thrilled. "Do they preach the gospel?" their dad asked Rebecca. "It's about doing what Jesus would do," Rebecca replied. "And it's called me supporting my sister. Period."

. . .

In a dream one night, Ben's youngest son, Theo, came to Rachel and climbed into her lap. "I've lost my community," he told her. Rachel's sense of profound spiritual loss persisted as 2022 began. A few days later, Rachel was driving when her phone rang. She picked it up to find Ben on the line with a question: Would she lead a new church? He wouldn't be a pastor. He wanted to follow Rachel and knew there were many other people who felt the same. She asked for time. She was praying her way through the first days of the year, still asking God for direction. Her husband, Jeff, was urging her to return to social work. Rachel had made more money as a social worker than as a pastor, and felt better about herself, without all of this bullshit and unnecessary suffering. Despite the wishes and guidance of Jeff and her old friends, she was still receiving the clear word "stay." She could feel the Holy Spirit moving, and a radical new vision being cast at the church, with people of color leading the way.

By March 2022, she had decided to remain at Circle of Hope. That winter, she weathered the anger of old members who told her that by staying she was being manipulated by Jonny Rashid.

Although she had her own struggles with Jonny, Rachel rejected this narrative. "It makes me into a dodo," she said. And Jonny was going through all kinds of changes that very few people knew about.

One night in March, Rachel logged on to Zoom along with Julie and Jonny and some queer members of Circle. That evening, the queer members were advising the pastors on practical ways that the church could live up to its new proverbs. As the meeting began, however, Jonny broke down, confessing that he, too, was queer.

"It's scary to come out," he told them. "You all have more courage than me because you came out. I couldn't, because I knew Circle of Hope wasn't safe and I couldn't even come out to myself."

Like Julie, Rachel wasn't surprised. She was delighted that Jonny was moving more deeply into the truth of who he was, a truth she'd long wondered about. But she wasn't sure about what happened next. As Jonny shared his emerging realization, the members of the queer affinity group put aside their agenda for the meeting and focused on caring for their weeping pastor. Listening in silence, Rachel worried that Jonny was centering himself, instead of the church. Later, she said,

"I feel like he is more into himself and his own process than shepherding and pastoring a body, a community."

Some in the queer affinity group felt similarly. Watching Jonny, Holly Meneses, a church administrator who'd been close to him for years, was frustrated with the timing of the admission, which derailed the meeting and seemed curated. "He was factoring in the performance and the impact of his image," she said later. This didn't mean that Jonny was faking. "He really went through the wringer these last two years," Holly noted. "Of course it's gonna bring out some of the worst in anyone."

Not long after, Holly joined the exodus of those leaving Circle of Hope. Her departure wasn't solely about Jonny, she told me one afternoon in reflection. With the community coming apart, the values that Circle of Hope had long held were also under question. "I'm grateful for the good parts: grassroots spirituality, motherly as opposed to fatherly spirituality, social justice being central, an openness to allow folks in who had all kinds of questions and critiques so we could truly be together without being judged." Then there were the parts that had come to trouble her. "Lack of boundaries, professional and spiritual. Emotional enmeshment, leaders, followers, staff, power plays and manipulation set as precedent by the Whites. Some of the flavors of cult are there—especially the fact we are different, special, not like everyone else."

For Rachel, Circle's cult of specialness was egoic delusion that needed to end and that required making friends with death. "I die daily," the apostle Paul said. But death in the abstract was terrifying: oblivion. How could they befriend a natural and inevitable process? Her son, Zach, told her about mycelium, a fungus that aided decay. At nineteen, Zach, an expert in foraging, spent days in the woods searching for wild mushrooms and fungi, selling them to high-end restaurants. Fungus breeds new life, Zach told his mom. If nothing dies, there's no room for growth. But how could the natural wisdom of a microscopic fungus be applied to Lent? One of her cell leaders, Mable Bakali, a Black artist and consultant who worked at an engineering firm, came up with an idea. Mable, twenty-six, was originally from Malawi and had grown up in the more staid Episcopal Church. She welcomed the funkier, Spirit-based practices that Rachel envisioned to South Broad.

"One of the most spiritual things you can do is create," Mable said. She and Rachel decided to hang rough black fabric on the sanctuary walls. During worship throughout Lent, they invited people to consider the fungus and to paint mycelium, which Mable discovered looked like microscopic jellyfish, on the fabric. By the time Maundy Thursday arrived, and South Broad welcomed the whole church for foot wash-ing, ghostly white jellies swam over the walls. Rachel invited people to head to the foot-washing stations. "Offer the gift to one another in that same spirit of humility and gratitude for God's surprising and shame-killing and hierarchy-destroying love," she said with an unruffled smile. She didn't notice Jonny and Julie moving off to the side to wash each other's feet.

That evening, however, welcoming death was difficult. Rachel couldn't get Zoom to work, and although the room was full of people from Marlton Pike, Germantown, and Fishtown, very few of her flock showed up.

In their one-on-one coaching sessions, Bethany was encouraging Ra-chel to share more of herself, her flaws, and fears, the mistakes she'd made. "If people can see your humanity, they tend to have more empa-thy," she told Rachel.

That night, Rachel told the story of a fall. An accomplished climber, Rachel had nearly died at the age of nineteen, tumbling sixty feet onto her head. "My hair was all matted with blood. And my Aunt Nancy took all this time to tenderly work around the wound, loosening and cleaning the blood and dirt out of my hair. It was uncomfortable to receive this gift because I felt bad and stupid for risking my life for adventure and falling off the cliff, and her gift was so tender." This was the nature of grace: it couldn't be earned.

In her sessions with Bethany, Rachel had also been exploring the terrible cost of perfectionism. She was coming to understand that the demands she inflicted on herself could leak onto other people, includ-ing her sister. Rachel was learning that her drive to produce, her fear of failure, and her sense of self-preservation were symptoms of a toxic whiteness that was poisoning her and hurting people in the church. By defending Rod unwittingly, she'd helped to push marginal people out. This included Candace McKinley, the Yale-educated lawyer who'd helped start Circle Mobilizing Because Black Lives Matter. With all that was happening at Circle, people who'd left had begun to call out the church, telling their stories online. Candace had posted on Facebook that before leaving the church, she'd turned to a pastor for help, and the pastor had disappointed her. Candace didn't name Rachel, but Rachel wondered if it might be her, since she'd been Candace's pastor and her friend. She also didn't remember the encounter, but she didn't deny it. It sounded like the kind of thing she might have done at the time: defend the church without knowing she was hurting others in the process. To Rachel, these issues affected people of color and white women. It all fit together: Rachel's evasion of conflict and unwillingness to speak directly, her disordered eating, her sister's struggles with alcohol and self-recrimination due to giving up her child—these wounds might feel self-inflicted, but they were cultural ways in which women learned to survive in a male-dominated society by diminishing their power.

The next day was Good Friday, and it sucked. "I've lost most of my congregation, and I can't get them back and I'm so ineffective," Rachel said. She fought with Jeff, got her period, and thought *Of course*. She took solace in a text from Bethany, who wrote to say she was glad that Rachel had survived her fall off the cliff. It was only a sliver of reconciliation, but Rachel was grateful for the small gesture. She could feel herself letting go of the tightness and control of the old ways.

That weekend, in preparation for Easter, and Circle's return to Lemon Hill, she didn't spend hours making traditional dough from scratch as she had in prior years, thanks to the ready-made. When she invited the slope of nearly two hundred people to break their cookie in two, it snapped just the same. Shattering the cross included liberating women from being bound to endless duty.

At their pastors' meeting the next day, Rachel hosted Jonny and Julie in her warm third-floor office, where she kept an electric kettle by a prie-dieu to make mugs of herbal tea. With ease and intimacy, the three sat close to one another on Rachel's soft chairs and couch.

"I'm finally opening up about my problems with race and sexuality in the church and in my marriage," Jonny said, sharing the state of his soul. "It's like water damage and the wall: when you open the wall you see the whole thing is fucked." Jonny reminded Rachel of a decade-old conversation they'd had in which she'd suggested that he wear women's shoes if he wanted. "I didn't think I was pretty enough," Jonny told her.

"You are, Jonny," Rachel replied. She asked him what he wanted to do with his marriage.

"All of us have to answer the question of who we want to be next," Jonny said. "All of us need to change and grow. It's been very hard, though."

"Do you think that you'll stay in the marriage?" Rachel asked.

"I don't know," he replied. Divorce seemed scary.

Then Rachel risked going further into a decade's worth of unspoken honesty. "I remember how much you cried at your wedding," she said. "And I wondered."

"I was wondering, too, and there were people wondering with me," Jonny said.

Until now, this conversation would've been impossible at Circle of Hope. Queerness might've been welcome in some theoretical way, but certainly not in a pastor who was wrestling with the future of his marriage. The church had always frowned on divorce. Rachel wanted to be clear that she wasn't pushing Jonny to stay married, as she and other pastors had done in the past. "I want what you want for yourself. I don't have some idea about what's right for the church. That's the stuff that we have to shed."

"Thanks for asking, because I wasn't going to talk about this," Jonny said. "This is very vulnerable. Things I never would've said in a pastors' meeting three years ago. Never. Off the table."

"This is a new kind of pastors' meeting," Rachel said.

. . .

Yet Rachel also harbored no illusions that the Easter, the celebration of Jesus's rebirth, solved everything. That wasn't the Christian ideal. In Scripture, it wasn't as simple as Jesus dying on the cross and returning to life three days later as a surprise party favor. Instead, the forty days following Easter was a time of uncertainty when death and life hovered in the balance for Jesus's early followers, who were living in hiding and trading incredible ghost stories and random sightings of their murdered teacher. The season culminated in the Ascension, and the task of building the early church. "It's similar to this liminal space where a lot of people are now, including the church," Rachel preached one Sunday after Easter. "It was this paradox of joy and grief, no one knows what's happening and what's next. You feel this hope for a new world coming, but you're carrying all these questions."

It had been nearly two years since the shake-up at Circle, and five months since Ben had resigned. Faced with some twenty newly emptied chairs staring at her most Sundays, Rachel couldn't avoid the crisis of diminishment. Despite the overwhelming and persistent grief, which kept leading Rachel to question her direction, as well as that of the church, she felt hope and joy for what was growing at South Broad.

The Spirit was fizzing and crackling around them as they acted together as one body. Rachel discovered that there was a name for this spiritual buzz, "collective effervescence," first defined by the early twentieth-century French sociologist Émile Durkheim. She opened worship up to informal conversation. It wasn't talkback, which sometimes resulted in masculine intellectual sparring and one-upmanship. It was a gentle and genuine soul-searching for what needed to change, mostly by returning to the simplicity practiced by Jesus's first followers. For too long, Circle of Hope had stayed isolated, "forming a clique," as Rachel said, believing they had the answers. Sitting together in worship, they decided to try something new.

Instead of offering a teaching that Sunday, Rachel suggested that they head into the streets to "walk in silence" with their eyes open. Let the world be their teacher. "You're going out to notice what's happening," she told them. "You can talk to people if that's how you feel led." This wasn't about growing the church or giving people answers; it was a humble effort to learn from outside their four walls. "You don't have to be a priest—this is the priesthood of all believers," she'd told her flock. "And when we come together, something bigger happens. It's like we are greater than the sum of our parts." People paired up, as Jesus's followers did, and ventured onto South Broad Street, walking past vestment shops and shady medical clinics offering "pain relief." Rebecca found an unhoused man wandering around South Philly after leaving treatment; she brought him back to the church and prayed with him. Rachel's suggestion began a tradition of walking around South Philly, inviting people into the church for spaghetti and a warm, well-lighted place.

Rebecca got a kick out of all the weirdness that was Circle of Hope. It was fun and distracting from her contentious divorce, and the support she found from sober people at Jimmy's Saturday cell encouraged her to give up drinking for a time. By the summer of 2022, she'd decided to make a covenant and join her sister's church. She wasn't going to be baptized, however, and certainly not at the gross dog beach in the Wissahickon Creek, where Rachel was going to dunk new members at their seasonal Love Feast in July. "I was already baptized when I was eighteen," Rebecca said firmly.

Rebecca met up with them after the dog beach baptisms, in Fernhill Park, across from Julie's home. The Germantown congregation was hosting the Love Feast, and when Rebecca arrived, Jasmine and Iboro Umana were setting up signs on paths and welcoming about thirty people. Many were carrying colorful bowls. Rachel brought a panzanella, an Italian salad of chopped tomatoes and chunks of bread, which Jasmine, in a pink sweatshirt, arranged on the table, giving her five-year-old daughter, who was holding a bottle of hand sanitizer, the job of squirting a few drops into guests' hands.

At 10:00 a.m. in a black romper and a white pedicure, Rebecca readied herself under a London plane tree, next to a Circle of Hope yard sign and a porta-potty. She stepped forward to make her covenant. Since so many who came to Circle were fleeing traditional evangelical spaces, new members were often self-conscious about avoiding the language of their childhoods. But Rebecca wasn't aware that such language was taboo. "I rededicate myself to the Lord daily," she began, "almost minute by minute." Onlookers smiled gently at the lack of Circle-ese. Rachel couldn't care less what words Rebecca used. As the outdoor service ended, and people welcomed Rebecca, Rachel cheered her little sister.

Two months later, to celebrate Rebecca's forty-second birthday, the sisters drove to Atlantic City. Rebecca "knew a tattoo guy" there, she'd told Rachel, and Rachel had imagined that they were headed into Rebecca's world of champagne flutes and white pleather couches. But when they arrived at Fat Kats Tattoo, the place was full of bikers. Rachel braved the table first, bracing for the needle's sting. In blue ink on the inside of her bicep, a velveteen rabbit appeared. The artist added the words "We become." Then it was Rebecca's turn.

In October, out of nowhere, Rebecca received her first Facebook message from her son. His profile picture showed a tall twenty-one-year-old with rust-colored curls and Rebecca's smile. She steadied herself. She could handle this. She typed her number into Messenger and waited to hear her son's voice. When he called, she told him that she'd been thinking about him every day for twenty-one years. He thanked Rebecca for "giving him life." He wasn't sure she'd wanted to hear from him, now that she had a family of her own. Rebecca realized that he had no idea how many times she'd tried to contact him, and wondered if he'd seen the box she and Rachel had made, with the photos of her family smiling in the Pocono woods. For the time being, she left the hard questions unasked. When she and her son hung up, she called Rachel.

PART IV

13

JONNY

*"Blessed are you when people insult you, persecute you,
and falsely say all kinds of evil against you because of me."*
—MATTHEW 5:11

Jonny was still shaking himself free of the Whites. "2021 was my hardest year as a pastor," he tweeted as the year drew to a close. In the safety of his therapist's office, Jonny was surfacing long-buried questions. "Now that the Whites have left, a whole burden on me is lifted," he reflected. "I can start seeing who I am." During one session in December, he realized that he felt trapped in his marriage. For a time, cooking elaborate meals and working long hours had allowed him to push down his feelings. New desires had awoken during the pandemic, and he didn't want to be married anymore, he went on, hinting at a truth he'd been withholding. When Jonny said nothing more, his therapist dropped the word the two had been dancing around for a while now, "bisexual." Jonny corrected him. "I'm queer," he said, preferring the term. The declaration was terrifying and liberating.

For the next two months, he didn't tell a soul. Instead, he exuded rambunctious joy and threw himself into celebrating Christmas. His defenses were descending, and some of the warm, funny Jonny who'd disappeared over the past year reemerged. At the pastors' annual party,

Jonny volunteered to lead the singing, but Rachel was irritated that she and Julie ended up doing everything else: cooking and running icebreaker games. The next day, she admonished him for "showing up smelling like a party." Jonny said it wouldn't happen again, but Rachel believed this was the same old patriarchal pattern in which male pastors did whatever they wanted, while she and Julie were left to make salsa and clean up the mess.

Jonny usually threw his own individual celebration for his leaders at Fishtown. He'd skipped 2020, due to the spiking virus. But this year, the numbers seemed safe enough to gather his friends and leaders in a Germantown yard on the evening of December 17. Near a boxwood hedge, Jonny set up his spread on a card table: Christmas crinkle cookies and muhammara, a red pepper and walnut dip, along with his signature aged eggnog, with various vintages dating back years. (As a seasoned home cook, Jonny allayed fears about expiration dates and potentially dangerous bacteria in the eggs and milk. The alcohol killed off both concerns.)

He hustled around the dozen guests huddled in puffy coats around a stainless-steel Solo stove, making sure that everyone had a beer, eggnog, or a cookie. Then he invited each guest to share the year's "Consolations and Desolations," a riff on a tradition of the sixteenth-century theologian Ignatius of Loyola. This practice, called the Daily Examen, entails reviewing quotidian events and asking God to reveal divine presence within them. When Jonny's turn came, he shared a troubling revelation. Someone at Circle of Hope had betrayed the church by calling Bishop Hoke in secret to confess that Circle was going to openly affirm queer marriage and pastors.

When Bishop Hoke told the pastors about the secret call, Jonny had demanded to know the name of the caller. But the bishop refused, saying only that it didn't matter, since the person "was leaving the church anyway." Still, it mattered to Jonny, and around the Solo stove, he ran through a list of suspects and how to smoke them out.

Jonny was right to claim that the implications of this disclosure were existential. According to BIC doctrine, Circle's violation gave the denomination the right to claim all of the church's assets. Though it had begun as a small rebel outpost of Jesus followers, Circle's holdings had grown significantly. In addition to more than one million dollars in the bank, there was another nearly $2.3 million invested in real estate properties: three churches and two thrift stores. All of this bounty was due to Rod's real estate savvy, which he attributed to the Holy Spirit, and the wild success of Circle's thrift stores.

Three nights later, the whole church was gathering to adopt the new queer-affirming proverbs, and Jonny volunteered to lead the discussion. To prevent another fight like the one a month earlier at Marlton Pike, the pastors made it clear that this wasn't going to be an open discussion about Scripture and sexuality. Circle of Hope was becoming affirming, full stop. In advance, they'd circulated a survey: if anyone opposed queer inclusion, they should say so and their pastor would contact them before the meeting. No one should stand up in real time and object. But the survey process hadn't gone as planned. A couple of respondents had voiced concerns about queer affirmation, and although they'd spoken to their pastors, it wasn't at all clear these discussions had changed their minds or that they wouldn't show up that evening to argue their opposition. To guard against potential disruptions, Iboro Umana and a handful of members pledged to step in and interrupt anyone who said hurtful, homophobic things.

Jonny ate nothing all day on December 20, in nervous anticipation of the evening's confrontation. He hadn't realized the untenable position he was putting himself in. No one in the room knew what had recently happened in Jonny's therapist's office. This referendum on affirming queer pastors was a referendum on *him*. Before the meeting began, he spotted two of the dissenters. Breathing deeply, and in his tone of boundless reasonability, he explained that Circle would no longer be sharing money with homophobic religious institutions. One lifelong Anabaptist with an old-timey beard objected. Surveys weren't how they did things at Circle. "Doing theology" required wrestling together in person over what Scripture entailed.

Jonny refused to indulge this complaint. There had been plenty of dialogue, he argued, and their new proverbs affirming queer marriage were "deeply rooted in biblical study." To stop the conversation and keep pushing forward, Jonny called for a vote, and the room rang with *yeas*.

Even though the proverbs had passed with overwhelming support, a second dissenter still stood to make his case against them. "I can't affirm the, um, the proverbs," he began, haltingly. "I—I've got some concerns." The member decried the new moral policing at Circle, which he labeled "a kind of fanaticism where we can't be together with people that disagree with us."

Naming people as fanatics crossed the line. Iboro Umana broke in over Zoom, calling into the room through his computer microphone. "This isn't about process, it's in people's bodies," Iboro warned. What seemed like theological "dialogue" to some was deeply insulting to those who were actually queer. That's why disagreement caused harm. By the meeting's end, the two dissenters had been shut down, and both were leaving the church.

"When homophobic people leave your church it's a good thing," Jonny tweeted the next day. Several people found his tweet alarming. Although they supported affirmation wholeheartedly, they feared a new pattern: if they ran afoul of Jonny, they might be named as homophobic or racist on his Twitter feed, accusations that could cost them their jobs. When Jonny heard these concerns, he responded with another tweet: "Can we stop with the idea that calling someone racist or homophobic is an insult?" The insult, he explained, was the racism and the homophobia—not being called out for them. Jonny was beginning to feel under siege by those on his side. "I can't believe how much abuse, defamation, and slander I faced for just trying to help a church live into its proclamation that it was antiracist," he tweeted in February 2022. The abuse was still happening, yet his faith remained unshaken and, if anything, stronger. "It's been two years of trauma and abuse in a church I grew up in both as an adult and as a pastor," he tweeted. "Started attending at 19; became a pastor here at 24. I became an Anabaptist here. Despite all of the horror, Anabaptism is still the Christianity that inspires me the most."

Rachel wasn't much for Twitter, but when she learned about some of these tweets, she felt uneasy about Jonny's use of social media. He seemed to be using Circle of Hope to threaten people and to build his personal platform. (At the end of one sermon, he'd asked his flock to preorder his forthcoming book, *Jesus Takes a Side*, as his birthday gift.)

Jonny defended himself: "Say what you will about me, but I don't fit the mold of Mark Driscoll. I'm not a big white yelling kind of guy."

He also began to argue on his pastor's blog and on Twitter that the old Circle of Hope had pressured people to get married. This was yet another form of abuse by a heteronormative culture. By the end of March, Jonny had told a handful of people that he was queer, including his wife. He was also trying to reach people who, like him, had been hurt by the church by weaponizing homophobia against themselves. "There are queer people in your Evangelical churches that are afraid to come out," he tweeted obliquely. "Some of them haven't even admitted to themselves they are queer because of internalized homophobia. The violence this does to a person's humanity and dignity is immense."

At 6:52 a.m. on April 27, he finally tweeted, "Purity culture turned me into a straight man who was supposed to be obsessed with sex. It turned women into sexual objects, and harmed my relationship with them. And more than anything it limited how I understood my bi/demisexuality. It abused and oppressed me." He was officially out on Twitter. Three and half hours later, while he was recording the pastors' podcast with Julie and Rachel, one follower replied. "This! It made me bury my bisexuality for 38 years," they tweeted, adding a "bi pride" high five GIF.

He was grateful he could help others, but he still hadn't come out directly to the whole church.

"If you can go on Twitter and tell people that you're queer, but you can't tell your congregation, you have no integrity," Audrey Robinson said.

But it was safer to come out to his followers on Twitter.

Soon, he called his dad in tears, saying that he'd failed and his marriage was ending. He said nothing about his evolving sexuality. Despite their dislike of divorce, his parents supported Jonny and helped pay his legal fees. For his dad, this was a way to make amends to his son. "He thinks I was too tough on him and I didn't express love to him," Samuel Rashid said.

Jonny finally came out at Circle in May, referring to himself, in passing, as "AAP," an internet acronym meaning "androgynous attracted person."

. . .

Now that Circle of Hope was openly affirming, the time had come to officially leave the Brethren in Christ. Soon, Jonny and Rachel wrote to Bishop Hoke and surrendered their licenses. (Julie still didn't have one.) Within hours, Hoke replied that he "was sad to see them go." He didn't mention the fact that the BIC still possessed the right to sell Circle's buildings and lay hold of their some $3.5 million in assets. Jonny believed, however, that Circle was in a strong position to negotiate. It had a couple of bargaining chips. First, he wagered, relying on his journalistic sensibilities, Circle could leverage the threat of embarrassing media coverage. Seizing buildings and driving progressive young Christians into the streets of Philadelphia in the cause of homophobia would garner appropriate empathy for Circle of Hope and be a pretty bad look for the BIC. For the time being, Julie and Rachel talked Jonny down from going to the press. Both felt it was better to keep the discussion civil; maybe the BIC would let them leave peacefully, and there was no advantage to going to war. They were pacifists.

Jonny kept strategizing. "Let's get this deal done," he told Julie. "Let's just keep as many buildings and as much cash as possible."

Rachel was harder to convince. She didn't want to fight over money and power. Talk about assets and buildings was more "church growth, capitalist-empire" thinking. She was finding the unwinding of the church's wealth and institution liberatory. But Jonny kept trying to convince her that it was their responsibility, as pastors and stewards, to guard as much money as possible so that they could plant something new. There was nothing shameful or craven in strategizing. "I'm talking about millions of dollars of assets, and I'm not going to lose that," he argued with Rachel.

While Jonny negotiated for the church, he was looking for a way out of Circle of Hope. He wanted to find a new job as an Anabaptist pastor in Philadelphia. Yet such positions were hard to come by; there were only seven thousand Anabaptist churches in the country, which made such positions exceedingly rare. Then he learned that West Philadelphia Mennonite Fellowship, an almost all-white congregation with many retired professors, was looking for a new pastor. The job felt like a long shot, but he went ahead and applied.

Jonny hosted a launch party at the Fishtown church to celebrate the May 2022 publication of *Jesus Takes a Side*. He invited his childhood friends from Lebanon County, Brandon and Bryan Peach, to come jam, playing alt Christian covers. This was the Jesus punk of their youth, which had led them to question the conservative evangelicalism in which they were raised. But it was really the r/Christianity group on Reddit, which the Peaches had introduced to Jonny, that challenged and transformed their thinking.

Brandon arrived around 4:00 p.m. in a tweed cap and Duran Duran T-shirt, ready to rock. The late afternoon was warm and the party-goers spilled out onto Frankford Avenue. While the Peaches warmed up, Jonny milled about among the conversation circles that clustered around different decades of his life. He was wearing a blazer, as he had on his very first visit to Circle, when he'd shown up clasping a Bible under his arm. Nearly twenty years later, he'd become the person he had dreamed of being: an author, a pastor, and a progressive theological influencer. Greeting people and working the room, he led friends to a stack of books, which he sold and signed.

"I love attention," he confessed. For so long, Rod had used Jonny's ego to shame him, and Jonny was done with shame. He joined Bethany Stewart and Andrew Yang at a folding table in the front of the room to record a live session of their *Color Correction* podcast. Jonny's eyes sparkled, and he was in his finest pundit form as he asserted that half the people in the United States were fascists because they belonged to the Republican Party. The Peaches capped the evening by tearing into one of Jonny's all-time favorites. "The guy, yeah, he's got style and it's plain to see," they sang, covering "Chick Magnet," a track by MxPx, a Christian punk band.

. . .

A lot had happened in the space of less than two months: Jonny had come out to the church, begun a divorce, and published his first book. On the last day of June, I sat on his office couch in Fishtown watching him chat to podcast hosts, while promoting *Jesus Takes a Side*. He took the familiar stance at his standing desk, shifting from leg to leg, deftly able to answer questions about theology while checking his email on a second desktop monitor. Aloud, he talked about Circle with a much higher degree of gentleness than he did in his Twitter quips and hot takes. "I want to be a pastor who is known for bringing the best out of people," he said. Afterward, Jonny wanted to try his first pedicure, so we headed to a nail salon. Playfully, he deliberated over colors, settling on white, the 2022 summer hue.

"Have you seen these yet?" Jonny asked his congregation one Sunday evening in July while he stood at his music stand. On the wall behind him, he clicked through images taken through NASA's James Webb Space Telescope: a billowing cloud of orange gas so thick it looked solid, a red rock cliff. "Here you're seeing young stars being born." NASA called this a stellar nursery. Each point of light was yet another galaxy. There had to be more life out there. "The point of this talk isn't to say that aliens exist," Jonny said, "but they do." He laughed.

The vastness of the universe was the vastness of Jesus, both all-

encompassing and indefinable. The point of religion was to put ourselves in some conceivable relation to the inconceivable—to taste,
touch, and smell it. To be together in its contemplation. "That's why
we have church," Jonny said. "When I contextualize this magnitude in
faith and in religion, I then have a chance to have some hope. And I
don't have to figure it out. We can hold on to the mystery of the sky.
We can hold on to the limitations or understandings of God."

Energy sparked off him: Jonny was still forming, swirling with potential like a young star. "No, you aren't the center of the universe," he
went on. "No, Philadelphia, as much as I hate to say it, isn't the center
of the universe. Neither is the United States or the earth, right? But
just as God's fullness was pleased to dwell in Jesus, God's fullness is
pleased to dwell in you and in all things." He concluded with a prayer
of gratitude: "Thank you, Lord, for your presence, for your magnitude,
and for our ability to rest in that magnitude that we're okay. You show
us the magnitude around us, show us the vastness of our relationships,
and may we treat each other with tenderness, too."

. . .

Jonny moved in with a cousin during the summer. On weekends, he
shuttled his kids to his mom and dad's house in Lebanon County. Parenting on his own, as a divorced dad, deepened his relationship with
his children and his awareness of his love for them. "They're my babies.
I'm going to keep being the best version of myself that I can be for
them," he said. They were a more important part of his identity than
being a pastor. "When people ask me to describe myself in one word, I
say 'dad,'" he said.

On August 4, he packed up the kids for the two-hour drive west of
Philadelphia to Hersheypark, the amusement park where he'd run the
Coal Cracker ride. That experience had shaped Jonny, who, with his
sideburns, had seen his first glimpse of his value beyond the limiting
world of his childhood. They were planning to meet his mother and
their cousins at the park later that morning. Jonny stopped on the way

at a Sheetz convenience store to pick up a chicken sandwich, a hoagie, and a copy of *The Philadelphia Inquirer*. Jonny flipped through the pages, until, on A9, he found a half-page op-ed under a banner headline: "I Let Homophobia Reign at My Church. I'm Deeply Sorry." It was his mea culpa for hurting queer people who'd come to Circle of Hope.

"Like many other evangelical churches," he wrote, "we wouldn't include LGBTQ people if they weren't celibate." By hurting others, he'd hurt himself. "The homophobia I purveyed crept into my own life," he wrote. "My actions in the church prevented me from coming out."

Seeing his first byline in the *Inky*, as locals called the paper, fulfilled a goal Jonny had held for almost all of his thirty-six years. He drove on in quiet triumph. By the time he pulled into the Hersheypark lot, Jonny's phone was buzzing with friends' notes of support. Near the entrance, Jonny spied his mom. He was wearing flip-flops that showed off his canary-yellow toenails, and he'd painted his fingernails black. Pointing at them, she asked, in Arabic, "Are you gay?"

"I wouldn't draw that conclusion just because of my fingernails," he replied, and shot back that she was wearing short shorts, an act akin to harlotry in their conservative Egyptian culture. Let her try to shame him.

But his mom, though diminutive, was tough. She pointed to the crotch of Jonny's jeans. "Is there anything there still?" she asked.

Attempting to laugh off her insult, he shepherded the kids through the gate. In the distance, they could see the milk-chocolate-colored loops of the Candymonium, the park's fastest attraction, which Jonny was itching to ride. A roller coaster connoisseur, Jonny coached his children on and off the park's most extreme offerings: the SooperDooperLooper, the Lightning Racer, Tidal Force, Hershey Triple Tower, and Laff Trakk.

At the Coal Cracker, he tried to chat up the ride's workers. Offering himself as a case study, he shared his personal history and assured them that greater things awaited. They seemed nonplussed. "None of them are as nice as I remember being," he observed. Still, neither his fight with his mom nor the dead-eyed disinterest of the carnies dampened his elation, and he drove home still on a high.

The next day, his dad called. A friend had sent him Jonny's *Inquirer* article. "What filth is this?" he asked Jonny in Arabic.

Next, Jonny's mother called. "Are you still a Christian?" she asked.

"Yeah, I am," he replied. Flipping the script, he foisted the shame his parents were trying to instill in him back onto them. So many queer Christians commit suicide, he told his mother, as a result of abuse from their families and churches. "I think that the fruit of your thinking is evil," he added. "I'm praying for you to change."

. . .

Thanksgiving, which Jonny spent with his parents at his sister's house in Lancaster County, was a trial. He tried to keep it upbeat, making a cranberry tart for his family, but his mother harangued him about his sexuality. "Are you proud of yourself?" she asked.

His divorce exacted heavy social costs, not only in his family but also at Circle. Jonny felt that Rachel was weaponizing his divorce to undermine his authority in the church. When she suggested to him and to leaders that, given all of his life changes, he take some time away from being a pastor, he grew angry. He didn't want to work with Rachel anymore. He floated the idea to Julie that maybe the two of them should partner up and leave Rachel on her own "with that albatross of a building."

Jonny was eager to leave Circle of Hope, but he still had nowhere else to go. "I don't know how valuable I am to this church," he said in a raw moment on Thanksgiving morning. "I don't have as much power as I used to for a lot of reasons." He knew that his screeds and polemics were beginning to draw more scrutiny. This wasn't the Gen Xers who'd supported Rod. Even some aligned with Circle's recent direction were referring to him, tongue-in-cheek, as "the new Rod."

. . .

As Jonny took the de facto lead in negotiating with Bryan Hoke and the BIC, the back-and-forth was taking forever. According to the contracts signed years earlier, Circle was entitled to zero percent of their assets once they'd violated BIC doctrine. Yet Jonny and others weren't willing to hand over some three and a half million dollars in combined cash and real estate. Jonny remained determined to hold on to as many assets as possible. That November, after seven months of conversation, the BIC finally conceded to allow Circle of Hope to retain about 60 percent of its cash, $600,000. But the BIC wasn't willing to give Circle back any of its real estate. The BIC would still own Circle's three church buildings and two thrift stores. Bryan Hoke and others thought that this offer was exceedingly generous. So Hoke was startled when Circle rejected it.

"I still have some fight in me," Jonny said, "and their offer sucks." With the approval of Circle's leadership team, he requested a meeting with Hoke and asked Rachel to go along.

"I'm willing," she answered. "But I do wonder if I'm the best person to negotiate. I don't feel like I'm a good negotiator at all. Well, I kind of give things away."

It was typical Rachel, thought Jonny. She was so averse to conflict that she was shirking her responsibilities as a pastor.

Instead, Jonny took along kindly John Londres from Marlton Pike and two other leaders. They had a new legal angle. They'd found pro bono attorneys who thought there was precedent to argue that the de-nomination was violating Circle's first amendment right to free speech. When Bryan Hoke heard this, he threw up his hands. Hardball wasn't in keeping with Anabaptist pacifism. What the BIC wanted, Hoke ex-plained, was to recoup its investment in Circle of Hope.

"What's your number?" Jonny asked.

Hoke didn't have one, nor was the BIC prepared to negotiate. This wasn't *Shark Tank*.

Jonny teared up. "I appreciate the investment you've given me," he told Hoke. He was grateful that the BIC had provided a pastor coach who'd helped see him through the conflict with the Whites. He also appreciated the investment the denomination had made in him in becoming a young pastor. "But I want you to appreciate the investment that I've made in you," Jonny added.

The meeting broke up with no resolution, except that they would communicate in writing going forward.

When Jonny called Bryan Hoke several days later to back-channel, the bishop didn't answer the phone. Instead, he sent an email reminding Jonny that all proposals should be submitted in writing. Eventually, Circle asked that, in addition to the $600,000 in cash, they be allowed to buy back their two thrift stores, so they could keep operating independently even if the church shut down. The decision was likely to take another six months at least, placing it deep into 2023, by which point Jonny hoped he'd be gone.

He was finding it impossible to heal within Circle and lead it at the same time, and he didn't want to pastor the church from his own woundedness. "I've been here in this church since I was nineteen," he told Rachel and Julie. "I'm working through that experience and sharing it as part of my own story so people know we're not unique. I have my own process of forgiveness and healing that I need to do just to live my life, you know? I don't expect the church to solve that for me."

However, he didn't tell them he was actively looking to leave. That week he scheduled his first interview to become the pastor at West Philadelphia Mennonite Fellowship (WPMF). He pulled on his tweed blazer and a forest green button-down shirt. He was so excited that he wore good shoes, brown leather Rockports, although the interview was on Zoom. Smiling nervously into his camera, he tried not to use his hands as he talked: his nails were still painted brown and orange for Thanksgiving, and he wasn't surprised to see that the interview committee was made up of half a dozen white and mostly older members of the church. As an icebreaker, they asked about hobbies. Two trays of a homemade dessert called millionaire's shortbread were cooling next to Jonny for a cookie swap that weekend, so it was easy for him to talk about cooking. "I'm also an avid sports fan," he said, adding that he sometimes called in to talk radio "to share my word." They laughed.

"Can you help us grow?" one interviewer asked Jonny. At one hundred people, the congregation was already twice the size of Fishtown during the pandemic, and Jonny had grown skeptical about the idea of growth. Carefully, he laid out how, in the past, he'd followed the methods and strategies of church growth. As a young pastor, he'd passed out flyers, created "Love Lists" of potential members, wheedled peoples' emails out of them, in addition to phone numbers, so that Rod could put them on blast. All of that could be "predatory," he explained. There were other problems with the church growth movement—how it was fundamentally racist and enabled characters like Mark Driscoll, whom many accused of taking advantage of his position of power. Winning, for Jonny, was no longer a matter of souls on a scorecard.

He was still in his interview outfit later that day, for a Circle Zoom, when Julie asked him why he was wearing a sport coat. He spun a quick story that his mother had given him an overcoat and he wanted to be sure that a sport coat fit underneath. She seemed to believe it.

Jonny was walking into Rachel's second-floor office in South Philly for a meeting with her and Julie several days later when he received an email invitation to a second interview; he was a top candidate. The starting salary was $63,000, based on his level of experience and education, around $9,000 more than he made at Circle, in addition to benefits.

"Hey, I've got to make a phone call," he told Julie and Rachel, ducking back downstairs to share the good news with a friend. Amped, he sat through the annual staff lunch at the nearby Mexican restaurant, imagining leaving. The position was ideal. Yes, he'd be leading another bunch of white people to do anti-racism work, but finally, he'd have more emotional distance, since the community he'd be leading wasn't the same that formed him.

Jonny wept through Christmas caroling with his Circle friends and, later at church, singing "O Little Town of Bethlehem" and "Come,

Thou Long Expected Jesus" for what he thought would be the last time with them.

On the second Sunday in January 2023, the Philadelphia Eagles were clobbering the New York Giants in a crucial game. "I'm so excited about this job that I'm missing the game," Jonny told the next round of interviewers, this time in person. Noting their laughter, he relaxed. Disarming an audience with easy charm was a talent as well as a survival tactic. For a bit of flair, he'd donned a purple blazer and a lavender shirt. As Jonny answered their questions and laid out his theology in greater depth, he relied on Circle's proverbs. This surprised him. He'd come to question so much at the church over the past several years that he hadn't accounted for the teachings in which he still believed.

"Buildings aren't sacred," Jonny heard himself say. When asked about his view of Scripture, Jonny explained that he saw reading the Bible as a group project and he had a historical critical approach. Long gone were the terms of his youth: that the Bible was "infallible" and "inerrant." Instead, he read the Bible through a historical lens, and with an eye toward whichever marginal group he was reading alongside—BIPOC, queer folk, and, more recently, Jewish people. One interviewer had read Jonny's recent blog about being tokenized, in which Jonny had called convincing people at Circle "a waste of time." He asked why Jonny thought WPMF wouldn't also be a waste of time.

"I'm not connected to you as I am to that body," Jonny answered. He'd planted a congregation and served as pastor for twelve years, and now he was ready to move on for his "third act," he added, borrowing language from Rod. In Act One, he'd moved from his parents' house to Philly; in Act Two, his life became Circle of Hope. "This is the Third Act," he said. "I'm leaving that system."

Would people from Circle follow Jonny to WPMF? the interviewers asked. "I won't stop them, but I won't encourage them," he said. He thought that kind of migration wasn't a good idea. There had been "no shortage of pain" already. "People will be happy for me, but they will be sad." He was thinking of Julie. Jonny knew that she didn't want to lead a church on her own, and for months they'd been talking about how to lead creatively together. She had no clue what he was up to, and he knew his departure would be hardest of all for her.

He crushed the interview, and shortly thereafter Jonny received an email letting him know that the following Sunday, January 15, 2023, WPMF wanted to announce that he was their candidate of choice.

. . .

Preparing for his trial sermon at WPMF, Jonny read the liturgical calendar wrong. He wrote a homily on the beatitudes, which began the Sermon on the Mount, and had been the previous week's gospel reading. No one cared. High-octane Jonny was at his authentic best when slightly flustered. Afterward, everyone descended into the basement for coffee and chocolate crinkle cookies, which Jonny had made for the Q&A session. Following the discussion, the congregation would vote on his becoming their new pastor. He breezed through replies, the thornier the better. When questions arose about the conflict at Circle, and Rod and Gwen White, he wasn't surprised. He spotted two former Circle members in the audience, Jill and Tim Schellenberg, the Kansas couple who'd left Bethany's cell after the impersonation fiasco. After feeling cast out of Circle of Hope, they'd found their way to WPMF.

Although Jonny wanted this job, he wasn't going to soft-pedal his assessment of the Whites. So, he explained that Circle of Hope favored "power families." Jonny was careful to add that he was certain there were power families at WPMF also. Rod and Gwen had committed "abuses of power," Jonny went on. Yet if Circle had had normative ethics, as WPMF already did, the Whites would've had clear guidelines requiring them to leave the church for a time when they stepped out of leadership, he said. As soon as the Q&A ended, Jonny spotted the Schellenbergs leaving. Sprinting after them, he caught them on the basement stairs. Tim was frank with Jonny: they didn't intend to vote for Jonny as pastor. But he didn't have to worry about their influence, they added; they weren't a power family and were planning on moving back to California soon.

Jonny asked if he could come over for lunch anyway, and they agreed. Later that week, he bought flowers for Jill, and lunch meandered pleasantly for two and a half hours over tostadas and pots de crème. Tim, Jill, and Jonny discussed theology and the "horrible things" that the Whites had said about him. Jonny didn't press for details. He didn't want to know. Jonny beguiled the Schellenbergs, and when he prepared to leave, they told him so.

"So, are you going to vote for me?" he asked.

"No," they answered.

And they didn't. A few days later, when the votes were tallied, he learned that 91 percent of the congregation affirmed him as pastor. Jonny did the math. If sixty-two people had voted in total, then fifty-six had voted for him. That left six who hadn't. Two of them he knew; four he didn't.

The Schellenbergs also called the Whites, sharing Jonny's comments from the Q&A about power families and egregious power grabs. Soon after, Rod wrote a post for his personal blog titled "Slander Divides: Six Ways to Overcome It." He wrote, "Not too long ago, I heard of an incident when someone again slandered me in public. Thank God they were doing it in a very small pond, but the nasty water lapped on my doorstep. I was angry. I think that's a natural response to being violated. I was hurt so bad I shook with emotion." Slander, he wrote, sowed division. "The Bible repeatedly teaches about the importance of words and the deadliness of slander," he wrote. "In Proverbs 16:28 it says '*A perverse [person] spreads strife / And a slanderer separates intimate friends.*'"

Without naming the transgressors, Rod listed other historical incidents of slander and defamation, including what sounded like a reference to the decade-old incident with Andy Stahler, who'd contacted the local newspaper reporter, Ryan Briggs, over homophobia at Circle. "One time a person felt slighted by the church and somehow got their dissatisfaction reported on in a local paper!" he wrote. "It caused a small cyclone of recrimination and fear about our reputation. That's what slander does and why it is such a favored tool among power-hungry people."

Though he had several times resolved to stop, Jonny still read Rod's blog, mostly to scan for sideways slurs like this one. He hated that they still stung so much. "It's the same old shit," Jonny said. However, he offered no counter-screed on Instagram or TikTok, where his sermons now garnered more views. He was determined to leave Circle of Hope on decent terms. "It's not some idyllic exit, but I didn't scorch the earth or hang on, tearing down the church on my way out, like Rod did," he said. "I'm happy with the work I've done and the people I've touched." Instead, resolving for the umpteenth time to stop reading Rod's blog, he quoted Ecclesiastes 1:9: "There's nothing new under the sun."

14

JULIE

"To he one who is victorious, I will give . . . a white stone with
a new name written on it, known only to the one who receives it."
—REVELATION 2:17

In 2022, Circle of Hope decided to throw out the proverbs. The list
of 105 sayings no longer reflected who they were or aspired to be.
They also got rid of Rod's amorphous "Amoeba of Christ," in favor
of creating a clear organization chart, and calling it that. And Circle
wasn't simply leaving the Brethren in Christ over its anti-gay position;
the community was willing to risk all that it had, in order to follow
Jesus's principles of radical inclusion.

But not all the church's goals for the year required hard work,
and that was the point. Circle of Hope was taking a collective rest.
"After two difficult years in a global pandemic, we are hearing a call to
new rest and liberation through Jesus," Julie, Jonny, and Rachel wrote
to the congregation. Beginning with the pastors, everyone was going to
chill out. To become "a healed and healing community," they needed
to "reduce the pace of our life together" (read: slow the endless slew
of Zooms) and "weave rest into our daily, weekly, yearly rhythm." This
goal reflected a millennial trend of self-care, but it wasn't New Age pab-
lum; it was an attempt to follow Jesus's invitation in Matthew 11:28–29:
"Come to me, all you who are weary and burdened, and I will give you

rest. Take my yoke upon you and learn from me, for I am gentle and humble in heart, and you will find rest for your souls."

Julie delighted in prioritizing rest and play. "The church is too much in our heads," she said. "Getting into our bodies will help us worship God." Germantown adopted new practices of "sabbath-keeping, and allowing beauty to flourish." They invited their children to lead them in Godly play, a teaching method developed by the theologian Jerome Berryman and based around "wondering" questions. And the community was playing in ways that had nothing to do with Scripture, with cells hosting game nights, tubing, a churchwide field trip to a daytime drag show, Big Wig Golden Girls Brunch at Punch Line Philly. They formed a cheering section at the Independence Blue Cross Broad Street Run, one of the fastest ten-milers in the country (on a downhill course), and planned a camping trip to Mauch Chunk Lake in the Poconos.

For Julie, the hardest work remained leading the church alongside Rachel and Jonny. In principle, they agreed on the new map's goals of liberation and anti-oppression, but when it came to how they might achieve these goals, they kept getting stuck. Julie and Rachel repeatedly butted heads.

"We mean different things by anti-racism," Julie said.

Rachel insisted that they include all voices of color, even those who hadn't experienced racism at the church. "I'm a pastor," Rachel reasoned with Julie. "I'm definitely called to serve *all* the people in our church. I can't dismiss any of them. Can we widen the room?"

What Rachel viewed as widening, Julie considered making room for whiteness. This risked derailing the process they'd agreed to: being led as a church by those who'd been harmed. "Not all BIPOC always agree on an experience," Julie told Rachel. "It's very common for white leaders to use that incongruence that comes up in communities and organizations as deflection." That's what Julie thought Rachel was doing: deflecting.

· · ·

As their anti-racism consultant, Bethany Stewart joined pastors' meetings at least once a month. Throughout the summer of 2022, she listened to Julie and Rachel face off in clipped tones week after week. "Anabaptists are polite even when they're mean," she observed. She was coaching the two white pastors in the practical tools of anti-racism, like how, as white leaders, to better handle racialized conflict. (She didn't coach Jonny, because he was a person of color.) Gender also played a role. For too long, Rachel and Julie hadn't been listened to in the same way that male pastors were. "It wasn't that the men at Circle had silenced women; the men were just louder," Bethany said. "Y'all have things to say!" she told them. Bethany suggested they slow down when conflicts flared, take a breath, and put a hand on their hearts. Don't arm up or get defensive, she instructed. Keep allowing your vulnerability to show.

Although Bethany wasn't assigned to coach Jonny, it bothered her that, when she offered guidance during the pastors' meetings, he usually looked at his phone. She didn't know he was actively job hunting. Since Ben had resigned nearly a year earlier, Bethany had hoped that by now, this trio might be able to move forward, but their lack of unity remained the impasse. It was plain to see that Julie and Jonny didn't share Rachel's vision for the church, and Rachel didn't share theirs. To Bethany, the solution was clear: let Rachel shepherd South Broad on her own as a separate church; Jonny and Julie could lead something new together.

Bethany was sick of listening to them fight, however politely, so, in October 2022, she decided to confront them with the question. "Do you want to keep leading the church together?" she asked bluntly one morning. This wasn't a casual matter: their answers could dissolve the church. She gave them a deadline of December by which to offer an honest response.

In the meantime, in one last-ditch attempt to help the pastors come to a shared vision, Bethany suggested they attend an advanced, forty-hour anti-racism training led by Roots of Justice, the Anabaptist organization where Bethany had worked as a consultant for two years. The training was specifically designed to help predominantly white organizations figure out where they were along a continuum of diversity, from exclusive, like the KKK, to inclusive, like so many progressive organizations were struggling to become. Bethany knew that this was harder than it looked and that the pastors' divisions were all too common. This internal turmoil was happening all over the country. Secular institutions and advocacy groups—including Planned Parenthood, the Sierra Club, the American Civil Liberties Union, the Movement for Black Lives, Time's Up, the Sunrise Movement, and the National Audubon Society—were riven by similar issues. Many were wrestling with the question: Were they to effect positive change in the world or focus first on changing themselves? Conversations and common efforts broke down over language, methods, proper terminology for shifting identities, and who had the right to speak, along with how and when. Some cited a generational divide over values—boomers, Gen Xers, millennials, and Gen Zers. Yet others said this analysis was ageist or racist, both, or something else.

Following Bethany's suggestion, Julie and Rachel signed up for the online training and recruited several other leaders to join. (Jonny skipped it to take his kids to doctors' appointments, but in his place another Fishtown leader attended.) They met at South Broad to sit together around a table together and share a screen. When the Roots of Justice trainer described how white people sometimes feared change and unwittingly helped sow divisions among people of color, Julie assumed that Rachel recognized herself. When he stressed the importance of coming to a shared understanding, Rachel assumed that Julie understood the importance of including all voices of color.

Finally, the trainer laid out the difference between agitation and celebration: since anti-racism work was never complete, it was important to celebrate victories along the way. There would always be problems, he added, but you couldn't just agitate, because this burned people out and made them give up.

Afterward, Julie and Rachel wanted to share what they'd learned with cell leaders at Circle in their next monthly training. Yet Bethany slowed them down. The pastors weren't qualified to lead any more sensitive, emotional conversations on racism, no matter how well-intended. "When we move with urgency, people of color get hurt," she warned them. Julie and Rachel submitted to her guidance, assigning Jonny the task of reworking the agenda for the cell-leader training. He ran his revisions by Julie and Rachel, who thought they looked great. He was also supposed to review these revisions with Bethany, but he didn't, and never told them otherwise.

The pastors invited some thirty people, including all members of color, cell leaders, and coordinators, to come to South Broad on the evening of November 21. The pastors asked people to come in person, since the conversation was sure to touch wounds. They were going to ask people to break into small groups to consider the question: "What would it take to come to a shared analysis of racism at Circle of Hope?"

Julie spent the afternoon of the meeting on the couch in Rachel's office at South Broad. She tried once again to explain to Rachel why this talk about listening to "all voices of color" was destructive.

Rachel, who was scrambling to get her daughter, Cori, to the orthodontist, heard more "shame and blame." She told Julie, "You're just trying to run these people out of the church."

"You're killing me!" Julie cried. Her stomach twisted in anticipation of the evening's meeting. She wished they were calling it off, as Bethany had advised.

That evening, Marcus Biddle, the public radio reporter, showed up in person at South Broad. He was scared, but he'd decided the time had come to speak out or just fade away like his friends who'd quietly left the New Jersey congregation. He'd already met with Rachel to tell her how he was feeling. "This isn't anti-racism work," he'd said. "It's becoming a cult of personality around Jonny. This whole situation is driven by Jonny's ambitions, Jonny's narrative, Jonny's feelings, Jonny's desire to be seen." Over the past several months, in addition to confiding in Rachel, Marcus had begun to voice his concerns with Black members from other congregations, including South Broad's Mable Bakali and

Germantown's Iboro Umana. These discussions gave him confidence to offer his dissenting opinion. When the pastors asked for feedback toward the end of the meeting, Marcus decided to share his honest thoughts. "What you're calling white supremacy culture, I haven't experienced that in the church," he said. Maybe, he offered, not calling Jonny by name, "some people were centering themselves a little too much." Marcus wondered if the church revolved around Jesus anymore. "I don't think that we even have the credibility as a church to do work that's God-centered," he said later. "What we've morphed into has been a church that has been personality-centered." This was more than a structural critique; it was a theological one. If a person, instead of God, stood at the center of Circle, then it was no longer a church.

The Fishtown seminarian exploded on Zoom. He'd avoided attending in person specifically to protect himself from this kind of racialized harm, which called into question the past two years of work they'd been doing. He didn't really know who Marcus was, or that Marcus had been a New Jersey member for seven years. This was part of the problem of trying to do such sensitive work across congregations. People in New Jersey felt left behind and judged as somehow being racists; Fishtown, heavily influenced by intellectuals, seminarians, and activists, sometimes felt held back. The seminarian informed Marcus that Circle still had a standing teaching to guard against conflict and gossip: Matthew 18:15–17, under which one believer went directly to another. This was an odd reminder. Jonny and the seminarian had spent months deconstructing that passage from Matthew, revealing its problems with power, when it forced people to confront pastors directly and in private. Yet the seminarian went on: To ask for "evidence" of racialized harm was another form of abuse. No one had to share their stories if they didn't want to. "It doesn't fall on the person who has been harmed to take off the bandage and show their stigmata around the group," the seminarian said later. As the meeting devolved along these now-familiar patterns, Jonny started to cry.

Bethany asked for the microphone. "Okay, I told you guys directly that a person of color would get harmed, and look at that!" she said, indicating the seminarian, who was Chinese American, and admonishing the three pastors. "A person of color just got harmed!"

Julie, remembering what Bethany had taught her about not receding, stepped in. Bethany watched as Julie took a breath and put her hand on her heart, as she'd taught her to. "We're glad that you haven't experienced this," Julie told Marcus. "But many people of color here have." Although Julie was speaking to Marcus, she also wanted to reassure those who'd been hurt that they were not going to be discounted once again.

From Marcus's perspective, however, Julie was "whitesplaining" to him, as a Black man, what racism was. Fed up, Marcus rose and walked out of South Broad. Sitting on a bench outside the church, he wondered, "Is this going to be the last time I'm at Circle?"

. . .

It was evident to Julie, as to most everyone else, that the community couldn't withstand any more of these meetings. The next morning, Jonny sent around one of his recent blog posts, in which he'd argued that Circle of Hope was stuck in the earliest stages of anti-racism work. To outline his claim, he cited the numbered stages from the Roots of Justice training he didn't attend.

A few minutes later, when she read his assessment, Bethany, who was at home in her living room, was apoplectic. "To say that the church is stuck is outrageous," she charged. It was the pastors who were stuck, and disruptions like this from Jonny kept the church from moving forward. It was also a slam on her as a consultant. In this difficult work it was essential to celebrate victories. And there was plenty to celebrate. Circle of Hope, now openly affirming, was taking the unprecedented step of leaving the Brethren in Christ, even if it ended up costing the church everything.

And in the white pastors, Bethany could see the results of her coaching: Julie led into conflicts with grace, hand on heart; Rachel was risking being more honest, repenting, and taking responsibility for past harms. Then there was Jonny. He was the one trapped in agitation. She wrote back to him directly: "I specifically spoke to you last week about how demoralizing and insulting it is to say that we're at Stage 2 still publicly after the TREMENDOUS amount of work I've put into the pastors team and this church." Bethany was quitting. "I'm done."

Within minutes, Jonny began to text and call her. Bethany didn't answer. She needed a break from the Jonny show. For months, although she agreed wholeheartedly with Jonny over what needed to change at their church, she'd been growing suspicious of his motives. "Jonny wants to be a celebrity pastor," she'd said. But the problem was deeper than his ambition.

"A pastor is a proxy for God," Bethany said. It was right for a pastor to be challenging, like a therapist, or even to piss you off. But leading the wrong way out of self-interest was a sin. "Not to be all evangelical about it," she added, slightly self-conscious about using the language of sin. But sin was real. "That's how people get hurt and the devil wins souls." Finally, she called Jonny back.

Pleading with her not to quit, he told her he'd been wrong. He should've listened to her much earlier when she said the church needed to come apart. Would she stay and help him divide the church?

She spent the next few days over Thanksgiving break considering his offer, but she couldn't get around the feeling she was being used. "I don't think Jonny wants me; he wants to win."

On Sunday, November 27, which marked the beginning of Advent, Bethany pulled out her Christmas decorations and set about decking her house for the season. Peering out her front door, she looked up and down West Gordon street. Over the past three years, since she'd moved to Strawberry Mansion, gun violence had worsened. Gunshots were no longer white noise. One afternoon, Bethany overheard a loud argument, and then, a double shooting resulting in a murder from her second floor bedroom.

She propped open her front door and began to cover it with foil wrapping paper, like a giant present. Setting to work with scissors and tape, she called Jonny. "You're my pastor, and you don't have respect for me as a Black woman," she began. He didn't listen to her, and he kept blowing up the church, causing problems that she had to clean up, costing her friendships. She got so hot she started dropping F-bombs, then realized her front door was still open. She worried what her neighbors might think, since she was clearly cursing out her pastor. Yet she went on streaming invective: Jonny was not an ally; he was lying to her. "I need you to know that I'm quitting because of you." She wasn't going to tell the white pastors, however, so as not to undermine him or the work. It was a blistering attack.

But instead of responding as a practiced debater, Jonny paused. He didn't want to react from a place of devastation. "I'm feeling defensive," he stammered. The sincerity of his rawness startled her. Then he apologized for disrespecting Bethany and not honoring her wisdom.

Later that Sunday, Bethany drove from Strawberry Mansion to Fishtown to record "Answer Me," the final episode of the season's *Color Correction* podcast. She was nervous about running into Jonny. "I'd just snapped on him," she said. But he wasn't around. When they'd finished recording and Bethany emerged from the studio, she found other members decorating for Advent. She joined them, rooting around in secondhand trimmings from Circle Thrift. Picking hairy fistfuls of red tinsel out of the box, she laughed to herself; nothing could be more Circle than well-meaning white people scavenging used tinsel. It was easy, and essential to poke gentle fun at their earnestness, but such unshakable conviction had also drawn her to Circle: the most genuine attempts at devotion she'd known. In this moment, she saw God's divine humor. Bethany had become the kind of curmudgeonly elder she knew well from childhood, the type who "cusses the pastor up one wall and down the other" and still shows up to decorate the tree.

. . .

For Thanksgiving break, Julie and Steve took Isaiah and Alliyah to Cape May, a seaside town in New Jersey dotted with gingerbread rows of pastel Victorians. They spent blustery days collecting flotsam on the beach, and stayed in a friend's cabin, which had no oven, freeing them from the obligatory ritual of cooking a turkey for Thanksgiving dinner. Instead, they ate stovetop chili. All day it rained, so Julie and Alliyah spent hours painting Christmas ornaments they'd purchased at the dollar store to make homemade gifts. They listened to music and talked. As Julie painted every detail, she realized that she had an answer to the question that Bethany had asked the pastors several weeks earlier: Do you want to keep leading the church together? Julie's answer was no. It was proving impossible to reach the visionary goals of their map together. Jonny and Rachel had moved from distrust to open dislike of each other. She and Rachel were nearly always at odds. "It has become clear that we are doing different things," she said. It was time to pull apart.

Clarity was agonizing. Julie loved Rachel. Without Rachel's example and reassurance, Julie might not have envisioned the path of being a pastor. Walking through the high grasses of Cape May's marshes, Julie contemplated the implications of her decision. She couldn't lead the church with Rachel anymore. Rachel could go forward on her own, and Julie and Jonny would continue to lead together in some form, since they and their congregations were so aligned.

The process felt to Julie a little like being a hospice chaplain. Sometimes family members fought against death, going to extreme measures to do battle with the inevitable. "People feel that it's unloving to accept death," Julie said. "I feel like my leaders and myself are finally in a place of saying, 'Let's die well.'"

Along the beach she searched for a totem, a tool she'd learned about through Resmaa Menakem's concept of somatic abolition. She needed an object that she could hold on to during hard conversations as a physical reminder to hold on to herself. She combed the wet sand picking up knobbed whelks, the spiral shells that littered Cape May's beaches, until she spied a white stone. Still cold from the sea, the small rock felt smooth in her palm. One edge was jagged, and as she ran her finger over its brokenness, she felt tremendous power in the tender reminder that she was broken, too. "Rubbing the broken part of the rock is a way to check in with the broken part of me," she reflected. "I'm attending to the part that really hurts."

There's a mystical promise from God in Revelation 2:17: "To the one who is victorious, I will give . . . a white stone with a new name written on it, known only to the one who receives it." Maybe, in time, Julie would find a new name. For now, it was enough to find herself.

On November 28, 2022, at their first pastors' meeting after Julie returned from Cape May, she told Rachel and Jonny that she could no longer work with the two of them as a team. "Um, we've been trying to do this for the last two-plus years," she began. Maybe this is what the new map—which had read in part, "As a church we are moving in a new direction which opens up new possibilities"—had foreshadowed. "I don't want to keep going together," she told them. They kept talking around patterns of harm at "the highest levels" of the church. Well, they were the pastors. "It's us," Julie said. Her implication was clear: Rachel was leading in a different direction, and that was hurting Jonny.

But Jonny offered a gentle correction, softening what Julie had said. "I wanna be clear about something," he said. "Most of the harm I've experienced in Circle of Hope in terms of racism happened well before this team." Yes, there had been ongoing problems, and he wasn't going to deny that. But, he continued, "We are ultimately trying to build structures to help racist stuff from happening. We didn't seem to ever really get to that place. It's hard to move forward in a situation like this that validates everybody's experience. And that's an appropriate place to be stuck at."

It was the most generous assessment he'd offered in a while, and maybe it was possible only because they were allowing themselves to unwind from one another.

Disentangling posed a practical challenge: as one body, the congregations shared nearly everything—theology, staff, money. In asking her question about staying together or splitting, Bethany had assigned the pastors the task of writing down their answers. Julie used Google

Docs to draft the end of their partnership, and to share her tentative response with Jonny and Rachel.

Rachel, who agreed with everything Julie was saying, thought the written statement should be shared with the leadership team. Reading it over, however, Julie felt that sending this statement was too huge an act. It was a declaration of divorce. So, instead, she dragged the document into the virtual trash. Without telling Julie, Rachel resurrected the statement and sent it to the leadership team core. When Julie found out that her personal musings, which she'd thrown away unfinished, had been shared, she was angrier than she'd ever been in her life. For the next three days, she tried to reach Rachel so that they could talk about it, but once again Rachel didn't respond, so Julie ended up venting to Jonny about what a sneaky, sideways maneuver it was and how it underscored her certainty that it was time to split.

None of this ongoing drama was apparent to the rest of the church. At their annual meeting that December, when the leadership team core updated the church on the process of separating from the Brethren in Christ, they announced, without further comment, that the pastors were going to spend the next three months focusing locally on their congregations. Germantown, Marlton Pike, Fishtown, and South Broad would each discern their own way forward.

· · ·

The new year began with the gift of no more pastors' meetings. Monday mornings Julie no longer had to rush back from dropping Isaiah at school and log on. Instead, she sat in her front room and prayed. "It's like finding a space to breathe," she said. As the church was finding new ways to rest, so was Julie. To deepen her spiritual reset, she was exploring new modalities. She'd found a Franciscan nun to be her spiritual director, and a therapist outside Circle Counseling to help her explore her growth away from the inherited system.

Jonny reached out to Julie in the early afternoon of January 9, 2023. He wanted to come over, and made up a story about needing a reimbursement check. Sure, she said, knowing he was lying but uncertain as to why. Within an hour, he was in her living room, oblivious to the fact that she was needed in the family hubbub of homework help and after-school activities. Julie led Jonny outside and across Abbottsford Avenue into Fernhill Park for her half-mile walk around the basketball court, under the highway to the place where the pavement suddenly ended. Julie had never heard the loquacious Jonny struggle for words, but twice he started to say something, then stopped. To encourage him, Julie looped her arm through his and kept her eyes straight ahead.

He stood still and looked at her. "This Sunday," he began, "West Philly Mennonite is going to announce that I'm the top candidate in their pastor search."

"Let's keep walking," Julie told him. "I don't want to stop." She felt hot tears stream down her face.

"I'm sorry," he told her twice, though Julie told him not to apologize. "I'm not leaving with animosity. I'm leaving for hope. I'm not waiting until I'm so angry I have to leave. I found an opportunity and I took it." Jonny went on to say that she was the first person he'd told—that he'd just received the call from West Philadelphia Mennonite Fellowship and driven right over.

Julie knew that, in his own way, Jonny was trying to tell her that she was special, but she also knew his story was a lie. What angered her more than his leaving was this kind of spin. "Jonny, stop," she told him. "I'm not the first to know. It's not honoring. It's bullshit." It was rare for Julie to swear. But she was bereft. For months, they'd been talking about building something reparative and collaborative, reimagining Circle of Hope. "I thought we could do something together, Jonny. I thought we could change how Circle of Hope worked."

But they'd reached the end of their walk. When Jonny returned to his car, he looked at his watch. The conversation had taken thirty-seven minutes.

Back home, Julie tumbled in the front door, where Steve was getting ready to take Alliyah to her cello lesson at the community center, where he boxed at the same time. Steve could see that Julie was distressed and disoriented, but they didn't have time to talk until after dinner. The family plan had been to take down the Christmas tree then, but Steve, in his quiet and unconditionally supportive way, could see that Julie wasn't ready. So they skipped it. "I need this tree up a little bit longer," Julie said.

. . .

It wasn't up to the pastors to shape the separate futures of their congregations. As Anabaptists and a priesthood of all believers, the congregations would determine their own directions. In the winter weeks that followed, the Germantown congregation met at the Presbyterian church where they still rented the auditorium for Sunday worship to discern their collective desire to move forward as one church with the three other congregations. Together, members of color and queer and disabled members led a caucus at which everyone sat in a circle and shared freely about their hopes for the church and the old patterns they were eager to leave behind. Julie said nothing, and was struck by everyone's laughter and ease as she took notes in tiny writing on a piece of paper. It was such a relief that none of this feedback had to go into a Google Doc to be noodled over by committees and teams. Instead, Germantown was free to follow however they sensed the Spirit leading them. They decided to worship together until Easter but then take a three-month hiatus. This was the best way to break old patterns; it was also the deepest form of rest they could discern.

"Discernment takes time, that's the idea, and we're all kind of messed up from the tumult of these past few years," Julie said.

A season without Sunday worship! Julie still had plenty to do. As they continued all kinds of activities, she was realizing that she'd neglected her congregation, by necessity, spending so much time and energy struggling to stay connected to the rest of the church. She looked forward to planning Holy Week and Easter with Germantown alone, so that she could honor the various wishes of her members. Her desire to go it alone surprised her.

. . .

But Jonny wanted to mark his departure with all four congregations coming together for one last Easter sunrise. "I want a proper send-off," he said. "I would like to be honored." Julie wasn't sure. Unwilling to disregard the needs of her congregation, she told Jonny that she would ask Germantown. Rachel weighed in with a reservation. Would Jonny mind "hanging back," she asked, and letting other leaders at Fishtown "run the show"?

"Of course I mind, Rachel," he replied. "It's my last Sunday ever at Circle of Hope. My dream was to do it together for the last time. So I would like the chance to help lead worship and preside for a final time. I am offended and hurt by your suggestion."

"This just confirms that it's about him and not the risen Lord," Rachel noted later. "Why would we make Easter Sunday, the biggest celebration of the year, about us? Let's focus on the risen Christ, maybe?"

Julie was conflicted. Maybe all of the pastors should step back.

Rachel agreed. "I'm fine with all the pastors stepping back, too," she responded in an email. "If we celebrate Easter together, I'd like to reflect the direction we seem to be headed (more collaborative, less top-down leadership) more than stay where we've been."

Fishtown decided to do their own thing for Easter, but Jonny still wanted a chance to say goodbye to Julie's congregation. On March 12, 2023, he arrived in Germantown for 3:00 p.m. worship wearing a Sixers jersey under a denim jacket. Jonny preached to forty-three people about that week's Bible passage: the story from John 8:3–11 of an adulterous woman whom Jesus saves from being stoned to death by the religious elite. "It was too easy, and wrong, to judge folks as dirty, either for their profession of faith, or their sexuality," Jonny said. "You know, I've been called dirty by people very close to me." Then he recounted the story of how he'd hurt the church by helping to keep queer people out, before helping lead the church to affirmation. "It's something I'm ashamed didn't happen sooner," he said. As he drew his talk to a close, Jonny referred to his argument in *Jesus Takes a Side*. "I hope that we continue to take a side with the oppressed," he said. "I leave you with that word. That's what I can give you. I'm sorry for the harm that I caused while I was here. I'm grateful for where we moved as a community and my part in it, and your part in it." He asked Julie if he should sit or stand while others offered talkback and remembrances.

"Sit," Julie said.

Yet Jonny stood as Julie, Iboro, and a handful of others shared encouraging words and formed a circle around Jonny.

Julie laid her hand on his shoulder. With all of his vibrancy and foibles, she cherished his leadership and the way he'd insisted on pointing out the church's necessary path. "Thank you, God, for the way that Jonny has illuminated Jesus and the gospel for me in all new, deeper ways that are changing my life and my faith and this church," she prayed. "I pray that he'll find space to rest and freedom to lead in his fullness."

From the church balcony, yellow, blue, green, and pink balloons tumbled toward Jonny, flung down by Circle's teens. They scudded over a folding table, on which sat the chocolate-and-vanilla sheet cake that Julie had picked up at ShopRite; it read, in blue icing, *Thank you for everything.*

Several months later, Jonny asked Julie to take part in his investiture at his new church. She declined.

. . .

The Fishtown congregation gathered on Easter morning in darkness on the bank of the Delaware River. In twos and threes, bike lights blinked like fireflies, slowing to a stop near the playground in Penn Treaty Park where William Penn was said to have forged a treaty with the Lenape people in 1682. Jonny arrived carrying trays of hot cross buns through a cloud of welcomes rising from picnic blankets heavy with sleepy children. By 6:15, some fifty people had come together in the park, a much larger number than had typically attended Fishtown lately.

With the cuffs of his petal pink pants peeking out from beneath the hem of his overcoat, Jonny, mike-less for the morning, laid out the historical context of the gospel reading in which Mary Magdalene, whom Thomas Aquinas, the thirteenth-century saint, named "Apostle to the Apostles," arrived at Jesus's tomb only to find the stone rolled back and his body gone. This wasn't so unusual at the time, Jonny explained, offering some historical context. Grave robbers and practitioners of witchcraft sometimes stole bodies for their nefarious purposes. "But we come with different news now," he went on. "Something different has happened. Jesus has revealed that life has triumphed over death. And he gives us hope to overcome our suffering and our death. That as we follow him in this new way, we're coming through. We're here, we're waking up together. We're listening to the birds. You see the light in the faces around you. It's new every morning."

A Corgi puppy wrestled with a toddler for a rubber ball as Jonny invited everyone to find the nearest baking sheet of hot cross buns. "Here's the idea," he said. "You and your neighbor are gonna take one and break it together, 'cause the power of sin is broken." Instead of cross cookies, Jonny said, he was trying something "a little different." Yet hot cross buns weren't so different; Gwen had baked them years ago. As the sun rose over the nearby power plant, they began to sing. The park rang with the words of the contemplative poet Wendell Berry alongside the hymn "Oh Happy Day."

Bethany Stewart was absent. She wasn't leaving Circle. However, she'd told Jonny that she wasn't coming back until he was gone and the Fishtown congregation determined its future.

Like the other three congregations, Fishtown's members were still discerning what came next. About half wanted to join Germantown in their Sunday-meeting hiatus; the other half didn't. They were exploring the idea that, like South Jersey, perhaps they didn't need a pastor. Others weren't sure they wanted to be a church any longer, and they wondered if they should disband. Bethany was clear: if they weren't going to be a church, then she was out. "What glued me to Circle was the way we talked about Jesus together," she said. "If we're not a church, then I'm not just hanging out with y'all."

Although he felt much the same as his friend Bethany did, Andrew Yang, the prescient visionary, did show up on Easter morning, as he had for nearly two decades. He stood at the edge near the river. Church was church; not another social gathering. Outside of Circle, he had other friends, and his nonprofit job as an attorney. "Church was supposed to be something different," he said.

Following Easter and Jonny's departure, the congregation at Fishtown started a weekly rotation in which people signed up to lead Sunday meditations, local service projects, or barbecues as their communal meeting. Andrew hung on, playing music, nurturing the congregation as it dwindled. Sometimes he wondered what he was doing, but for the time being, he was still here. "We made music together and we supported each other's lives and businesses and family lives, and babysat each other's children, and moved into houses together," he said. "The dream of committing to that kind of mutual life in mutual love because we love Jesus together, I don't think I can let that go until I'm the only one left."

· · ·

A dozen miles north, before the sun rose on Easter morning, Julie's phone rang.

"Julie, the people who killed Jesus are here in the playground!" a member of her congregation whispered urgently into the phone.

It took Julie a minute. "Do you mean the police?" she asked.

"Yes!" the caller told her, worried that people of color were gathering for church.

Julie hurried to the playground, yet by the time she arrived, the officer had completed his rounds without incident. That morning, Julie preached about change. "I have heard from some of you that stopping cells and Sunday meetings disrupts what has essentially felt like home for two decades for some of us!" she said. "While that is true for me, it is also true that my privilege, my social position, whiteness, has shaped my experience of home here as well as my theology and the structures and practices of Circle of Hope more than I ever realized." Julie didn't want to hit too hard on the parallels between their community dying and being reborn and the death and resurrection of Jesus. That felt a bit on the nose, and their story was still unfinished.

At 3:00 p.m., the congregation met in the auditorium of the Presbyterian church for a potluck of vegetable curry and to watch their children engage in Godly Play. A member of the congregation had painted a series of arresting watercolors depicting Jesus's life and death, and the children considered the images laid out in a line on the wooden floor. They were choosing which moments of Jesus's life were essential to telling his story. "You need the beginning," a girl of six said, selecting the picture of Jesus's birth, which showed Mary and Joseph's terrified eyes peering down at the swaddled infant. "And you need the ending," she added, pointing to a gray wash of Jesus's face on the cross. But a line wasn't the right shape, the children decided, pushing watercolors around on the floor. "The ending's a beginning." The story was a circle.

15

RACHEL

"No one can serve two masters."
—MATTHEW 6:24

For the past two years, I've really absorbed my close coworkers projecting their assumption that I'm doing Rod's bidding, telling me how racist I am," Rachel said. "It's gotten to me." Rachel was feeling pretty beat-up from the troubles with Julie and Jonny. There had to be a better way to lead them out of this cycle. "God, if there's something you want me to do differently, please show me," she prayed. When she asked for guidance about remaining at Circle of Hope, she no longer heard the word "stay."

Instead, an ancient ocean shimmered in her mind's eye: the Red Sea, which God had parted so that Moses and the Israelites could flee Egypt. On Sunday evenings that fall of 2022, South Broad was studying liberation theology, which Rachel taught from the Old Testament. Each week, she shared stories in which God had delivered people from impossible situations. But in her meditations, she didn't see the Red Sea parting. Instead, she was trapped on the bank.

One of their 2022 goals involved "shedding the expectations of the dominant culture," which Rachel still saw all over the church. "There's still so much of the system to keep up: the survival of the fittest, the amount and length of internal meetings, which take up so much time

300

and energy—a strand of capitalism work-you-to-the-bone religiosity and institution," she said. She was so done with these outmoded systems. "I don't have to be the general on top of the hill that Rod told me I had to be," she said. Yet Jonny seemed intent on placing himself at the pinnacle of the hierarchy they were trying to leave behind. "I think he's just gonna keep going consciously or unconsciously trying to run the show around his pain," she said. "We tried to acknowledge his pain for two years at the expense of others." And for some reason that Rachel couldn't fully fathom, Julie was "one hundred percent willing to do that." For so long, Rachel had believed that staying together—remaining one community—was innately good. But Rachel didn't want to twist herself into knots anymore repairing a system that needed to be torn down. "Swirling around to patch up this old thing is just so not what I wanna do," she said one afternoon following a tense pastors' meeting in December. "I just don't want to get caught up in these stupid internal conflicts around ego—I'm just, I'm just not interested anymore. I've gotta just . . . I've gotta get free."

So when Julie returned from Thanksgiving break and called for an end to working together, Rachel readily agreed. "I think this is where we need to make some decisions," she said. South Broad was ready to go out on its own. But Jonny offered a different model of how churches remained part of a network. "I'm sorry to say it this way, but they're like McDonald's, where there is a sole owner of the McDonald's store, that's kind of like how a denomination works." Rachel wanted no part in being McDonald's. She was finished with the business of church.

Jonny offered an alternative. There was a biblical model that would allow them to disagree without questioning one another's Christianity. Maybe this was their Paul and Barnabas moment, Jonny offered. Paul and Barnabas traveled around Cyprus and Turkey together from 47 to 49 AD chatting with villagers and making disciples until they fell out over inviting along Barnabas's relative John Mark. When they couldn't agree, Paul and Barnabas each went their own way.

To help South Broad discern its path forward, Rachel hosted

stakeholder meetings once a month after Sunday worship, framing a positive inquiry, "What do we love about being the church?" Participants' answers didn't surprise her: "Jesus, cells, being able to do things as a community that are bigger than what they could do on their own, being part of a church that no longer asked them to 'pray the gay away.'" Yet when she asked a second question—"How do we want to relate to one another as different congregations?"—the members of South Broad drew a blank.

. . .

Breaking up had another unexpected benefit: paradoxically, when leading their own congregations, the pastors were much freer to follow the map: "Build a rhythm of communally ceasing from work and productivity in our meetings." Once the decision to split was made, the tension eased among the pastors. "My Henri Nouwen devotional told me to make a pizza," Rachel said, laughing with Julie and Jonny for the first time in a long while.

Since Advent was the season of birth, Rachel was practicing contemplation using Henry Ossawa Tanner's painting *The Annunciation*, which hung above her desk. She focused on the incredulous Mary peering at a patch of light searing through the wall of her hovel. Mary looked freaked out in the extreme. So often, as Rachel well knew from the calm and blissful figurines of Mary in her collection, the mother's terror and pain was airbrushed out of the Nativity. Jesus's birth may be cast by America's consumer culture as cute and easy, but in reality, it was dangerous and difficult. So, too, was the birth of the church.

"The birth of the church is always impossible," she said. Something new was being born at South Broad, she told Jonny and Julie. Their growing pains were, by extension, natural, and there were more to come. The Brethren in Christ's forthcoming decision on the fate of Circle's assets was nearly certain to include the sale of South Broad, the building she'd scrubbed and blessed and lovingly nurtured. She was okay with that—the church was its people—but that didn't mean it wouldn't be painful. "If the BIC takes my building, all I want is my art and my plants," Rachel told Jonny and Julie.

"I don't have any religious art in my basement office," Julie replied, sounding annoyed. "I don't even have a wall."

. . .

Despite her positive messaging about South Broad, the truth of Rachel's future was uncertain. Yes, something new was growing, but after three nearly impossible years, Rachel wasn't sure that God intended her to be the gardener. For the second Christmas in a row, she was considering quitting. The hostility and mistrust of her two fellow pastors, over time, had caused her to doubt herself. She wondered if God wanted her to hand South Broad over to a new pastor. "A good shepherd of color," she said, "who might have us, you know?" On the morning of New Year's Day, she went to worship at the Church of the Redeemer, a Black Baptist church pastored by a friend of hers. Bethany, in her coaching sessions, had suggested that Rachel find a person of color outside of Circle to mentor her in her efforts at anti-racism: an "accountabilibuddy." Rachel, however, saw the Black Baptist pastor not only as a mentor but also as a friend. Over the past couple of years, she'd shared the struggle at Circle with him, and he had supported her, reassuring Rachel that she shouldn't give up on being a pastor, or on anti-racism. She was so grateful for him that she found herself weeping through the New Year's Eve service. At the end, she walked up to the altar and placed all the money that her family had given her for Christmas onto the offering plate.

When her husband found out, he was angry. Rachel was always giving too much of herself. How, he wondered, could all of her struggling at Circle be worth it? She needed some space to get away from Philly's biting winter and to ask God, once and for all, what to do. So she found a $50 plane ticket to Florida on JetBlue and decided to go visit her dad at his condo in the new year.

Before leaving, she scheduled a meeting with Jimmy Weitzel in January 2023 to discuss her likely departure. She also reached out to Calenthia Dowdy, the former Circle member who directed faith initiatives at Philadelphia FIGHT, a nonprofit organization that provided primary care to people with HIV. The previous month, for World AIDS Day, Rachel attended a prayer breakfast, where she was surrounded by people she'd known for twenty-five years. It felt like she was home. There, among progressive interfaith groups and Philly FIGHT, she was delighted to see how the movement she'd been an early part of had grown. It would be good to get back into this work, she thought. She emailed one organization to let them know that she might be in the market for a new job. The executive director emailed right back and asked Rachel out to lunch.

Yet before Rachel had a chance to reply, Jonny called with the news that he was leaving.

When Rachel hardly reacted, Jonny grew hurt. He took her lack of response as a sign that she didn't care. But that wasn't it. So many people had warned Rachel that Jonny would do exactly this: blow Circle up and then leave in search of a bigger platform. "Okay, God, is this the deliverance that I've been waiting for?" she prayed. The relief seeped into her gradually, like sunlight. No longer needing retreat, she canceled the trip to Florida. "I could pinch myself, I feel so free," she said. "For the first time in my eleven years of pastoring, I don't have these big, narcissistic, aggressive male personalities hanging over me."

She buzzed with so much excitement she couldn't sleep. A new space opened around her, the Holy Spirit pouring in. The worship services she led took on a Spirit-filled strain. No one was speaking in tongues, but the flavor was changing as their map grew from intention to incarnation. They actually "embodied community care in the form of art making and music, cultivating joy." In the middle of the sanctuary, her congregation constructed an enormous tree, cutting hundreds of leaves out of green construction paper. The canopy shivered with joy, and the congregation kept growing. Some Sundays, the room filled with as many as ninety-seven people—many of them queer and people of color. And the welcome extended online; when an HIV-positive gay man wrote into the Circle website, Rachel eagerly replied. "I feel free to connect to people and to connect to what God is actually doing in our neighborhood," she said. An old Italian man had taken to coming irascible and drunk. They welcomed him. A homeless chef hung out in the building during weekdays. They welcomed him. "They are the church," Rachel said.

She still invited people to come forward and share comments and questions during worship. "What's really exciting is that the first people to talk aren't white," she said. For decades, Circle had welcomed questions in the middle of worship, ostensibly from everyone. But this was dominated by mansplainers in porkpies. "I signed up for a way more collaborative life," Rachel said. There was nothing here to marshal or muscle, only God revealing Herself through Her divine creation.

Rachel simply didn't care about power, and she rejected any effort to struggle over it. While Jonny was in the final rounds of interviews for his new job, Rachel received an inquiry from Jill and Tim Schellenberg, Rod and Gwen's friends who'd left her flock after their incident in Bethany's cell and gone on to join WPMF. As part of Jonny's vetting process, they wanted to raise questions about his actions at Circle. Rachel refused to engage, and suggested they ask Jonny directly. No matter how she felt about Jonny these days, she wanted no part in causing him trouble.

As her days freed of drama and difficult meetings, she could return to what she loved best: the one-on-one pastoral care that her colleagues had told her was a waste of time. She had space for people again, for long walks and conversations over herbal tea and cold brew. Some encounters required Rachel being willing to repent of her role in the past. The map explicitly called for Circle to "recognize and confess the harm in our history; tell the story of where we were and where we are going."

She knew the church had a history of failing women, especially those who were seeking divorce, which Circle of Hope opposed. Over the years, one or two had come to Rachel asking for help, but she'd offered little. The women ended up leaving both their marriages and the church. Among them was Rod and Gwen's former daughter-in-law

Sarah, who'd come to Philadelphia from California to attend Eastern University for college and fallen in love with the Whites and Circle of Hope. At twenty-two, she married Rod and Gwen's second eldest, Luke. From the start, she found herself profoundly unhappy. Over the next four years, she realized she was stuck: there was no way out of her unhappy marriage without losing her beloved community. At twenty-six, she screwed up the courage to sit the Whites down and ask for permission to end the marriage. They counseled her to stay, as Sarah recalled, explaining her misery as an aspect of love. "I followed their guidance," Sarah told me. "I stuck it out for nine more years." Yet Gwen and Rod had no such memory of the meeting. Over the next decade, nothing got better. By thirty-six, she was committed to leaving the marriage, but she didn't want to lose the church, which was her spiritual center as well as her chosen family. Twice, she came to Rachel, who she thought might be able to listen to her, asking for guidance. The first time, Rachel listened with an open heart and told Sarah honestly she didn't know what she should do. The second time, however, after the Whites had spoken to Rachel, she counseled Sarah to stay, telling her that "Christ's miracle was just around the corner."

Sarah thought otherwise. "Leaving was Christ's miracle," she said.

Rachel hadn't spoken to Sarah in five years, since that day in 2017, until she received an email requesting a face-to-face conversation. Rachel accepted immediately.

They met up at La Colombe near city hall. When Rachel arrived, Sarah was already sitting at a table. She looked just the same: flowing clothes, long blond hair piled atop her head, thick-framed hipster glasses. Before Rachel sat down, she told Sarah, "I'm sorry."

They got right into it.

"I felt betrayed by you," Sarah said.

"I betrayed you," Rachel replied.

Sarah was stunned by Rachel's willingness to be open and honest. Yet Rachel didn't stop at a one-line confession. She let Sarah lead her step-by-step through the past, through every slight that she'd experienced as rejection and shunning. Rachel told Sarah she was correct.

This, Sarah thought, was anti-gaslighting: owning harm and making amends for it. Afterward, the women became close friends.

When Jonny came out and divorced, he also called Sarah. He wanted to tell her that he now understood how Circle's heteronormative culture pushed people into marriage. Although Sarah didn't consider returning to Circle of Hope, she went to visit her old congregation at Fishtown when she learned the church might soon lose its buildings. She hadn't been to a worship service at Circle since she was shunned five years earlier. Walking in, she spied Jonny wearing a mask over his beard and a wireless mike, although he was preaching to only nineteen people. Despite the trappings of evangelical culture—its cadences, poses, and microphones—Jonny was sharing a very different and intimate message. Since adolescence, he'd assumed that God was leading his life in a certain direction, he told the tiny group. When that life shattered, Jonny had realized that God's love wasn't out there somewhere to be sought after. It was within him, and already within everyone sitting in the room, no matter how they chose to go forth into the world.

. . .

At South Broad, Rachel kept flinging open the doors, forging relationships with those she called neighbors and friends. For so long, Circle of Hope had held itself apart from other Anabaptists in Philadelphia, believing itself to be special. Of all of the bonds Rachel wanted to shake loose from the church, this sense of superiority topped the list. Rachel began to build new partnerships. Joining POWER Interfaith, a grassroots effort to tackle climate and justice issues, she helped the faith-based group successfully lobby the city council for a funding initiative. She also joined the executive committee of Kingdom Builders, which represented a diverse group of fifty Anabaptist organizations around Philadelphia. Kingdom Builders included Vietnamese, Haitian, Hispanic, and Indonesian communities, among others, and Jonny and Julie also joined. Soon, Rachel was asked to become vice-chair.

. . .

Along with the rest of Circle, Rachel was still awaiting the final terms of the settlement with the BIC, since it was a near-certainty that South Broad would have to surrender its building. An Indonesian Mennonite church offered to share their space if South Broad needed a place to worship.

Rachel found their differences in belief, mission, and worship exciting. "The acceptance of diversity in worship is like water to my soul," she said. "It's showing me the cultish fundamentalism that I've been part of for so long." Not all of these churches, however, were affirming. The intersections between racial and sexual diversity could be messy in places, especially with Anabaptists and other people of faith from around the world. But to affiliate only with people who believed the same things, and judged others harshly, felt limiting to South Broad. Perhaps there was a way to claim an authentic unity through Jesus while different strains of faith continued to evolve.

"The Kingdom of God is going to sprout in different, beautiful ways," Rachel said. The most exciting transformation at South Broad was collaborative leadership. Early that spring, Mable Bakali, along with other women, invited Rachel to a potluck brunch. Around the table, the women asked Rachel what kind of support she, as their pastor, needed. At Circle, the language of "support" had often implied screwing up.

"Do you think I'm doing a bad job?" she asked them, nervously.

Of course not, they told her. Instead it was time for her to let go of self-abnegation. "That's exactly why you need this," one replied.

Rachel proposed that, instead of her leading the church as its pastor, South Broad could form a vision team of elders. "Not just old people," she explained. "Spiritually wise people who really pray." At brunch, the women volunteered to join the vision team. Soon, Rachel was following them—stepping back from decision-making and moving into a role of facilitating what the vision team and others decided. Most of the time, the people leading up front at South Broad were women. This was true in all congregations.

But the church wasn't even sure of its name anymore. With the settlement looming, people stopped sharing their money with Circle of Hope. It might end up in the coffers of the Brethren in Christ. And although the four congregations were moving apart from one another in spirit, they had to hold their assets in common until the Brethren in Christ announced the terms of the settlement. So the leaders created a new legal nonprofit as a container for their assets in the interim. Jimmy Weitzel kept track of donations so that they could eventually be divided according to congregation. They called this new entity Safe Place Church.

. . .

South Broad was still trying to make sense of the past. The question, as Rachel put it, was "What the heck had happened?" Lent 2023 marked three years since the church began to implode. Rachel thought it would help South Broad if they could tell themselves a shared story. An image that reflected the arc of their journey would help. Lighting a candle she kept in a bowl of pine cones at her prayer spot, Rachel picked up a pen and asked God for direction. She traced a circle in her journal.

But the closed shape wasn't right. "It needs to be more open than a circle," she thought. Their journey wasn't about ending up once again in the same place; the archetypical circle had to break. "This is going somewhere else." When she looked down, she realized that she was drawing a spiral, like a nautilus or a knobbed whelk. On the open end of the spiral she added an arrow; they were moving onward. At its center, she wrote, in red, "pandemic" and labeled the spiral as it began to unwind, "A Call to Change." She thought, "We're not as inclusive as we set out to be!" Then, along the descending line, she labeled a series of trials: "loss of mentors," "conflict and confusion," "allies and enemies." She kept the archetypes general, although she knew the specifics: Rod's departure, the gutting of her congregation, Ben's quitting, irreconcilable conflict with Jonny. All of these led to the abyss. "The belly of the whale," she said, labeling these tests as "intrinsic aspects of the Supreme Ordeal, which culminated in death." Then the line began to gently curve up again into new life: "The Spirit of God over religion."

This was the story of their liberation: a crisis had forced the members of Circle to ask questions, revealing the gap between who they'd meant to be and who they'd become. Despite their best intentions, they'd become rigid and institutionalized. As the spiral continued to open, fights began. "Church was supposed to be a movement of people revealing love to one another," Rachel said. Transcending the "Supreme Ordeal" required despair, until, like Jonah in the whale, despair became a doorway through which she crawled into a new, more authentic world and way of being closer to God, as yet unfinished. They were still asking questions, like "What's happening? Are we breaking up?"

At first, when she drew back from the spiral she'd drawn, Rachel saw a hero's journey, a trope she knew well from watching her son play video games and devour anime. Yet a hero's journey involved a killing—a stand-in for an oppressive God. "We're doing the opposite," Rachel said. "We're killing religion, so we become dependent on the Spirit again." The magical change agent they needed, "the elixir," Rachel saw, "is God Herself—that's our magic potion, which isn't magic, but is real love, consciousness, and awareness."

When Rachel shared her spiral with Mable, her partner in creative play on the newly formed vision team, Mable was astonished. Recently, on vacation in Hawaii, Mable had battled a migraine that lasted for days, and as she came out of it, she felt her body unwinding. To celebrate and express her relief, she, too, had sketched a spiral as the image of her soul experiencing freedom.

Mable saw God in mathematical patterns and ratios, above all, in the Fibonacci sequence, a series of numbers in which each following number is the sum of the two that precede it (0, 1, 1, 2, 3, 5, 8 . . .). This sequence can be drawn as a spiral that reflects what scientists, philosophers, and theologians call the golden ratio (denoted by the Greek letter phi, an irrational number equal to around 1.618) or the ratio of beauty. In some ways, Mable saw the golden ratio as the structure of faith: an intrinsic belief in divine design. "It's one of the most practical models for growth," Mable said. "It's iterative."

As the archetype for Circle of Hope's difficult journey, Mable and Rachel decided to draw the spiral with all of South Broad. After worship one evening during Lent, Rachel sketched the spiral on a whiteboard as Mable laid out the mathematics and theology on PowerPoint. "As we move outward in that spiral shape, we're going to grow," Mable explained, clicking through images of a pine cone and an unfurling leaf to demonstrate how the ratio existed in nature. She paused on the inner workings of a sunflower. "We're going to expand into that shape and we're going to be different every time we move outward."

. . .

Rachel handed Holy Week to the vision team. For the first time in years, she didn't lead foot washing, and the vision team decided to skip it. Instead, the congregation created a collage representing the hair of the woman who washed Jesus's feet with her expensive perfume, and is named Mary in John 12:1–8. South Broad decided to skip the rigors of meeting before dawn to welcome sunrise, gathering at 10:00 a.m. instead. Rachel wasn't ready to let go of the cross cookies, but she gave them her own spin, making an Italian recipe her family called viscuits: 1 cup of butter, 1½ cups of sugar, 3 eggs, 2 cups of ricotta, et cetera. Viscuits were so rich that Rachel made them only once a year, on the day before Easter, and usually just as a gift for her family. This year, however, she decided to share them with the congregation, icing a vanilla cross on top.

At the front of the room stood a large wooden cross half covered with silk lilies, roses, and tulips. Most years, Rachel decorated the whole thing herself, so it was perfect before anyone arrived; in 2023, she'd left it unfinished. "We usually meet at five p.m. on Sundays, so people get to sleep in and go to Target or do your laundry, whatever needs to be done," Rachel told the fifty people who filled the sanctuary. "But today's a special day. We're waking up early to greet the risen Lord, the one who came through death to show us the way through it. And so we're coming through, too." Stragglers peeped through the doorway. "Welcome, friends. Come on in. Happy Easter! There are some seats up front," she went on. "We can move the guitar."

She shared George Herbert's poem "Easter Wings" and then turned the service over to the congregation, to read John's account of Mary Magdalene arriving at Jesus's tomb to find it empty and mistaking Jesus for the gardener. "Even if you feel stuck in confusion and grief this morning, you're not alone," Rachel said. "God sees you and wants to meet you there, just like he met Mary in the garden, in her grief."

Then she asked people to tell their stories of struggle and resurrection, a Circle tradition worth keeping. A neurologist from Puerto Rico shared first. It had been a hard year. Her mom had died unexpectedly, and her home was being ravaged by climate change. "I often wonder, where is God in all of this? . . . I'm a Christian because I happen to be born in the eighties in my specific context with my specific family," the neurologist said. "And I can't say that I have any answers to any of the good questions of faith that I still carry, except that every time I have been distant or wishy-washy or walked away, God's love keeps and keeps and keeps showing me the way back home."

Next Rachel's sister Rebecca came grudgingly forward. She was pissed, she told everyone. She'd been at the gym earlier in the week when Rachel had asked her to talk in front of the whole church. "My life was a mess," Rebecca said. "So I was like, sure, why not? It can't get any worse."

Everyone laughed.

She spoke about giving up her first baby, now a young man who'd recently found her on Facebook, bringing up feelings she'd spent her life stuffing down. She'd only been part of the church for a year. "I do have to say the moments of peace I feel and the moments of Jesus's presence I feel have made it worth it in a small way, even though it's still hard at times," Rebecca said. She then thanked everyone, including her sister, and took her seat.

Mable spoke next. Despite her eloquence and spiritual intelligence, she, too, had felt reluctant about addressing the entire congregation, so she'd shared her reservations with her therapist. "The cool thing about my therapist is she knows Scripture," Mable began. "So she said, Paul said that to the Corinthians: 'For when I am weak, then I am strong.' It's an undeniable paradox." She told the crowd, "I also came to Circle at one of the darkest times in my life. I feel like there's this theme that not everyone but a lot of us show up here. We're, like, going through stuff; it's just really cool that we can share that together as we figure it out."

As the storytelling finished and the congregation prepared to sing, Rachel offered the viscuits. "They do have dairy," she said. "But we wanna break the cross together. We're gonna eat the cross together like our communion this morning. We wanna break it and enjoy the sweetness of Jesus's victory over death. As we're doing right now, our hearts and our lives can break open to each other and to love in new ways this year." She added, "We'll feel our weakness again and again, like Mable was saying, and we'll need to keep coming back, suffering lasts for the night. But joy comes in the morning." Rachel invited anyone who wanted to come forward and add a flower to the wooden cross. "Stay and eat with us. There's plenty of food over there on the tables," she said. "We do have welcome lists, I think, under chairs somewhere. So especially if you're new to us, please sign in, so we can say 'Hi.' But God bless you. He is risen. He is risen. Amen."

. . .

The church ran out of money in September 2023. The pastors were still waiting to hear about the terms of their settlement, but there wasn't enough left to keep paying Julie, Rachel, or the rest of the staff, so September became Rachel and Julie's last month as pastors.

"It feels strange to be moving out of formal pastoring," Rachel reflected. "Especially in this moment, where it's finally freer of the unhealthy stuff. But I have a sense that my role was to help get us here and birth a church that is truly communal internally and integrated within the larger community of our neighborhoods."

Asking permission to take the month off, Rachel handed leadership entirely over to the vision team. Then she road-tripped to California with Zach, to set him up for a move out west, and settled Cori into her first year of college in Philadelphia. Late in September, when the BIC finally offered terms for the settlement, the outcome was close to what Rachel and everyone else had expected. South Broad, along with Fishtown, would have to surrender their buildings. But the BIC was still willing to give Circle about $600,000 in cash, as well as sell them the two thrift store buildings at a discounted rate of 40 percent of their market value, which amounted to $660,000. Circle accepted the deal, and the thrift stores began to shop for new mortgages, so they could stay open on their own. However, as of January 1, 2024, Circle of Hope, as a church, would officially cease to exist.

Rachel was ready to stop being a pastor, likely for good. She and Rebecca were headed off to Sicily for an adventure of their own—"to mark endings and hold our hands open to new beginnings," as Rachel put it. The trip was a celebration of Rachel's losing her job and Rebecca's newly finalized divorce. Sometimes, there was freedom in loss.

16

BEN

"Truly I tell you, they have received their reward in full."
—MATTHEW 6:5

Without traffic, Ben's daily commute to his new job in Wilmington, Delaware, took at least thirty-five minutes each way. He didn't mind. He used the drive to practice his Spanish, tuning in to the podcast *Radio Ambulante*, or to chill out to Philly sports radio. As a hospice chaplain, he was ministering in Spanish to kids sick with cancer and to their frantic parents. It was hard to imagine more challenging human circumstances than theirs. During his first week at Nemours Children's Hospital, a nurse mistook Ben for an interpreter and pulled him into a conversation. He had to translate simultaneously for a doctor explaining a high-risk surgery to a family who spoke no English. "I'm not the interpreter, I'm the chaplain," Ben protested, but the doctor and family ignored the distinction. The conversation was urgent: a five-day-old baby bore fatal genetic conditions, and even though the operation had a low probability of success, the doctor needed to operate if the family wanted to try to save the baby's life. No, the father told Ben. Almost certain to fail, the surgery would do little other than prolong an excruciating death. The mother stayed silent, so Ben checked in with her separately to make sure she agreed. No surgery, he confirmed to the doctor.

When the family realized that Ben was a chaplain, they asked him to stay close as they readied themselves to turn off the machines. Waiting among a crowd of white coats and clipboards, Ben surveyed the baby's private room in the NICU. It reminded him of a spaceship: futuristic, white and chrome. And yet, despite the technological advances, nothing could save this baby. In the quiet, a nurse asked him to pray. Ben hadn't expected this. Amid the medical professionals and scientific minds, he was nervous that he might offend someone with too much Jesus, so he launched into an ecumenical prayer, translating line by line between English and Spanish:

God, you are big, and you are here in the room. *Dios, eres grande y estás aquí en este cuarto.* So that means you must be here, and we need you right now. *Eso significa que tienes que estar aquí, y te necesitamos ahora mismo.* We need you to be here, because we are in great sorrow. *Necesitamos que estés aquí, porque tenemos una tristeza grandísima.* We stand at the edge of life and death, and that is a holy place to stand. *Estamos al borde de la vida y la muerte, y estar aquí es estar en un lugar sagrado.* But it is difficult to stand here. *Pero es difícil estar aquí.* We are gathered here around this child and his family. *Estamos reunidos aquí en torno a este niño y su familia.* All of us, nurses, doctors, the whole medical team, and of course the family. *Todos nosotros, enfermeras, médicos, todo el equipo médico, y por supuesto la familia de él.* We are sad because it is time to say goodbye. *Estamos tristes porque es hora de decir adiós.* Though his time with us was too short, we know his life matters. *Aunque su tiempo con nosotros fue demasiado corto, sabemos que su vida importa.* It matters to us, so it must matter even more to you. *Es importante para nosotros, por lo que debe ser aún más importante para usted.* What happens next is a great mystery. *Lo que sucede después es un gran misterio.* But we want to believe that there is nowhere this child can go where you are not. *Pero queremos creer que no hay adónde pueda ir este niño donde tú no estés.* So hold him, God, in your arms when we can no longer hold him. *Así que sostenlo, Dios, en tus brazos cuando ya no podamos sostenerlo.* And hold the family in your arms in their immense grief. *Y sostén a la familia en tus brazos en su inmenso dolor.* His mother and his father have loved him well. *Su madre y su padre lo han querido mucho.* And they are loving him in letting him go. *Y lo están amando al dejarlo ir.* But their love will continue. It will continue forever. *Pero su amor continuará. Continuará por siempre.* And if love goes on, then you must be holding him. *Y si el amor continúa, entonces debes estar abrazándolo.* Because where would their love go if this child weren't there with you? *¿Porque adónde iría su amor si este niño no estuviera allí contigo?* Bless them, bless us. *Bendícelos, bendícenos.* Give each one here a sense of your presence as we go from this place. *Dale a cada uno aquí un sentido de tu presencia cuando nos vamos de este lugar.* We are asking you to be with us. Amen. *Te estamos pidiendo que estés con nosotros. Amén.*

To Ben, the prayer felt disappointing because it didn't center on Jesus. He was relieved when the father launched into a fiery oration about Christ. "He just bathed this kid in tears and blessing and prayer and hope in the Resurrection," Ben recalled. When the father had finished, Ben placed his forehead against the man's, and thanked him for focusing on Jesus, as Ben had feared doing. "You prayed for me," Ben told him. "For all of us."

"We can't handle watching him die," the baby's father told Ben.

The parents filed out of the room and Ben followed. For the next two hours, he ducked in and out. A nurse kept vigil, holding the baby as his breathing shallowed and slowed, hanging on. Finally, Ben offered to take the baby into his thick arms so that the nurse could leave and tend to other patients. The bundle weighed nothing. For nearly an hour, Ben sat in a recliner and tried to ease the baby's passage. He'd attended many terrible deaths, grinding through them, feeling diminished and useless. But this was different, as if he were being initiated into a more profound role than he'd known, a guide of sorts, whispering in Spanish, "You can go. You can die. Go into the arms of the Lord. Your parents and your brothers and sisters love you," until the baby slipped away.

. . .

Being useful helped Ben to heal. His life had shrunk. And so had his salary. At the hospital, he took home $50,000 a year. Without the clergy tax breaks and with a higher health insurance premium, he estimated that his family was losing about $18,000 a year. For the first time since the boys were born, Gwyneth had to go back to work. She found a job as an executive assistant at a dental practice. At home, power was shifting between them. Ben had so much free time that when Gwyneth asked for his help, he was always free to offer it, saying, "Yup, I can do it." Part of him hated this, but instead of wallowing in insignificance or thinking that he wasn't working hard enough or living up to his potential, he tried to see the positive. Mornings he poured bowls of Froot Loops and Frosted Mini-Wheats, toasting the occasional frozen waffle, before hustling Ollie and Theo to the bus stop. His evenings, too, were suddenly free. Instead of being stuck on Zoom at least three nights a week—or at cell, in leadership meetings, or embroiled in other bureaucratic entanglements required by the Amoeba of Christ—he read the Harry Potter series aloud with the boys. After only three months they were into the sixth book, *Harry Potter and the Half-Blood Prince*.

"I'm living through a humbling season where I just have to learn to be small, and that's a good thing," he reminded himself. Ben waited for Lent, the season of reflection and repentance, to turn to his journal and make forgiveness a discipline. "Right now, I live the Sermon on the Mount by forgiving Jonny, Julie, and Rachel," he said. As a practical application of Jesus's admonition in Matthew 6:26 to "look at the birds of the air," he picked up *The Bird Guide to New Jersey* and read an entry every day. He kept a pair of binoculars atop a stack of yellow-spined *National Geographics* in their front bay window, from which he tracked robins and orioles flitting over the goose pond across the street.

He loved birding so much that Gwyneth and the boys gave him a T-shirt that read BIRD NERD. Ben was partial to New Jersey's geese, who, with their awkward tummies and loud, unwelcome honking, sometimes felt to Ben like kin. Back at Eastern University, they'd scared him a little, and during the pandemic in Camden, he'd had to drive them away from the park lawn that served as his church. He'd learned a few years back that the Irish considered the goose a symbol of the Holy Spirit.

Along with the bird guide, each morning he read from Robert Alter's translations of the Bible's book of Psalms, which his dad had given him as a gift. Many dated back to the tenth century BC, and some, like Psalm 3, were pretty visceral, invoking God to smash teeth, for instance:

> Rise, LORD! Rescue me, my God.
>   For You strike all my foes on the cheek,
>   The teeth of the wicked You smash.

He decided to write a psalm of lament. Finally, on the day he'd marked in his journal, March 26, 2022, he sat down to let loose his fury. Yet all he felt was relief, love even. He missed Rachel, Julie, and Jonny. For so long, he'd lived what he called "a buoyed life," bobbing along sheltered by his family. "I'm out of the boat, and I expected it to feel bad, but I feel free," he said. Or mostly free. "It should've been my discipline to not read Jonny's tweets for Lent," he added. "I should've washed him out of my hair, but I didn't."

· · ·

Gwen White wasn't finished with forgiving. On New Year's Eve, at the cabin in the Poconos, she wrapped herself in fury and headed into the night. Raging against the community she and her family had lost, she stalked around the lake. Rod waited at home, worried; later, when he told her he feared she'd been eaten by a coyote, she retorted, "That would've been perfectly fine with me." She needed other people. That was the whole point of Circle of Hope. "It was written into the DNA that we talk to each other," she'd said. "When we disagree, we do it together. That's why Circle of Hope died. Jonny Rashid took our church and turned it inward against itself, and in the name of inclusion, they became the most exclusive."

. . .

Rod was further along than Gwen and Ben in the process of letting go. During Lent, he blogged about Jesus's famous words to Mary Magdalene: *Noli me tangere*, in Latin, meaning "Don't hang on to me." Rod explained, "Don't hang on to the Jesus that was—as wonderful as that experience was. There is more to come for you and them." He and Gwen kept themselves busy seeing clients at Circle Counseling and running retreats at the Hallowood Institute, named for their Poconos subdivision. Rod also offered spiritual direction to seven clients. "In the Christian life, we don't talk about failure," he said. "Sometimes things end, and then there's a beginning." The end was behind them now, and something new was beginning. Rod was considering getting the band back together: gathering once a month to worship.

This terrified Ben. He knew that his parents wanted nothing more than for him to be a pastor again, but this move felt totally counter to peacemaking: it felt like raising a rebel force. "I don't wanna be Braveheart for this group," Ben said. He wanted to tell Rod, but he couldn't find the courage and feared further breaking his parents' hearts. Instead, it was time to admit that Circle of Hope just wasn't that unique. "I had this great idea for a church that was different, and it turned out to be a pretty basic church in the end," Ben said. "And I was part of that."

. . .

Then there was Easter. For the past fifty-two years, since the age of sixteen, Gwen had risen before dawn to celebrate the Resurrection.

"I'm going to be up at sunrise somewhere," she said. So Gwen made her own plan, organizing friends who'd left Circle—about twenty-five "rag-tag, beaten-up people." They were meeting Ben and his brothers Joel and Luke, along with their families, at dawn on Strawberry Mansion Bridge. (Jacob and Aubrey didn't attend.) No one was going to lead the gathering, and there was no real plan other than bringing something of themselves to offer. "It's potluck worship," Gwen told Gwyneth and Ben. "Bring spiritual food to share."

So, at 5:30 a.m., Ben and Gwyneth bundled up Ollie and Theo and headed for Philly with the cross cookies Gwyneth had baked as her offering. When they arrived in the snapping cold, two dozen tired-looking people were setting up portable camping chairs on the bridge. On Gwen's instructions, each had brought something to present from their spirit; most were offering something they wanted to let go of. One woman, who'd suffered multiple miscarriages, tossed flowers into the black void of the Schuylkill River rushing below.

The ceremony was small and gloomy and cold, and in that way fitting for the vulnerable dawn of the rising Christ. Worshippers came forward one by one, offering songs, stories, and poems. Ben shared a parable about a wise man who saved a drowning scorpion. The wise man knew that the scorpion would sting, but rescued him anyway. He quoted the wise old man, saying, "My friend, just because it is the scorpion's nature to sting, that does not change my nature to save."

Dawn broke.

"He is risen," Ben said as he greeted his dad.

"He is risen indeed," Rod replied, beaming.

Ben's son Theo handed him a crayoned picture of a cross covered with vines and blooms. "Jesus has overcome the cross," he told Ben. The boy showed his picture to Gwen. Moved beyond tears, she could see in it new life sprouting, and she could feel, in her body, the solace she'd been longing for. Some people started to dance in the cold. Forming a circle, people moved in and out, even the teenage boys, who risked the embarrassing awkwardness, moving from death to new life.

Gwen's son Luke, who was on the bridge, put it pointedly: "My parents were crucified on the cross of wokeness."

Among her friends and family, Gwen saw their place in a larger cycle. Churches die, as people do. "If Christ calls you, he calls you to come and die," she said.

Ben watched his mom hand out cookies. Despite his fears about this morning, he felt none of the wrath he'd anticipated.

. . .

In his more tortuous moments, Ben still felt he'd failed his parents by losing Circle of Hope. He worried most about what his departure would cost his kids. "My whole parenting idea was to let them experience a beloved community, and let them choose their own path," he said. "And now it's gone, and they're bereft of that."

On his own, he curated his boys' encounters with the sublime. For Father's Day, he drove them north for a father-son trip to Niagara Falls, where he'd gone when he was seven. He remembered a moment on the boat, *Maid of the Mist*, when, approaching the falls, Ben had clutched Rod's legs tightly, only to discover that he had the wrong grown-up in his grasp. There was something about the disorientation of that moment that stuck in Ben's consciousness, and he'd returned to the boat in his meditations. Once, years later, while practicing an Ignatian exercise of imagining himself meeting Christ, he had a vision of swimming beneath Niagara Falls with Jesus. He saw himself approaching the boat's gunwale, then glancing back at his dad, who gave him a thumbs-up. Ben stripped off his plastic poncho and dived in, swimming forward against the push of the water, trying to reach Jesus. But Jesus came up behind Ben, tapping him on the shoulder. He was wearing a Speedo and a 1970s snorkel mask.

Ben didn't need to interpret it. He was pretty sure that his vision foretold that he'd have a mystical encounter when he took his boys on *Maid of the Mist*. But when the time came to board, his younger son refused and grew hysterical. "I can't leave you," Ben told him. "If

Mom were here, you could stay behind, but she's not, so you have to come." Ben managed to coax Theo onto the boat, but he didn't calm down, and as they approached the falls, sheets of water poured onto them. Ben held the drenched boy tightly. "This *is* scary," he repeated. In fact it *was* scary, and much more intense than Ben had remembered. Forget contemplation. Instead, he hung on to the deck with the boy in his arms.

They left the boat soaked, stopped in Buffalo to catch a 3:45 p.m. showing of *Dr. Strange*, and then drove south toward Cherry Springs State Park in northern Pennsylvania. It was one of the best places in the United States to see stars. Ben had studied the forecast, trying to game the night that would provide the clearest window. He hadn't counted on the summer solstice, however, and so when he pulled into the park, around ten, Ben had to wait an extra two hours for the sky to darken. The boys slept in the back of the Prius until Ben woke them around midnight and led them over a berm and into a field. To the boys, he'd advertised that they'd be able to see the Milky Way in its entirety, but mostly he hoped they'd encounter "the wonder of the universe." As they lay in the grass, Ben used an app to identify the constellations, and soon the boys grew more engrossed in the glow of the screen than in the actual stars. So much for engineering an encounter with the sublime. Ben studied the horizon, searching for a constellation with a scorpion in its center. He bore three regrets. He should've stood up to Jonny, he thought. He also wished that he'd told people what was going on instead of keeping it to himself until it was too late. The last regret ate at him most. "I wish I'd mastered my anger," he said.

. . .

Without a pastor, Marlton Pike was flourishing. In the two years since Ben departed, the congregation functioned as a true priesthood of all believers, with every one of its forty-some members pitching in to run mutual aid and to keep the doors open, welcoming whoever came along in need or whoever came to pray. They took turns leading worship. There were practical advantages to being pastor-free, including saving $53,000 a year in salary. On Sundays after the Circle of Hopers went home, Victory Temple Deliverance Center hosted lively charismatic healing services. Eventually, the members of Circle decided to sell the building to their neighbor, The Work Group, a nonprofit job training organization, for $327,000. Marlton Pike could pay off the $302,000 mortgage in full, and they could keep meeting there on Sundays for free.

The sermon at Marlton Pike frequently fell to Christy Randazzo, a Quaker theologian who wore dangly earrings, a sundress, and a bushy beard. They'd first arrived at Circle at the height of the church's turmoil in 2021. However, struggles and fights didn't spook them. They believed that most serious religious communities wrestled, in one way or another, over how to follow Jesus, and sometimes the best humans could do was to set this question in terms of binary answers. Christy, who'd written a dissertation on Quaker theology, preached about common scriptural misreadings that were also homophobic. Consider the story of Sodom and Gomorrah (Genesis 19), they preached one Sunday. God punished the people of Sodom not because they engaged in anal sex, but because they raped angels. This act, by all measures, violated ancient codes of hospitality, which was a sin.

Christy, who loved to preach, visited other Circle congregations to talk about queer theology. This was about much more than gender, or sexual identity, they explained one July evening to Rachel's flock at South Broad. "Queering" involved seeing through false dichotomies and not dividing the world into binaries like good and evil, saved and damned. Maybe it was possible to abandon binary theology in favor of something more expansive and inclusive, with a more boundless quality, like love. Queering the Bible required a different kind of close scriptural reading: considering who was left out of a story entirely.

"God is always with the oppressed, focused on both their needs and on alleviating their oppression," Christy said. "And with all due respect to Jonny Rashid, Jesus didn't need to take a side. There is no choice.

God is simply born this way." Laughter of gentle recognition rippled through the sanctuary.

Although Marlton Pike remained without a pastor by choice for two years after Ben left, the community kept up some of Circle's traditions, including the Easter sunrise service. In 2023, they pitched tents in a member's backyard in Deptford, New Jersey, rising at dawn to share a breakfast of French toast, eggs, vegan sausage, and crema catalana.

Ben had honored the agreement to stay away from Circle of Hope for a year. Then another. Time slipped forward.

Ben and Gwyneth returned to Strawberry Mansion Bridge to celebrate a second sunrise in 2023. Crocuses and cosmos were in bloom. Rod and Gwen had invited the same cast of twenty-some former Circle of Hopers to reconvene for a spiritual potluck. This year, Ben felt much more relaxed. There was no rebellion on the horizon, and he would never be Braveheart. With his distance from his old congregation, he didn't know that they were still rising at dawn to celebrate Easter. He'd assumed that the sunrise tradition had fallen away, along with his family. When he learned about the tents and the vegan sausage, he was delighted and surprised. It was cool they had no pastor.

A BENEDICTION

To bless means to wound.
To wound means to mark as one's own.

Each week, as worship drew to a close, the pastors of Circle of Hope offered a blessing: "Go in peace." Jesus spoke these words to one of the six hundred unnamed women in the Bible. We know her only by her illness: she had been bleeding for twelve years. Scripture doesn't specify the ailment, and it doesn't matter. According to Jewish law, she was unclean and so had been cast out of the safety of communal life and into the dangers of isolation and shame.

By healing her, Jesus was welcoming her into a new community. Yet admission comes with a price: a radical commitment to love and service. (A fuller version of the benediction is "Go in peace to love and serve the Lord.") What was Jesus asking of the woman he healed? What does peace entail? The New Testament employs the Greek word *eirene*, which means "prosperity" or "reconciliation." The more ancient word for peace in the Old Testament is the Hebrew *shalom*, which also connotes a flourishing soul. What is asked of any of us when we are told, "Go in peace"? How do we receive it? What if God is commanding us, "Go and flourish"?

When my father offered the benediction at the end of the hour-long service, I heard only the "Go" and felt the attendant surge of relief that I would soon be free of itchy white tights and the dig of their elastic around my middle. There was always the half beat in which people greeted one another in the pews before the organist hit two overzealous chords, rendering conversation impossible and releasing us to the world.

Until I began to follow the four young pastors at Circle of Hope, I never thought about the "in peace" part of the benediction. The idea that Christians were called to live in some superior way was anathema in our home. My dad's Episcopal theology hewed closer to mystical traditions in which the line between all three Abrahamic faiths, along with many Eastern practices, remains extremely thin. Many evangelicals would critique this form of Christian witness as weakened by universalism. Instead, the underlying principle is one of humility: Who are any of us to presume that we know who it is that God does and doesn't choose?

Despite being cautious about what a reporter might make of their faith and, later, their fights, Ben, Julie, Rachel, and Jonny allowed me to witness the many things they lost—ego, friendship, career, marriage, community, and, ultimately, their church. And yet, in the midst of each blow, they continued to lay bare as much of their mess as they could to me, because the Spirit had led them to say yes. Each, in their own way, honored the commitment they'd made, even as so many others dissolved around them.

. . .

As I was reaching the end of my reporting, and Circle of Hope was coming apart, my father developed a mysterious health problem. His lungs were drawing in plenty of oxygen but holding on to carbon dioxide rather than releasing it. The carbon dioxide was poisoning him, causing narcosis marked by vivid hallucinations. In the hospital, he slept and woke and drifted off again, returning with otherworldly tales of where he'd been. He was coming and going from his place in line in a long wait for heaven. Their processing times were far too slow, he groused. How could they not have a better system? Slipping away, he returned again from elsewhere: this time a battlefield where good was wrestling with evil, an epic spectacle. "Wait until you hear what I've seen," he told me, my sister, and my mom. His blue eyes fluttered open. They were growing milky. He carried urgent messages impossible to understand from beneath the plastic mask he wasn't supposed to remove. He kept trying. He was pointing out the forces of evil crawling up the wall when a young pulmonologist stepped into the room, asking if my dad was on opioids. No, I told him. He's just a man of God. What were any of us to make of the unknown realms in which my dad seemed to be traveling?

At one of his lucid moments, he asked me to fetch a small gray flannel satchel with two metal buttons from his bedside table. Inside was a Bible, bound together in red leather with the Book of Common Prayer. Dad was a liturgy guy, meaning he cared a great deal about the prayers and practices of the Episcopal Church. His concern with arcane-seeming things, like where a crucifer stood, reflected his attention to the formal order of the ancient rites. He asked me to read the Scripture for that coming Sunday, the third in Lent. Called in the ancient church the *Pericope Adulterae*, this is the story of elders who test Jesus by bringing to him the adulterous woman. According to the law set down in Deuteronomy, she is to be sentenced to death by stoning. Will Jesus follow the law, or will he break it by letting her go? Instead of choosing, Jesus bends down and writes in the dirt with his finger, uttering to the elders the famous injunction against human judgment: that whoever among them is without sin should cast the first stone. Then Jesus bends again and writes whatever he writes on the ground, which we never learn, and the elders, foiled, grumble away, leaving the woman with Jesus. "Go, and sin no more," he tells her.

Reading aloud to my father, I recalled a Circle member, Jenn Shannon, recounting this story to me as the foundation of the third way. We were driving around Camden delivering boxes of food for mutual aid. Casting aside the old laws, Jesus breaks the limited dialectic of salvation and damnation, and comes up with a creative solution. Mercy. This was the point of the story, my dad wanted to tell me that afternoon. God doesn't *choose* to forgive, or to love; God *is* mercy, and love. How many times have I seen the words GOD IS LOVE—stitched on a felt banner or printed on a well-intended ecumenical greeting card—and found them empty? I've mistaken the limits of my understanding for the limits of the statement's meaning.

It isn't that the woman didn't sin, my father mumbled from his hospital bed. Jesus tells her, "Go, and sin no more," but whether or not she does change is immaterial to God's love for her. If she causes more suffering, then she causes more suffering, but this has nothing to do with the all-pervasive love that surrounds her, the testy elders, and Jesus on that hillside outside Jerusalem. And what of the elders, who are forced, by Jesus's question, to interrogate their lives and search their souls until they surrender their judgmentalism and acknowledge that they, too, are flawed humans, that none is without sin? They aren't simply defeated by some Jesus-y mind game. They are transformed by understanding that they are implicated by the law they seek to enforce against others. Once we acknowledge our mutual vulnerability, we are less willing to wield the weapon of condemnation. This is the truth of empathy, a word too often bandied about in self-help and pop psych as simply meaning "feeling for others." Empathy is transformative, because through it we acknowledge a shared brokenness.

But what of the dirt? What did Jesus write in it? Maybe he doodled in the dirt to allow a moment for the elders to realize they'd screwed up. Maybe, biding his time, he scrawled "What jokers!" or "Jesus was here." Or maybe he was recording the names of the condemned in the dust, fulfilling the Old Testament prophecy of Jeremiah. I couldn't ask my dad what he thought, since he'd slipped away again and didn't return to consciousness except to murmur "Home!," ordering us to spirit him out of the ICU and back to his familiar bed so that he could wait comfortably for his number to come up in heaven. Five days later, he died in the ICU, not in an apotheosis of mystical and beatific peace, but in terror, pain, and rage at those intent on delaying his journey away from us. To love is to grieve.

A BENEDICTION

. . .

Churches are messy places where people seek many things, among them a common understanding of something larger than they are, of God. This can be a beautiful, courageous endeavor that, in its effort to do right, usually goes wrong. Maybe churches need to die, to rid themselves of their old bodies, their advanced pathologies, to make themselves new again. To be free of the weight of a past none can carry. This cycle is, after all, the foundational principle of the faith. The theologian G. K. Chesterton said, "Christianity has died many times and risen again; for it had a god who knew the way out of the grave." Yet the notion of a circle doesn't fully satisfy. Death and rebirth, death and rebirth: the cyclical nature goes nowhere, doomed to repeat itself. This may be an honest assessment of the universe's affairs; however, it isn't very hopeful. In Rachel's spiral, in Julie's knobbed whelk, in Jonny's realization that leading Circle and healing himself were two separate endeavors, in Ben's acceptance of erasure and return to being humbled by grieving strangers—in all of these, there are hints of moving forward by breaking a circle and not repeating it.

The four pastors humbled one another, or perhaps "harrowed" is the better word: raking one another's souls, like fields, and freeing them to grow. It's uncomfortable to accept our flaws, let alone having them pointed out to us, hearing how we hurt one another and ourselves by clinging to received ideas. In some ways, this is the work of the exegete: to examine a story or an experience for what it reveals not only about the world, or God, but also about ourselves and what, in our embodied consciousness, must grow, or die.

Dying is difficult, even when welcome. There's no controlling what our bodies say and do in their final hideous and terrifying paroxysms. It's a curious thing to be an observer of human beings in the midst of their great struggles, and it's easy to forget that, as observers, we exist as humans alongside.

My father died during Lent in 2023. As I was leaving the church at the end of my father's funeral, I glanced into the forest of mourners and was startled to catch sight of Julie in a black blouse and pants, more formal than anything I'd ever seen her wear. She cracked when I saw her. So did I. I hadn't imagined her visiting my world, and yet there she was, mourning the loss of a man she'd never met, as this, among so many other unseen acts of service, is what a pastor does.

METHODS AND SOURCES

Excerpts from the following sources appear in this book: T. S. Eliot, "The Dry Salvages"; the Bible, New International Version; Margery Williams (1880–1944), *The Velveteen Rabbit; or, How Toys Become Real* (1922; reprint, New York: Doubleday, 1991).

This is a work of nonfiction. It relies on the techniques and methods of immersion journalism, which include multiyear observation and direct engagement with primary subjects. Over four years, I sat in on more than one thousand hours of Zoom meetings, in addition to visiting church events, worship services, firepits, hikes, and people's homes to interview 119 current and former members of the church, along with their families. Almost all chose to participate as named sources. The many who willingly spoke and are not named in the book contributed integral material to the narrative and character of Circle of Hope.

Every church is more than the sum of its pastors, and Circle's existence as a collective rendered it difficult to tell the story primarily through the experiences of Jonny, Julie, Rachel, and Ben. I chose this interlinked structure of four primary subjects because it reflected the challenges facing the church, and because all four granted me permission to enter into their daily lives without asking for control over what I would write.

In addition, this project required extensive historical research, as well as secondary source interviews. I worked with a team of religious scholars, researchers, and fact-checkers. This group of talented and committed colleagues was headed by Katherine Ellis and included Jess Rohan, Natalie Meade, Vienna Scott, Noah Daley, and Clara Mc-Michael. All offered their keen attention and limitless resilience to a project requiring the highest levels of ethical and professional commitment and rigor.

ACKNOWLEDGMENTS

When we began this project in 2019, neither the pastors nor I had any sense of how events would unfold, or what would be required to set them down, accurately reflecting their differing perspectives, over the next five years. In the course of reporting, writing, and fact-checking this book, Julie, Rachel, Jonny, and Ben spent untold hours in person and on the phone, reliving these sometimes excruciating events. As their loyalties to one another and to the church changed, there were moments that called into question their desire to continue with this project, and yet each, out of a deep sense of integrity, remained committed to its completion.

The same held true for Rod and Gwen White: as the church shifted its focus inward, they found their legacy under scrutiny not only in the community they'd given their lives to creating, but also, by extension, within these pages. I am grateful to them, and to the White family: Jacob, Aubrey, Luke, Joel, Kathy, Ben, and Gwyneth, for their contributions, and I hope among the chorus of voices and points of view they find their own.

There were many at Circle of Hope, and beyond, who shared their perspectives and varied accounts in the course of this reporting: Bethany Stewart is first among them. Her intelligence, acuity, and faith guide these pages. Others include, in alphabetical order, Stephanie Adams, Lucille Alexander, Roby Anstet, Jeremy Avellino, Mable Bakali, Marcus Biddle, Diane and Curt Bitterman, Ryan Briggs, Katy Jo Brotherton,

Anita Grace Brown, Art and Mary Bucher, Jordan Burge, Shane Claiborne, Scott Clinton, Rebecca DeMara, Susan and Dennis DeMara, Leonard Dow, Calenthia Dowdy, Debra Fileta, Greg Fuguet, Tricia and Adam Fussaro, Martha Grace, Dasia Griffin, Scott Hatch, Nelson Hewitt, Brice Hewlett, Bryan Hoke, Steve Hoke, Greg Jehanian, Nicole Jordan, Josiah Kephart, Blew Kind, Nikki Kleinberg, Tracey and Paul Kohl, Becca and Andy Koval, Scotty Krueger, Rob Larrimore, John Londres, Heather Machal (Wax), Sister Margaret, Ashley Martin, Elizabeth Martin, Mikey Masters, Pete McDaniels, Marguerite McDonald, Andrea McIntosh, Joel McIntosh, Candace McKinley, Eden McLendon, Rebekah McLendon, Holly Meneses, Will O'Brien, Jonathan Olshefski, Danny P., Caz Tod Pearson, Christy Randazzo, Samuel and Rebecca Rashid, DeeDee Risher, Sarah Robbins, Audrey Robinson, Aly Rogoff, Megan and Ben Rosenbach, Robin Ryan, Claire Ryder, Bobby Saritsoglou and Christina Kallas-Saritsoglou, Tim and Jill Schellenberg, Jenn and Scott Shannon, Jessica Shoffner, Dawn Smelser, Lauren and Joel Smith, Kristin Snow, Naomi Sonne, Andy Stahler, Nathan and Sarah Swanson, Sarah Taylor, Christina Thompson, Oneita and Clive Thompson, Matt Tice, Jasmine and Iboro Umana, Ashley Walliser, Jon Wear, Jimmy Weitzel, Gerry West, Rand Williamson, Anita Wood, Rae Wright, Amy and Andrew Yang, Kyle Zieba, and Jonathan and Danielle Ziegler.

I am grateful to *The New Yorker*, New York University, Princeton University, and the Templeton Foundation. John Cunningham, David Nassar, Ben Carlson, and Kristen Johnson offered essential guidance and research support, and convened a panel of expert readers to review an early version of this manuscript. Led by Jeff Chu, these experts included Tessa Desmond, Kristin Du Mez, Drew Hart, Mihee Kim-Kort, Kenji Kuramitsu, and Kathryn Lofton. Many friends and colleagues also offered thoughts along the way: Michael Wear, Beth Allison Barr, Nadia Bolz-Weber, Father Dave, Michael Luo, Richard Rohr, and Jemar Tisby, to name several.

The editorial support of FSG, as ever, is invaluable. Deep gratitude to Eric Chinski for his early enthusiasm, Jenna Johnson for her overwhelming commitment and guidance, Martin Mraz for his technical prowess and patience, Janet Renard for her editorial attention, and Steve Weil for shepherding this book into the world. Additional thanks at FSG to: Gretchen Achilles, Janine Barlow, Caitlin Cataffo, Thomas Colligan, Lianna Culp, Daniel del Valle, Nina Frieman, Diana Frost, Sam Glatt, Debra Helfand, Henry Kaufman, Isabella Miranda, Sheila O'Shea, Joshua Porter, Nicholas Stewart, Hillary Tisman, Sarita Varma, and Jonathan Woollen. And, as ever, Jonathan Galassi, whose integrity and encouragement will always be my lodestar.

Without Tina Bennett, I would be under a desk, and not coming out anytime soon.

To wonderful friends in Philly and London: Camilla Baker, Lucy Barzun Donnelly, Katy and Jason Friedland, Sarah Fuld, Suzie Kondi, Heather and Mark Levine, Emily McDonnell, Amanda and Shaun Raad, Denise Withey, and Gerry Wolf. With gratitude to the entire village of Colls and Goldbergs, most of all to Susan, for embodying welcome.

For my mom, Phoebe Griswold, and my sister, Hannah Griswold, and my nieces, Louisa and Gigi—goddesses all.

And for my precious Steve and Robert. You guys!

A NOTE ABOUT THE AUTHOR

Eliza Griswold is the author of six books of poetry and nonfiction, all published by Farrar, Straus and Giroux. Her book *Amity and Prosperity: One Family and the Fracturing of America* was awarded the 2019 Pulitzer Prize in General Nonfiction. She writes for *The New Yorker*, is the Ferris Professor and Director of the Program in Journalism at Princeton University, and lives in New Jersey with her husband and son.